D1526679

Federal Union, Modern World

Peter Onuf &
Nicholas Onuf

FEDERAL UNION, MODERN WORLD

*The Law of Nations
in an Age of Revolutions
1776–1814*

MADISON HOUSE

Madison 1993

Peter Onuf & Nicholas Onuf
Federal Union, Modern World
The Law of Nations in an Age of Revolutions, 1776–1814

LIBRARY OF CONGRESS CATALOGING-IN-PUBLICATION DATA

Onuf, Peter S.
      Federal union, modern world : the law of nations in an age of
revolutions, 1776–1814 / Peter Onuf & Nicholas Onuf. — 1st ed.
        p.   cm.
      Includes bibliographical references and indexes.
      ISBN 0-945612-34-6 (acid-free paper)
      1. International law—History. 2. Federal government—History.
3. United States—Foreign relations—1783–1815. I. Onuf, Nicholas
Greenwood.   II. Title.   III. Title: Law of nations in an age of
revolutions, 1776–1814.
    JX2435.U6O58   1993
    341'.09—dc20   93–6038
                                                    CIP

Designed by William Kasdorf.
Printed in the United States of America on acid-free paper
by Edwards Brothers, Inc.

Published by Madison House Publishers, Inc.
P. O. Box 3100, Madison, Wisconsin, 53704

FIRST EDITION

Contents

Acknowledgments

Earlier and much different versions of chapters 4–7 were delivered by Peter Onuf as the Merrill Jensen Lectures at the University of Wisconsin in November 1990. He thanks John P. Kaminski and his associates at The Center for the Study of the American Constitution for their warm hospitality. In the context of a long planned collaborative work, now conceived of as a sequel to this one, Nicholas Onuf had agreed to contribute an introduction to the published lectures. His exploration of republican theory, now constituting chapters 1–3 as well as a large part of the Introduction, prompted a thorough rethinking and revision of the Jensen Lectures and accounts for their belated publication.

Peter Onuf wishes to acknowledge helpful critical comments by Lance Banning, Steve Innes, James Lewis, Jack Rakove, and John Stagg; special thanks to Mel Leffler and Herb Sloan for extraordinarily thorough and penetrating readings of successive drafts. Much of the reading in British sources was undertaken at the Royal Irish Academy during Peter Onuf's tenure as Mary Ball Washington Professor at University College, Dublin. A generous fellowship from The Center for the Study of the History of Freedom at Washington University in St. Louis supported further research. Many thanks to David Konig and Richard Davis. A generous sabbatical support award relieved Nicholas Onuf of teaching duties at The American University for the 1991–92 academic year. He thanks Kurt Burch, James Farr, and Jeffrey Reiman for critical help and Betsy Cohn for research assistance.

The book was completed at the Virginia Foundation for the Humanities and Public Policy where the authors shared a summer fellowship in 1992.

Peter Onuf
Nicholas Onuf

Charlottesville and Arlington, June 1992

dedicated to our mother
Barbara Greenwood Onuf
and to the memory of our father
Bronis Onuf

Introduction

The World of Vattel

Federal Union, Modern World is the general title for a pair of books. The first, entitled *The Law of Nations in an Age of Revolutions, 1776–1814*, takes a time of extraordinary change as its frame of reference. Yet it is not an historical monograph. Its substantive focus is the law of nations, as international law was then known, but it is not a treatise on the law of nations: we pay little attention to specific doctrinal developments, or to the invocation or application of its precepts by publicists and jurists in America or Europe. This book is instead meant to be a contribution to the new history of "conceptual change," drawing selectively on the history of diplomacy, political theory, and legal doctrine to identify and relate some important themes in the emergence of the modern world.[1]

Few scholars define modernity in the same way or agree on the date

---

[1]For an introduction to this literature, see Terence Ball, *Transforming Political Discourse: Political Theory and Critical Conceptual History* (Oxford, 1988); Ball, James Farr, and Russell L. Hanson, eds., *Political Innovation and Conceptual Change* (Cambridge, 1989); and, with specific reference to the American founding, Ball and J. G. A. Pocock, eds., *Conceptual Change and the Constitution* (Lawrence, Kans., 1988). In the last volume, see esp. Farr, "Conceptual Change and Constitutional Innovation" (pp. 13–34).

of its arrival. Most would agree that the emergence of a world we customarily call modern was a drawn-out process of interactive and accelerating changes in material conditions, social arrangements and popular attitudes. Assigning dates to any such process is inevitably arbitrary. It helps, however, to think of modernity as markedly and distinctively *reflexive*: "the reflexivity of modern social life consists in the fact that social practices are constantly examined and reformed in the light of incoming information about those very practices, thus constitutively altering their character."[2] To claim a particular importance for the years of revolution between 1776 and 1814 makes sense if we see modernity as a product of reflection, choice, and design—though hardly the product any one of its makers had in mind. It makes particular sense if we see modernity as having been propelled by efforts to implement Enlightenment ideas—ideas about progress and reason, law and politics, commerce and civility—on the scale of whole societies.

We plan a second book, also an essay, to be called *Federal Union, Modern World: International Law and the Rise of Liberalism, 1815–1848*. After 1815 the reflexivity so conspicuously present in the revolutionary decades became less self-conscious and more routinized. The universalizing and rationalizing impulses characteristic of the Enlightenment became dissociated. If universal truths were still professed, they were increasingly uncontested, and soon unexamined. Rationalization centered on reform; reason disappeared into technique; law as human activity displaced law as nature's bestowal. The law of nations, long and inextricably associated with the law of nature, came to be known exclusively by Jeremy Bentham's neologism—international law—and to be understood as positive law, made by sovereign states, acting collectively through authorized means, for their progressively more complex needs.[3]

More than anyone else, Max Weber is responsible for the view that modernity, as a process of rationalization, is peculiarly reflexive. In religion rationalization took the form of a sustained, worldwide process

[2]Anthony Giddens, *The Consequences of Modernity* (Stanford, 1990), 36–45, quoting 38.

[3]Bentham introduced the term in 1789. M. W. Janis, "Jeremy Bentham and the Fashioning of 'International Law'," *American Journal of International Law*, 78 (1984), 408–10.

of "disenchantment."[4] In law Weber identified two phases of rationalization: first came the formality and universality of natural law doctrine; then followed "anti-formalistic tendencies," substantive development of the law in response to social and economic demands, and the professionalization of legal practice.[5] Doctrine lost its coherence and importance, as rationalization centered on government, through which positive law is created and applied. Weber's scheme suggests a shift in the process of rationalization from the Western world as a whole to its major societies organized as sovereign units. Neither he nor later scholars have paid much attention to the conceptual implications of this shift from whole to parts, or to the relation between the shift and the practical politics of a revolutionary age and its aftermath.

The two essays comprising *Federal Union, Modern World* deal with these matters from what is at first glance an unusual perspective. They relate the emergence of the modern world of state-societies to a remarkable experiment in reflection and constitution at the margins of the old world. *The Law of Nations in an Age of Revolutions* shows how the formation of the United States as a federal union expressed Enlightenment impulses toward doctrinal rationalization more fully than any contemporaneous developments in Europe. It then shows how efforts by the new nation's leaders to secure a tenable position for their creation in a world of change fostered a movement from natural legal doctrine to the positive law of states. In so doing the federal union expedited, perhaps decisively, the shift in the process of rationalization from the old world—"the republic of Europe"—to the liberal states of what we now know as the modern world. *International Law and the Rise of Liberalism* continues the story by showing the extent to which the United States, by its example and the actions of its government, shaped a newly constituted world in its image and to its needs.

---

[4]See for example *The Protestant Ethic and the Spirit of Capitalism*, trans. by Talcott Parsons (New York, 1930), 105, 221–22, n. 19. See also Jürgen Habermas, *The Theory of Communicative Action, Vol. 1, Reason and the Rationalization of Society*, trans. by Thomas McCarthy (Boston, 1984), 186–215, on disenchantment and "the emergence of modern structures of consciousness" (quoting section title).

[5]Max Weber, *Economy and Society*, ed. by Guenther Roth and Claus Wittich, 2 vols. (Berkeley and Los Angeles, 1978), 2:865–900; Habermas, *The Theory of Communicative Action*, 1:243–71.

I. YEARS OF REVOLUTION

We turn now to the time of the American Revolution and to the vicissitudes of the United States under the Articles of Confederation. In 1789 this league of substantially independent republics reconstituted itself as a federal union that could act together, effectively and energetically, in the larger world while preserving the autonomy of its member states. Yet that world itself was on the verge of epochal transformation. The French Revolution destroyed the diplomatic system which the united American states had sought to join.

Emmerich de Vattel called this system "a sort of republic."[6] Vattel's republic was not the cosmopolitan, universal society that Europeans had imagined over the centuries, but a progressively more stable and benign system of sovereign states. Vattel, occasional diplomat and man of letters from Neuchâtel, and his law-minded contemporaries saw the European system as one of the great achievements of modern times. The collapse of the old regime and its disruptive consequences for the European system inevitably precipitated a crisis of faith in the system's very existence, not to mention its continuing progress. For all the hopes the French Revolutionaries inspired, their triumph called into question Enlightenment values of law, commerce, and civility for an improving world.

Between 1776 and 1814 the world—the Western world as leading political and intellectual figures understood it—changed dramatically, epochally. Students of the American and French revolutions typically ignore their common context—both the diplomatic system of Europe and an intellectual legacy that reached from Classical Greece to the Enlightenment.[7] Classical republicanism, with its strong conviction that

---

[6]E. de Vattel, *The Law of Nations or the Principles of Natural Law Applied to the Conduct and to the Affairs of Nations and of Sovereigns*, Translation of the Edition of 1758 by Charles G. Fenwick (Washington, 1916), III, iii, § 47, 251.

[7]But see Albert Sorel, *Europe and the French Revolution: Political Traditions of the Old Regime* [1885], trans. and ed. by Alfred Cobban and J. W. Hunt (London, 1969); Robert R. Palmer, *The Age of the Democratic Revolution*, 2 vols. (Princeton, 1959–64).

nature has a purpose, provided the American founders with a rich lode of ideas about how to organize a republic of republics to function as a sovereign among sovereigns. Vattel's modern republicanism was more diffusely teleological. Premised on the legal autonomy and moral compunction of many sovereigns, Vattel's European republic depended on a natural tendency toward balance and moderation, and not on the design of institutions according to Classical principles. At the same time, Vattel's support of commerce and diplomacy under the rule of law served as a conceptual foundation and working template for a liberal world. As a crucial link between liberalism and republicanism in international thought, Vattel enjoyed enormous prestige and influence in Europe and America. His one great work, *The Law of Nations or the Principles of Natural Law Applied to the Conduct and the Affairs of Nations and of Sovereigns* (1758), opens a window on the emergence of the modern world.

We begin this book with a brief account of Vattel's republic of Europe and follow it with an equally brief account of the prevailing view of nature, which Vattel shared, as governed by law in accord with higher purpose. This review of Vattel's world illuminates the conceptual context for the Americans' republican revolution. Once independent, the American states found their precarious position in the European system a source of constitutional crisis. The founders responded to a dangerous and deteriorating situation by adapting Classical republican conceptions of political design to new and unusual circumstances. These innovations enabled the founders to locate republican institutions in a federal framework.

In Part One we recapitulate the long historical development of *federal* republicanism in a tradition of thought dating back to Aristotle. Few scholars question the pervasiveness of Classical ideas in Revolutionary America. Of course, even the most Classically minded American had only a fragmentary and derivative acquaintance with Aristotle, whose works provide the first systematic exposition of republican principles. Through Polybius, Cicero, and innumerable later commentators, Aristotle's ideas had entered the mainstream of Western thought. For Americans, a variety of ancient texts—many of them poorly translated, others bowdlerized, none as comprehensive as Aristotle's—nonetheless converged to illuminate the deeper logic of the Aristotelian system. To define and secure a place in Vattel's world, Americans reached back to Aristotle's world for conceptual resources. In so doing they recovered Aristotle's crucial distinction between *polis* and *politeia*, polity and government, and bridged it with the federal Constitution.

Aristotle's world was much closer to the founders' conceptual world than to ours. For this reason we need to read Aristotle's texts more closely than the founders could or ever did, in order to recover a way of thinking they took for granted. The Aristotelian sources of American federal republicanism are manifest in a number of familiar phrases, each pointing to the answer to a conceptual problem the founders encountered on the way to federalism. For the purpose of reconstructing federal republican logic, we focus on three such phrases, one from the Constitution and two from *The Federalist*: "to form a more perfect union," "the compound republic of America," and "the extent and proper structure of the union."

For Aristotle *perfecting* a polity meant securing the common good. For the American founders the common good depended on creating a more energetic federal government in the face of disintegrative tendencies and external threats. For Aristotle the purpose of politics could only be secured by *compounding* human associations, organized in ascending, more inclusive layers. For the founders a higher level of organization in a federal republic would secure the liberty of citizens and sustain republican self-government in the states. For Aristotle material conditions imposed territorial limits on political association. *Extending* the polity beyond these limits would necessarily sacrifice the common good. Aristotle's contribution was to identify the problem of a polity's size, not to consider the conditions for its resolution. For the founders a dynamic political economy solved the problem of limits, enabling the union to add new states without affecting the republic's composite character.[8]

If the central ideas of federal republicanism reach back to antiquity, they reach forward as well. Their contemporary importance is widely proclaimed but little appreciated. In the process of reconstructing those

[8]Peter S. Onuf, "Liberty, Development, and Union: Visions of the West in the 1780s," *William and Mary Quarterly*, 3rd ser., XLIII (1986), 179–213; Cathy D. Matson and Peter S. Onuf, *A Union of Interests: Political and Economic Thought in Revolutionary America* (Lawrence, Kans., 1990).

ideas, we show how they continue to matter. Federal republicanism reflects the universalizing impulse of the eighteenth century while accommodating the last two centuries of rationalization—in legal and, increasingly, in functional terms—within the United States and among the state-societies constituting the modern world. While our primary concern is the shift to a world of competing states, rationalizing societies and positive law, we comment on more recent developments in the concluding pages of chapters 3 and 4.

In Part Two we proceed from our reconstruction of federal republicanism to a consideration of circumstances driving conceptual change, beginning with the efforts of American Revolutionaries to secure their independence and promote their interests in a Vattelian world. The eighteenth-century European system, according to Vattel and other progressive internationalists, was becoming more rational, predictable, and tractable because an increasingly refined balance of power supported a developing regime of law among nations.[9] This was the world the American Revolutionaries aspired to join as sovereign equals. This was a world to engage, even to improve, through diplomacy.

American diplomats directed their energies toward negotiating treaties, not just to secure military support crucial to the success of their revolution, but also to promote trade and foster more civilized standards of conduct. These efforts were frustrated, both at home and abroad. After European powers formally acknowledged American independence in 1783, the new states found themselves at odds with each other and unable to fulfill the promise of their Revolution. Forming a federal

---

[9]From the vast literature on the balance of power, historical and analytical, the following are particularly useful: Edward Vose Gulick, *Europe's Classical Balance of Power: A Case History of the Theory and Practice of One of the Great Concepts of European Statecraft* (Ithaca, 1955); Ludwig Dehio, *The Precarious Balance: Four Centuries of theEuropean Power Balance*, trans. by Charles Fullman (New York, 1962), 91–180; Inis L. Claude, Jr., *Power and International Relations* (New York, 1962), 11–93; Martin Wight, "The Balance of Power," in *Diplomatic Investigations: Essays in the Theory of International Politics* (Cambridge, Mass., 1968), 149–75; Alfred Vagts and Detlev F. Vagts, "The Balance of Power in International Law: A History of an Idea," *American Journal of International Law*, 73 (1979), 555–80; "Special Issue on the Balance of Power," *Review of International Studies*, 15 (1989), 75–214; "*AHR Forum*" on the balance of power, *American Historical Review*, 97 (1992), 683–735.

union would strengthen their position in the global balance and their hand in negotiating favorable terms for American commerce. The United States then could contribute to the creation of a better world— a world of prosperity, at peace, under law.

How did the American federal republic, newly energized but on the periphery of the European system, respond when balance-of-power diplomacy failed to contain the expansive thrust of Revolutionary France? We turn to this question in Part Three. In the 1790s Federalist administrations forged closer ties with Britain and the emergent Republican opposition vainly sought to sustain an independent course in a deteriorating international situation. When Jeffersonian Republicans ascended to power in 1801, their hopes for France finally shattered by the rise of Bonaparte, they abandoned internationalist predilections and attempted to protect the federal union from European entanglements.

In Vattel's world, the balance of power constituted an orderly system conducive to Enlightenment ends. Yet there was no balance or stability—or any place for neutral powers, however peripheral—in the anarchic world of the Napoleonic Wars. For Jeffersonians the balance became a mockery of itself, the antithesis of federal union. Jefferson and Madison insisted on neutral rights in order to keep a still tenuous union at a safe distance from the European conflagration.

The collapse of the European diplomatic system precipitated conceptual as well as political turmoil. The balance of power had failed in its vital role of foundation for a lawful world. Some writers, including Edmund Burke and Friedrich von Gentz, idealized the old balance but doubted that it could ever be restored. Others questioned the possibility of sustaining, much less developing, a law of nations. More optimistically, writers such as Henry Brougham projected a revived balance to support the system of law and diplomacy he called, echoing Vattel, "the great European Republic."[10] For most Britons the overriding imperative

---

[10]Edmund Burke, "Letters on a Regicide Peace" [1795–96], in Paul Langford, ed., *The Writings and Speeches of Edmund Burke*, 9 vols. to date (Oxford, 1981–), vol. IX (ed. R. B. McDowell): 44–119, 187–386; [Friedrich von Gentz], *A Vindication of Europe and Great Britain from Misrepresentation and Aspersion. Extracted and Translated from Mr. Gentz's Answer to Mr. Hauterive* (London, 1803); Henry Brougham, *An Inquiry into the Colonial Policy of the European Powers*, 2 vols. (Edinburgh, 1803), 2: 207–62; quotation at 2: 2.

was self-preservation: the defeat of France justified abandoning all other legal restraints.

American diplomats could not wait for the end of an apparently endless war to secure the rights of a nonbelligerent state under the law of nations. A stable system of law and diplomacy, responsive to the rights of all sovereigns, demanded a more reliable constitution than the balance could ever supply. For Secretary of State James Madison the challenge was to provide an alternative to the balance of power. In Madison's unjustly neglected legal brief, *An Examination of the British Doctrine, Which Subjects to Capture a Neutral Trade, Not Open in Time of Peace* (1806), what we now know as "the sources of international law" perform the historic constitutive function of the balance.[11] This was the conception of the world that redeemed Vattel's Enlightenment optimism and relocated the progress of civilization in the quotidian world of commerce and diplomacy.

Ironically, the success of the founders in constructing a dynamic federal system coincided with the destruction of the Vattelian world. Foreign policy responses to dramatically changing circumstances solidified the conceptual development of federal republicanism. As the European system collapsed, union came to be an end in itself and no longer a means for the progress of civilization on a global scale. Jeffersonian conceptions of union and antipathy to the balance of power redefined America's relation to the world of states and, of more lasting importance, promoted a distinctively modern conception of that world as a legal order reflexively produced and maintained by its indubitably sovereign members.

[11]Gaillard Hunt, ed., *The Writings of James Madison*, 9 vols. (New York, 1900–10), 7:204–345. On sources in international legal doctrine, see Nicholas Greenwood Onuf, "Global Law-Making and Legal Thought," in N. Onuf, ed., *Law-Making in the Global Community* (Durham, N.C., 1982), 14–31.

II. THE EUROPEAN REPUBLIC

In the wake of the French Revolutionary wars, polemicists argued about whether or not the balance of power had in fact developed progressively over the course of the eighteenth century. Supporters of the embattled British government argued that the French Revolutionaries had destroyed European civilization by destroying the balance. In response, French writers—and their British sympathizers—insisted that the balance was a sham, that it had been verging toward collapse *before* the French Revolution and that, in any case, it did not and could not support a working law of nations. In America, Jeffersonian Republicans also inveighed against the balance of power, "that European Hydra," as a corrupt system of entangling alliances that had kept Europe in a perpetual state of war.[12]

Thirty years before, American Revolutionaries had looked at the balance of power with less jaundiced eyes. Indeed the Americans knew their success depended on their ability to manipulate a progressively developing balance. The idea that the balance of power enabled Europe to function as a single great republic came into vogue in the 1740s and 1750s.[13] Europe had long been thought of as a whole, thanks to Classical cosmopolitanism and its absorption by the medieval Church. With the emergence of many sovereigns and the correlative decline of the Church as a political force and of Christendom as a political idea, writers such as Montesquieu, Voltaire, Fénelon, Callières, Rousseau, Hume, Burke, and Gibbon all treated Europe as united by Enlightenment values.[14] Not least of these values was an appreciation of balance and moderation, even in matters of power. But among all such endorsements of the idea of

[12]Orasmus Cook Merrill, *The Happiness of America. An Oration Delivered at Shaftsbury, on the Fourth of July, 1804* (Bennington, Vt., 1804), 9. See generally the discussion in chapters 5 and 6.

[13]F. H. Hinsley, *Power and the Pursuit of Peace: Theory and Practice in the History of Relations between States* (Cambridge, 1963), 161–64.

[14]For relevant quotations, see ibid.; Terry Nardin, *Law, Morality and the Relations of States* (Princeton, 1983), 62–63.

a European republic, only Vattel's systematically linked the traditions
of European thought to the pressing circumstances of European political practice—a context familiar to all well-educated Europeans as the
law of nature applied to nations.[15]

Vattel prefaced his celebrated description of Europe as "a sort of
republic" by noting that the Continent "is no longer, as in former times,
a confused heap of detached parts." He attributed this development to
the "constant attention of sovereigns to all that goes on, the custom of
resident ministers, the continual negotiations that take place"—a complex of activities which binds European nations together and "gives rise
to the well-known principle of the balance of power, by which is meant
an arrangement of affairs so that no State will be in a position to have
absolute mastery and dominate over the others."[16]

Written in French, the language of diplomacy, instead of the Latin
customary for learned discourse, Vattel's *Law of Nations* was a rapid and
lasting success.[17] Translated immediately into English, it was unrivaled
among such treatises in its influence on the American founders.[18] Vattel
brought to the task of writing his treatise some experience in diplomacy,

[15]Altogether inappropriately, Hinsley detached the "specialised field of writings
on international law" from what he took to be a more general discussion of European
affairs. *Power and the Pursuit of Peace*, 164. No European of the time considered these
writings "specialised."

At least in English, doctrinal history of the law of nations is sadly neglected.
Arthur Nussbaum's general study, *A Concise History of the Law of Nations*, rev. ed. (New
York, 1954), is much too concise, especially on the Enlightenment era (pp. 150–64).
More useful are Peter Pavel Remec, *The Position of the Individual in International Law
according to Grotius and Vattel* (The Hague, 1960), 127–200; Francis Stephen Ruddy,
International Law in the Enlightenment: The Background of Emmerich de Vattel's Le Droit
des Gens (Dobbs Ferry, N.Y., 1975). None of these studies is sufficiently situated in the
intellectual and cultural history of the time.

[16]Vattel, *The Law of Nations*, III, iii, § 47, 251.

[17]Albert de Lapradelle, "Introduction," in Vattel, *The Law of Nations*, xxvii–
xxxiii; Ruddy, *International Law in the Enlightenment*, 281–310.

[18]Charles G. Fenwick, "The Authority of Vattel," *American Political Science Review*,
7 (1913), 370–424; Daniel George Lang, *Foreign Policy in the Early Republic: The Law of
Nations and the Balance of Power* (Baton Rouge, 1985). Vattel's influence on contemporary international thought has been negligible. See, however, Peter F. Butler's
suggestive essay, "Legitimacy in a States System: Vattel's *Law of Nations*," in Michael
Donelan, ed., *The Reason of States: A Study in International Political Theory* (London,

an agreeable style and an interest in philosophy. His plan had been to digest an eagerly awaited work by Christian Wolff, a "great philosopher," which promised to extend Wolff's voluminous writings on natural law to the law of nations.[19] When Wolff's treatise appeared in 1748, Vattel found it "a very dry work," written as an integral part of Wolff's system and "after the method and systematic form of treatises on geometry." Although Vattel liberally borrowed from Wolff's treatise to execute his own more manageable work, he could not accept Wolff's foundation for the body of rules that writers from Grotius on had called "voluntary." "Mr. Wolff deduces" the voluntary law of nations "from the idea of a sort of great republic (*Civitas Maxima*) set up by nature herself, of which all the Nations of the world are members." Rejecting one sort of republic, a "fiction" that "does not satisfy me," Vattel went on to propose another—a sort of republic from which law and order are implicitly deduced. Vattel offered an empirical description of his republic. It is from the dealings of sovereigns and their agents that rules of conduct and the balance of power arise. Wolff offered nothing comparable. Instead his passive voice insinuates that any reasonable person would know of the great republic: "*Civitas, in quam Gentes coivisse intelliguntur, & cujus ipsae sunt membra, seu cives, vocatur* Civitas maxima"—"the republic into which nations are understood to have combined, and of which they are members or citizens, is called *the great republic*."[20] This great republic is democratic in form, because its members are nations, "free and equal to each other."[21] Since nations cannot actually convene,

1978), 45–63; Andrew Linklater, *Men and Citizens in the Theory of International Relations* (New York, 1982), 80–96.

[19]Vattel, *The Law of Nations*, Preface, 6a. All quotations in this paragraph are from the Preface, 6a–9a.

[20]Christian Wolff, *Jus gentium methodo scientifica pertractatum*, Vol. One, *The Photographic Reproduction of the Edition of 1764* and Vol. Two, *The Translation* by Joseph H. Drake (Oxford, 1934), § 10, 4 (Latin), 13 (trans.). The translation's rendition of "*civitas maxima*" as "supreme state" is wildly inappropriate. Vattel's "*la grande République*," or in English "the great republic," is the best choice among the many translations to have appeared over the years. Scholars have frequently noted but never considered Vattel's repudiation of the *civitas maxima* in any detail.

[21]*Jus gentium*, Vol. Two, § 19, 16.

they require a "*rector*" to act on their behalf.[22] By way of explanation, Wolff claimed that "all moral persons," including the great republic, "have something fictitious in them." The rector is presumably a natural person and must either be identifiable as such or, as Wolff appears to have conceded, wholly fictitious—in Wolff's words, "*Rector . . . fictus civitatis maximae.*"[23]

Wolff's conception of a great republic may owe its inspiration to Stoic cosmopolitanism. A celebrated passage from Marcus Aurelius's *Meditations*, surely known to Wolff, speaks of the "highest city"—in Latin, "*civitatis supernae*"—"whereof all other cities are like households."[24] Another passage states that "the Universe is a kind of Commonwealth [again, *civitatis*]." From it comes "our mind itself, our reason and our sense of law."[25] A careful examination of Wolff's characterization of the great republic suggests that it is more than a source—or invention—of reason. It is evidently mundane, specifically and not just metaphorically social, and possessed of its own moral personality. Wolff's *civitas* is not the highest conceivable, not the "heavenly city," but the largest that is physically possible, encompassing all other human undertakings and linking them with what reason tells us must be higher.

Wolff's great republic has a virtual reality.[26] Unobservable itself, it functions with observable effects, which Wolff identified as the voluntary law of nations. Although "equivalent to the civil law," voluntary

---

[22]*Jus gentium, Vol. One,* § 21, 7. The *Oxford Latin Dictionary* (Oxford, 1968), 1586, gives five meanings for "*rector*": helmsman, guide, someone in charge of other people or a sphere of activity, ruler or governor, preceptor or tutor.

[23]*Jus Gentium, Vol. One* and *Vol. Two,* § 21 Commentary, 7 (Latin), 17 (trans.).

[24]Written in Greek, *The Meditations* was first printed in 1558 in Latin translation. *The Meditations of the Emperor Marcus Antoninus,* ed. with Translation and Commentary by A. S. L. Farquharson, Vol. I, Text and Trans. (Oxford, 1944), III, § 11, 45–47; *Marci Antonini imperatoris eorum quae ad seipsum libri XII* [ed. by Richard Ibbetson] (Glasgow, 1744), 51.

[25]Ibid., IV, § 4, 55 (English trans.), 52 (Latin trans.).

[26]And its rector represents nations virtually. On "virtual representation" as a matter much debated in late 18th century England and America, see Gordon S. Wood, *The Creation of the American Republic, 1776–1787* (Chapel Hill, 1969), 173–81; John Philip Reid, *The Concept of Representation in the Age of the American Revolution* (Chicago, 1989), 52–62.

law is not voluntary in the usual sense.[27] Instead this law is derived from "the law of nature applied to nations," which Wolff called "the necessary law of Nations."[28] Nature is thus responsible for "a society among all nations," just as it is for a society "among individuals."[29] The purpose of this "natural society" of nations is "mutual assistance" for "the promotion of the common good by its combined powers."[30] If this is so, then the great republic is rendered superfluous, except insofar as it is a device for relaxing obligations derived from natural society which nations may find unduly restrictive.

Vattel expressly accepted Wolff's conception of natural society.[31] He also concluded that "the changes which must be made in the strictness of the natural law when applied to the affairs of Nations may be deduced from the natural liberty of Nations, from considerations of their common welfare, from the nature of their mutual intercourse," that is, from natural society itself.[32] In Vattel's reasoning, natural society is not the fiction that Wolff's great republic is, because it is manifest in the content of the relations of European nations. Those relations reflect even as they relax the requirements of natural law; they constitute Europe as a republic even as they make the great republic superfluous.

Not only is the great republic unneeded in Vattel's system, its presence would create a problem.

---

[27]Wolff, *Jus gentium, Vol. Two*, 22, 18. It is not voluntary in the sense of arising from "the deeds and customs and decisions of the more civilized nations." Ibid., § 22 Commentary.

[28]Ibid., § 6, 10.

[29]Ibid., § 7, 11.

[30]Ibid., § 8, 11.

[31]Vattel argued in *The Law of Nations*:

> We deduce a natural society existing among all men. The general law of this society is that each member should assist the others in all their needs, as far as he can do so without neglecting his duties to himself— a law which all men must obey if they are to live conformably with their nature and to the designs of their common Creator; a law which our own welfare, our happiness, and our best interests should render sacred to each one of us.

Vattel, *The Law of Nations*, Introduction, § 10, 5. On the parallel between Wolff and Vattel with respect to natural society's properties, see Ruddy, *International Law in the Enlightenment*, 100–10.

[32]Ibid., Preface, 10a.

> It is essential to every civil society (*Civitas*) that each member should
> yield certain of his rights to the general body, and that there should be
> some authority capable of giving commands, prescribing laws, and
> compelling those who refuse to obey. Such an idea is not to be thought
> of as between nations. Each independent State claims to be, and actually
> is, independent of all others.[33]

While individuals "could scarcely get on without the assistance of civil
society and its laws," this is not so for nations, precisely because they are
organized as civil societies.[34] Instead, "independence is necessary to a
State, if it is properly to fulfill its duties toward itself and its citizens to
govern itself in the manner best suited to it. Hence, I repeat, it is enough
that Nations conform to the demands made upon them by that natural
and world-wide society established among all men."[35]

Vattel accepted the great bulk of Wolff's substantive formulations of
nations' obligations, whatever "their primary sources," because they
seemed to be reasonable applications of natural law principles to the
situations of nations.[36] Both Wolff and Vattel affirmed the moral and
legal equality of nations no less than of people, whether small or large.[37]
Both declared that the first duty of nations is self-preservation.[38] Both
asserted the right of nations to be free from interference in their affairs.[39]
Yet Vattel insisted on the independence of nations and coupled independence to sovereignty: "the Law of Nations is the law of sovereigns;
free and independent States are moral persons."[40] Wolff did not. For

[33]Ibid., Preface, 9a.

[34]Ibid., Preface, 9a.

[35]Ibid., Preface, 10a.

[36]Ibid., Preface, 12a.

[37]"Just as the tallest man is no more a man than a dwarf, so also a nation, however
small, is no less a nation than the greatest nation." Wolff, *Jus gentium, Vol. Two*, § 16
commentary, 15. "A dwarf is as much a man as a giant is; a small republic is no less a
sovereign State than the most powerful Kingdom." Vattel, *The Law of Nations*, § 18, 7.

[38]Wolff, *Jus gentium, Vol. Two*, § 27–34, 20–24; Vattel, *The Law of Nations*, I, ii, §§
13–19, 13–14.

[39]"A perfect right belongs to every nation not to allow any other nation to
interfere in any way in its government." Wolff, *Jus gentium, Vol. Two*, § 269, 137. "It
clearly follows from the liberty and independence of Nations that each has to govern
itself as it thinks proper, and that no one of them has the least right to interfere in the
government of another." Vattel, *The Law of Nations*, II, iv, § 54, 131.

[40]*The Law of Nations*, I, i, § 12, 12; the first phrase is also a sentence in the Preface,
12a.

him, sovereignty is a property of civil society, internally exercised by nations and, if only virtually, by the great republic.[41] Independence goes unmentioned, except as a motivation for nations to participate in the balance of power.[42]

Wolff and Vattel were republicans. Yet their republics could never be confused. Wolff saw the European world in terms descending from Aristotle and informed by Roman law and medieval experience, as if the world itself were a European legacy, virtually complete, needing only to be formalized. Wolff understood his life's work to advance, even complete, this project. It is hardly an exaggeration to say that Wolff's treatise on the law of nations *was* the great republic, and he its rector: "he can be considered rector . . . who, following the leadership of nature, defines by the right use of reason what nations ought to consider as law among themselves, although it does not conform in all respects to the natural law of nations, nor altogether differ from it."[43]

Vattel saw the European world, not as a legacy to be rationalized, but as a collection of independent, and independent-minded, nations nevertheless bound together by a system of rules both reflecting and relaxing the requirements of natural law. This law of nations acknowledges their independence but does not absolve them of the duty of mutual assistance that nature imposes on individuals. "Each State owes to every other State all that it owes to itself, as far as the other is in actual

[41]*Jus gentium, Vol. Two*, § 102, 60. "Some sovereignty [*imperium*] over individual nations belongs to nations as a whole." *Jus gentium, Vol. One* and *Vol. Two*, § 15, 7 (Latin), 15 (trans.) Wolff explained that "this sovereignty has a certain resemblance to civil sovereignty," and must accord with the law of nations. Ibid., § 15 Commentary.

[42]"Equilibrium among nations is especially conducive to their liberty and disturbance of the equilibrium is very dangerous to liberty. Nor is there any reason why European nations should struggle so fiercely for the preservation of equilibrium, save of course that the liberty of those which are less powerful may not be endangered." *Jus gentium, Vol. Two*, §§ 642–44, 646–51, 330–36, quoting § 644 Commentary, 331. Far from seeing equilibrium as the source of stability in European politics, Wolff implied that its preservation might deprive nations of rights they are entitled to exercise, by force, "even if the equilibrium among nations is destroyed." § 647, 332. Not surprisingly, Wolff discussed equilibrium in the context of just war. Vattel's remarks on the balance of power and the republic of Europe occur anomalously in the same context.

[43]Ibid., § 21, 7 (Latin), 17 (trans.); "*Rector civitatis maximae*" rendered "ruler of the supreme state" in the translation.

need of its help and such help can be given without neglecting its duties towards itself."[44] Civil society keeps the balance between duties to self and others. In the absence of the civil society above nations postulated by Wolff, duties to self will tend to prevail over duties to others, individual rights over the public good. Beyond appeals to conscience, to an internalized legacy of republican values, Vattel's only hope for keeping the self-interest of nations in check is the balance of power. Instead of Wolff's elusive rector, the republic rests on fleeting moments of equilibrium.

As republicans, Wolff and Vattel both dwelt on the problem of the public good and the requirements of citizenship, or its equivalent among nations. Wolff did so with majestic indifference to the world around him—a world of sovereigns, as Vattel noted, and of self-interest.[45] Wolff was, after all, a philosopher, a systematizer, and his republic, a republic of letters. Vattel showed considerably greater sensitivity to a rapidly changing world, at commensurately greater cost to republican principles. Vattel was not just the more pragmatic of the two, a popularizer, a man of affairs: he was a man of liberal tendencies who saw no reason why liberalism and republicanism could not be reconciled in law and statecraft.

Liberal internationalism before the French Revolution was grounded in a widespread faith in the perfectibility of the balance of power. The rise of the new great powers—first Prussia, and then Russia—and their relatively equal coercive capabilities encouraged a more calculating and rational diplomatic regime. As F. H. Hinsley has written, "the great characteristic of the international politics of the *ancien régime*, especially after 1750, was the strong contrast between the realistic and limited nature of the objectives of foreign policy and the acute avidity with which these objectives were pursued."[46] Frenetic diplomatic activity to gain or neutralize marginal advantages fostered the idea of Europe as a

---

[44] *The Law of Nations*, II, i, § 3, 114. See also Linklater, *Men and Citizens in the Theory of International Relations*, 86–89.

[45] As we saw, even Wolff was bound to acknowledge the balance of power. "Certainly among us Europeans you may always hear a discussion of equilibrium, especially when there is talk of allies for war and a treaty of peace." *Jus gentium, Vol. Two*, § 643 Commentary, 330.

[46] *Power and the Pursuit of Peace*, 177.

complex system of forces subject to rational manipulation. War itself was subject to the rationalizing impulse, as sovereigns and their agents pursued increasingly circumspect policies and legal writers argued against belligerent excesses and for the rights both of noncombatants and neutral powers.

For the most enthusiastic exponents of the balance of power, diplomacy conducted in accordance with its principles promised to rationalize, even domesticate power. But its greatest contribution to the progress of European civilization was to promote peaceful, mutually beneficial exchanges across national boundaries. The enlightened self-interest of sovereigns converged with their subjects' to serve the common good of all humanity. "Since one country is better adapted for growing one product than another," Vattel wrote, "if trade and barter take place between them, each Nation will be assured of satisfying its wants and will use its land and direct its industries to the best advantage, so that mankind as a whole will gain thereby."[47] The liberal equation of interest with prosperity, of rationality with a preference for maximal over relative gains, resolved all conflicts in an ultimate harmony of interests. Enlightened statecraft worked toward this resolution by dismantling artificial impediments to trade.

As the collapse of the old regime soon demonstrated, liberal complacency about the progress of European civilization rested on fragile foundations. Even before the French Revolution, skeptics wondered whether alliances more often dragged states into war than kept them safe and peaceful. The first partition of Poland in 1772 provided the most serious challenge to the assumption that the balance guaranteed the independence of small, weak states. The discrepancy between promise and performance raised questions about the putative enlightenment of Europe's rulers and the state system's "natural" tendency toward equilibrium.

Frustrated by deeply entrenched mercantilist policies at home and abroad, radical economists doubted that states' leaders would ever see the light. By exacerbating conflicts among hostile regimes, balance-of-

---

[47]Vattel, *The Law of Nations*, II, ii, § 21, 121. On the liberalizing effects of expanding trade, see Albert O. Hirschman, *The Passions and the Interests: Political Arguments for Capitalism before Its Triumph* (Princeton, 1977).

power diplomacy retarded liberal reform efforts. The ultimate challenge to liberal internationalism came with the destruction of the European system itself in the French revolutionary wars. By then the idea that the balance of power functioned as the constitution for the European republic, a foundation of law and order and a source of peace and prosperity, seemed fanciful, if not absurd.

Yet in 1776, American Revolutionaries could look hopefully across the Atlantic. Whether or not the operation of the balance of power was inherently progressive, American independence was made possible by the clash of European powers, and the Revolutionaries understood that success depended on manipulating the balance effectively.[48] As Congress's Plan of Treaties of July 18, 1776, announced to the world, the American leadership had every intention of exploiting diplomatic opportunities for progressive purposes.[49] Here was a paradigmatic case for the enlightened statecraft promised by liberal internationalists. By challenging Britain's mercantilist regime, the Americans appeared not only to serve their own interests, but also those of prospective trading partners and of the trading world generally. Because the Revolution resolved the historic contradiction between arbitrary government and the need for rational diplomacy, American leaders were able to transcend the narrow and selfish policies of their European counterparts.

Optimistic Revolutionaries believed in the progressive possibilities of the balance of power. Embracing Vattelian logic, they relied on treaties with foreign powers to secure American independence. They also depended on statecraft to perpetuate their league of free states. Fearful of concentrated power and convinced that their republican state governments were naturally peaceful, Revolutionary leaders hoped that a treaty of confederation would guarantee union. Events proved this a vain hope. During a period of diplomatic and constitutional crisis, reformers sought to construct a new, more perfect political system. Much more than a treaty of alliance, the federal Constitution founded a state better able to cope with the other states of Vattel's world without sacrificing the republican heritage of the Revolution.

[48]James Hutson, *John Adams and the Diplomacy of the American Revolution* (Lexington, Ky., 1980); Lang, *Foreign Policy of the Early Republic.*

[49]The so-called Model Treaty is discussed in chapter 4 below.

III. NATURE'S DESIGN

The eighteenth century was a time of transition, with Classical republicanism on the wane and liberalism on the rise. Recent scholarship on the American founding identifies the same discordant tendencies we find in Wolff and Vattel, and sets them in opposition.[50] Drafting the Constitution clarified these tendencies and occasioned a "great national discussion," a great debate pitting republicans against liberals.[51] Scholars today see this debate as ideologically driven, and they tend to pick sides according to their own ideological predilections. Neo-liberal scholars argue that liberal concerns for individual autonomy and rights dominated the founding period; their neo-republican opponents find republican convictions about virtue and citizenship to have been the driving force.

The current debate has no clear winner. Even its structure has broken down, as participants and positions proliferate. This impasse suggests two possibilities about the founders' debate. It is possible that the debate was inconclusive and that current scholarship fairly reflects this discursive confusion. It is also possible that today's scholars misconstrue the terms of the earlier debate because of unexamined propensities in their own discourse.

There is little reason to think that ideology provided the founders with specific guidance in devising new political arrangements. Instead they took advantage of a permissive environment of offsetting ideologies to adopt extraordinary institutional innovations and invent a new political language to describe them.[52] If scholars in our own time improperly construe the terms of the earlier debate, then it may not have been an

[50]See Peter S. Onuf, "Reflections on the Founding: Constitutional Historiography in Bicentennial Perspective," *William and Mary Quarterly*, 3rd ser., XLVI (1989), 344–53, for a review. On republicanism as an historiographical paradigm, see Daniel T. Rodgers, "Republicanism: the Career of a Concept," *Journal of American History*, 79 (1992), 11–38.

[51]Isaac Kramnick, "The 'Great National Discussion': The Discourse of Politics in 1787," *William and Mary Quarterly*, 3rd ser., XLV (1988), 3–32.

[52]Cf. Onuf, "Reflections on the Founding," 350–56.

ideological debate at all. Discussion of institutional reforms would have been just that: discussion, presupposing what we might today call a broad ideological consensus. To the extent that scholars have fashioned the discussion of specific proposals into a debate about large ideological choices, they read their own ideological preferences back into history.

Contemporary scholarly discourse is pervasively liberal. At minimum, liberalism involves a judgment about human nature. Individuals act with calculating self-interest in an environment of equally self-interested calculators. Once individuals organize into groups for self-interested reasons, groups act no differently from individuals. Ontological support for this conclusion comes from positivism, which dates from the nineteenth century. Positivism is commonly identified with its methodological implications, because it radically individuates whatever the observer is able to separate systematically from a larger environment. Individuals stand apart, as do their traits and artifacts, both physical and social.

Liberal ideology presents itself first in terms of individual character and then in the minimal institutional terms of individual rights. It little matters whether such rights are found in nature, as Locke insisted, or are social artifacts, as positivists presume. Ironically neo-republican scholars tend to present republican ideology the same way. In their liberal-minded rendition, virtue comes first, as a matter of character, and civic duty follows as its institutional realization—a sequence suggesting that eighteenth-century republicanism was somehow a *response* to liberalism. This sequence renders the eighteenth century exactly backwards, however much it may describe the ideological odyssey of contemporary neo-republican scholars. Two centuries ago, republicanism was an ample tradition of political discourse and practice, liberalism the newcomer.

Especially when joined with positivism, liberalism offers a way of looking at the world that we mistakenly impute to the founders. Their attraction to Enlightenment values—achievement over ascription, the rule of reason, civility nurtured by prosperity—*seems* liberal in retrospect because liberalism is the Enlightenment's chief inheritor. Yet these values comport just as well with a republican disposition. Liberalism and republicanism did not represent radical alternatives to the eighteenth-century mind. If self-interest and civic virtue were seen as divergent

tendencies in human conduct, the universal human faculty of reason
more than compensated for their dissonance. With reason came an
understanding of nature's laws and the capacity to organize human affairs
accordingly. Faith in natural law, the universe as a lawful order, gave
Wolff and Vattel a common point of departure. The premises of natural
law gave their contemporaries, even those of lesser faith, a common
frame of reference.

The natural law tradition is central to the Western experience. The
idea that humanity should look to the natural order for moral guidance
was deeply embedded in Greek thought. Aristotle expressly invoked
natural law, the Stoics made it central to their cosmopolitan philosophy,
and Cicero lent it his elegant voice. Roman jurisprudence honored it.
Aquinas made naturalism integral to Scholastic theology; Grotius,
Pufendorf and Leibniz expounded natural law at length; Hobbes, Locke
and Kant worked within its terms. All these writers construed natural
law as a rational and universal system of principles, which gradually came
to be seen, from the point of view of the individual, as conferring rights
unaffected by political arrangements.[53]

Neither liberalism nor republicanism actually depends on natural
law. Liberals could invoke natural principles that make individual
human beings free and equal in their rights but they could also soon find
support for their position in positivism's radical individualism. Those
with an interest in the distribution of virtue and its institutional realization could look, with Machiavelli, to the laws of history instead of
nature. Nevertheless, the natural law tradition granted liberals and
republicans alike an ontological basis for understanding the world and
their place in it. Naturalism operates on a plane between God and
government, accessible through reason and ideally suited for reflecting

[53]On the difference between claiming to know what is (naturally) right and
claiming to have a (natural) right, see Friedrich V. Kratochwil, *Rules, Norms, and
Decisions: On the Conditions of Practical and Legal Reasoning in International Relations and
Domestic Affairs* (Cambridge, 1989), 162–66. Natural rights thinking emerged in the
fourteenth century and fully developed in the seventeenth. Richard Tuck, *Natural
Rights Theories: Their Origin and Development* (Cambridge, 1980). Outside of the natural
law tradition, rights long figured prominently in English justice, and English writers
were especially prominent in seventeenth century developments.

on the purpose of human existence, positing desirable social arrangements and evaluating general patterns of conduct.

On this plane the *purpose* of human existence must be considered
independently of the question, are human beings sociable in a state of
nature? Or are they driven into society by the adverse consequences of
their unsocial natures? Hobbes most famously took the latter position,
variations of which Locke, Montesquieu and Rousseau also affirmed.[54]
The former position was a Classical commonplace, reaffirmed by Grotius
and then by Pufendorf, countering Hobbes, and then by Vattel, countering Rousseau.[55] Not to be confused with individuals' motivations and
their social consequences, purpose refers to the design of the cosmos
(which subordinates society to nature). Sociable or not, human beings
and their artifacts are necessarily implicated in a design vastly greater
than themselves.[56]

---

[54]This is, or leads to, a liberal conception of human nature, which supposes that
instrumental rationality motivates human behavior. According to Leo Strauss and his
followers, it resulted in the "momentous change" from Classical naturalism to modern
natural rights thinking. In this change, Locke is the major figure. Leo Strauss, *Natural
Right and History* (Chicago, 1953), 165–294, quoting 166, and Thomas L. Pangle, "The
Philosophic Understanding of Human Nature Informing the Constitution," in Allan
Bloom, ed., *Confronting the Constitution: The Challenge to Locke, Montesquieu, Jefferson,
and the Federalists from Utilitarianism, Historicism, Marxism, Freudianism, Pragmatism,
Existentialism* (Washington, 1990), 9–76. Strauss clearly implied that the liberal conception of human nature cannot be reconciled with a view of nature as ordered by
purpose. *Natural Right and History*, 166. His famous demonstration that, despite
appearances, Locke divorced his naturalism from scriptural authority hardly makes his
case. Nor does Locke's testimony that "no rule of the law of nature is 'imprinted on the
mind as a duty,'" for reasons noted forthwith. Quoting ibid., 226; source of quotation
from Locke not given.

[55]Hugo Grotius, *De jure belli ac pacis libri tres, Vol. Two, The Translation* by Francis
W. Kelsey (Oxford, 1925), Prolegomena, § 6, 11: "but among the traits characteristic
of man is an impelling desire for society, that is, for the social life . . .; this social trend
the Stoics called 'sociableness'." Samuel Pufendorf, *De jure naturae et gentium libri octo,
Vol. Two, The Translation* by C. H. and W. A. Oldfather (Oxford, 1934), I, iii, § 16,
210–13; Emmerich de Vattel, "Réflexions sur le discours de M. Rousseau touchant
l'origine de l'inégalité parmi les hommes," *Mélange de littérature, de morale et de politique*
(Neufchâtel, 1760), quoted in Ruddy, *International Law in the Enlightenment*, 83.

[56]On the perception of nature's harmony and the inference of design, see
Clarence J. Glacken's monumental study, *Traces on the Rhodian Shore: Nature and
Culture in Western Thought from Ancient Times to the End of the Eighteenth Century*

This is a teleological vision, one that insists on the organic unity of nature—and of society, however formed, by its nature. If Hobbes's state of nature is difficult to reconcile with such a vision, we should note, with Pufendorf, "the ambiguity of the word nature."[57] Hobbes's liberal successors also exploited this ambiguity, though less obviously, for their more benign conceptions of the state of nature. Nature has a design which human beings acknowledge, whether by living in natural society or leaving nature for society.

The founders embraced the teleological conception of nature.[58] Whatever their differences, they commonly acknowledged that the nature of society demands consideration of the "public good," a term fraught with the sense of larger purpose in human existence.[59] If individuals have rights as a matter of human nature, they have duties as members of society; otherwise, the public good is thwarted, along with nature's design. Nature as a whole, in its larger design, accounts for human nature and society—for humanity's "asocial sociability," as Kant wrote 1784. This is "the propensity of men to enter into a society, which propensity is, however, linked to a constant mutual resistance"—includ-

---

(Berkeley and Los Angeles, 1967). Typical of the eighteenth century is Buffon, who held that nature, in Glacken's paraphrasing, 519, is

> a system of laws established by the creator for the existence of things and the succession of beings. It is not a thing, for then it would be everything; neither is it a being, for then it would be God. . . . It is at the same time cause and effect, means and substance, design and the finished work. Unlike human art whose productions are composed of dead things, nature herself is a perpetually living worker unceasingly active, who knows how to use everything, who works always on the same foundations, whose store is inexhaustible. Time space, matter, are the means, the universe its object, the movement of life its end.

[57]Pufendorf, *De jure naturae et gentium,* II, iii, § 16, 210. Pufendorf continued: "that no one should be led to make the same mistake it should, first of all, be observed, that self-love and a sociable attitude should by no means be opposed to each other." Less charitably, we may see Hobbes's ambiguity as a deception required by just such an opposition. Hobbes's alternative would have been to abandon the idea of a lawful nature accessible to reason—something he was not prepared to do.

[58]Consider, for example, Jefferson's well-known criticism of Buffon "for assuming," in Glacken's words, "that nature did not operate uniformly," after Buffon had alleged the natural inferiority of life in the new world. Such an assumption is simply incompatible with Buffon's teleology, as just noted. Ibid., 681–85, quoting 685. See also Daniel J. Boorstin, *The Lost World of Thomas Jefferson* (Boston, 1960), 100–04.

[59]Cf. Wood, *The Creation of the American Republic,* 53–65.

ing claims of right—"which threatens to dissolve this society."[60] The more liberal of the founders might have changed Kant's formulation from "*a*social sociability" to "social *a*sociability." Given the organic unity of nature, which comes first mattered little.

A concern for the public good, for society's place in nature's design, leads back to Aristotle. The more liberally inclined thinkers of the founding period were surely skeptical of claims, like Aristotle's, that society precedes the individual and, by implication, individual rights. Yet they had no such qualms about the claim, also Aristotle's, that human beings associate in predictable ways for a variety of purposes.[61] If human association did not imperil individual rights, there would be little reason to derive those rights from nature directly. A multiplicity of associations, many working at cross purposes, forms society. How then to reconcile purposes? By nature's design, through political association, with its purpose of securing the public good.

Nowhere in these pages do we wish to suggest that the founders knew the fine points of Aristotle or the long and often complicated history of their transmission. They did not. Nevertheless, reading as widely as they did, they could hardly have avoided Aristotle's presence.[62]

[60]Immanuel Kant, "Idea for a Universal History with Cosmopolitan Intent," in *The Philosophy of Kant: Immanuel Kant's Moral and Political Writings*, ed., with an Introduction, by Carl J. Friedrich (New York, 1949), 120. Kant went on:

> This propensity apparently is innate in man. Man has an inclination to *associate* himself, because in such a state he feels more like a man capable of developing his natural faculties. Man also has a marked propensity to *isolate* himself, because he finds in himself the asocial quality to want to arrange everything according to his own ideas. . . . Without these essentially unlovely ideas of asociability, from which springs the resistance which everyone must encounter in his egoistic pretensions, all talents would have remained hidden germs. . . . The natural impulses, the sources of asociability from which so many evils spring, but which at the same time drive man to a new exertion of his powers and thus to a development of his natural faculties, suggest an arrangement of a wise creator.

(120–21, emphasis in text.)

[61]"We thus see that the polis exists by nature and that it is prior to the individual. . . . The man who is isolated . . . is no part of the polis, and must therefore be a beast or a god." *The Politics of Aristotle*, trans. by Ernest Baker (New York, 1962), I, ii, § 14 (*1253a*), 6. The next chapter deals with purposive association in Aristotle's work.

[62]Consider Thomas Pangle's polemic against neo-republican "fashion," in the course of which he observed that the founders made far fewer references to Aristotle's

The founders need not have been intimately familiar with Aristotle's work to have absorbed its sense.

With Aristotle, the founders uniformly believed that people associate for many purposes relating to their own good. That people do so necessitates political association for higher purpose, which is the public good. With higher purpose in mind, the founders could ask, what arrangements bring out the good in these people and bring good to them? Rights aside, the individual can never be understood apart from society. Human association enables individuals and institutions to fulfill the purpose of making each other, and society, what they finally are. This way of thinking is increasingly alien and unfamiliar in the modern world. Most scholars in our time do not think teleologically about politics: they do not know how.

This book chronicles the eclipse of the Aristotelian conception of political life, a conceptual change inextricably related to modernity's arrival. Part I shows how Aristotle's vision of politics gave the American founding its form and rationale. Part II locates the founding in a Vattelian world. That world is recognizably modern—a world of states. At the same time it is a world unlike our own—a world in which the federal union, as an implicitly Aristotelian improvisation, solved all kinds of problems while avoiding others. Not least among the latter is the problem of sovereignty, which so beleaguers the world today. Part III examines the collapse of Vattel's world as it affected the federal union. In such circumstances, Aristotle's vision could no longer be sustained, even as the federal union survived—and continued to expand across the North American continent.

Politics than to "Xenophon, Plutarch and other classical sources." Yet Pangle's defense of the neo-liberal position has Locke and the founders actively rejecting Aristotle: "Lockean constitutionalism . . . tries to overcome the hierarchy that is at the core of the traditional or Aristotelian concept of society." Thomas L. Pangle, *The Spirit of Modern Republicanism: The Moral Vision of the American Founders and the Philosophy of Locke* (Chicago, 1988), 29, 253. Hierarchy or, more specifically, "quasi-patriarchical" rule is Pangle's simplistic characterization of "*politeia*," which Aristotle set apart from "*polis*," or political society. Whatever the genealogy of the founders' thoughts about rule in relation to rights, they were profoundly influenced by Aristotle's conception of political society, as the next chapter demonstrates at length.

Part One

FEDERAL UNION

Aristotle's *Politics* begins with the *polis*, the one human association whose purpose is the good life for all. In Aristotle's recurring formulation, the *polis* is "perfect" for this purpose—inclusive and sufficient. Capped by the *polis*, associations fulfill nature's design. Nevertheless, people give associations their form, which for the *polis* are forms of rule, or *politeia*, subject to evaluation by reference to the purpose of the *polis*. The distinction between *polis* and *politeia* ordered Aristotle's empirical and normative concerns in a comprehensively teleological context. Modern writers have not always appreciated the distinction, even as they appropriated his language.

When the founders undertook "to form a more perfect Union," they implicitly adopted the distinction between *polis* and *politeia*. Medieval political thought had reached a conclusion that Aristotle could not have anticipated: the *polis* is not the ultimate association. In a graduated natural order all kinds of things have their place. More perfect than the *polis* is a union of such associations dedicated to a common good, in form a republic of republics. The federal Constitution is the instrument by which the American people established the union and its form of rule.

Because the Constitution is "unalterable" by the ordinary processes of government, it also confirms the distinction between nature's design and positive law, between *polis*—the purpose of rule—and *politeia*—the conditions of rule.

For Aristotle the *polis* was a whole, compounded from but not reducible to its parts, which are wholes themselves. The relation of whole and parts organizes human association into levels, each qualitatively different from the others. Medieval law endowed associations with corporate personality, their rights and duties linking levels of association in relations of rule. In this context, Bodin defined sovereignty as a property of the highest level of political association, while Althusius located sovereignty in the people, who delegate it to associations above them. Pufendorf then demonstrated that sovereignty is indivisible and compound arrangements are weak and irregular. Sovereignty resides with those associations in which membership is involuntary; levels disappear. Vattel's world is the only one possible.

In creating a "compound republic" the founders revived the view that political associations occupy positions in a framework of ascending levels, none of which can claim the ultimate, unlimited sovereign authority. The union obtained powers suiting the needs of a state without eliminating the republics composing it or drastically changing their character. Ignoring the early modern political discourse that Bodin precipitated, the founders invoked Montesquieu to call their creation a federal republic, as if it were conceptually indistinguishable from a mere confederation of sovereign states. To this day, federalism is consistently understood to split the difference between a confederation and a unitary state. Such a view misconstrues the founders' success in drawing on a tradition of discourse in which sovereignty is irrelevant.

The founders responded to internal disarray and external threat with a new level of political association—one that could be effective in dealing with foreign powers, capable of extension by the addition of new members on equal terms, and republican in its form of rule. Because the Constitutional Convention was dominated by the negotiation of representative institutions that would balance the interests of large and small states, most writers presume that the founders were wholly preoccupied with the nature of the republic and not the union. The usual reading of Madison's legendary *Federalist* No. 10 supports this view. Yet when Hamilton's *Federalist* No. 9 and Madison's Nos. 10 and 14 are read together, it becomes clear that "the proper structure of the Union" provides the framework for a defense of arrangements to which a republican label is affixed. As a compound republic, "the extended republic" of *Federalist* No. 10 is first of all a union of states, to which new states may be added. Between the level of the federal union and the level of the states a new, functional level of activity has also emerged, replete with its own distinctive complex of institutions. Although the founders hardly anticipated this development, it is nevertheless consistent with the founders' intentions.

Chapter One

"A More Perfect Union"

I. "POLIS" AND "POLITEIA"

"To form a more perfect Union": few phrases are more familiar and less the subject of argument, or even examination. If something is "perfect," how can it be improved? The idea of relative perfection, of perfection as a comparative condition, may seem puzzling when we stop to think about it, and the words themselves an empty flourish. Yet to the authors of the Constitution of the United States, the idea that perfection comes in degrees was immediately intelligible. Applied to the union, it provided them with a conception of historical development and thus a teleological context within which to work.

The American founders ransacked the past to establish their place in world history. None did so more assiduously than John Adams, chief architect of the Massachusetts Constitution of 1780 and author of *A Defence of the Constitutions of Government of the United States of America*, a "bulky, disordered conglomeration of political glosses" published in 1787 and 1788.[1] Throughout the *Defence*, Adams examined the relation

---

[1] In Charles Francis Adams, ed., *The Works of John Adams*, Vol. IV (Boston, 1851, reprinted New York, 1971), 271–588. Quoted is Gordon S. Wood, *The Creation of the American Republic, 1776–1787* (Chapel Hill, 1969), 568, who also called the *Defence* "the finest fruit of the American Enlightenment."

between mixed constitutions and the balance of orders in society—"the consuls, senate and people," in Rome and their equivalents thereafter.[2] In assessing the Roman constitution, Adams quoted many pages of material translated from Polybius' *The Histories*, including this important passage: "'such being the power of each order to assist each other, their union is adapted to all contingencies, and *it is not possible to invent a more perfect system.*'"[3] Here Adams disagreed with Polybius. At least in theory, the English Constitution "is a system much more perfect. The constitutions of several of the United States, it is hoped, will prove themselves improvements both upon the Roman, the Spartan, and the English commonwealths."[4]

By 1787 Adams's preoccupation with mixed constitutions as a way of representing and balancing the "three natural orders" of society had become anachronistic.[5] Where in republican America were three naturally distinct, unequal orders to be found? Nevertheless, Adams's more advanced contemporaries readily accepted his broader conception of constitutional development proceeding from Classical antecedents, even if they dismissed his elaboration of this conception as incorrigibly medieval and empirically irrelevant to their new world. By way of Polybius and a host of other writers, this conception derived from Aristotle's description of the *conditions* of political life. Aristotle also introduced the language of perfection in Western political thought, but he did so in his description of the *purpose*, not the conditions, of political life.[6] For Aristotle purpose came first, conditions followed; these are the

---

[2]*Defence*, 440.

[3]Ibid., 439, emphasis in Adams' text, quoting Polybius' *History*, Book VI, "as translated by Edward Spelman, at the end of his translation of *The Roman Antiquities of Dionysius Halicarnassensis*," 435.

[4]Ibid., 440. In Paine's opinion, "a mixed government is an imperfect everything, cementing and soldering the discordant parts together by corruption, to act as a whole." Thomas Paine, *Rights of Man*, with an Introduction by Eric Foner (New York, 1984), I [1791], 141.

[5]*The Creation of the American Republic*, 589–92.

[6]In Greek the terms for "end" or "goal," and for "perfect" or "complete" are *telos* and *teleios* respectively. They have as a common root the word for "far off," "at a distance." In *The Physics*, trans. by Philip H. Wicksteed and Francis M. Cornford (London, 1963), Vol. I, III, vi (*207a*), 254 (Greek), 255 (trans.), Aristotle said "nothing

two dimensions of politics, related in practice but distinguishable to the observer.

In the *Politics* Aristotle held purpose and conditions apart by discriminating between *polis* and *politeia*. The *polis* is a "species of association" among people and the site of their activities aimed at fulfilling the association's purpose.[7] The first form of association is the household or family, and the next, "which is the *first* to be formed from more households than one," is the village.[8]

> When we come to the final and perfect association, formed from a number of villages, we have already reached the polis—an association which may be said to have reached the heights of full self-sufficiency; or rather . . . it *exists* for the sake of a good life.[9]

---

is complete [*teleios*] unless it has an end [*telos*]."

Plato spoke of perfection in *The Republic*, but as an ideal property, beyond reach in this world: "we cannot admit any imperfection in divine goodness or beauty." *The Republic of Plato*, trans. with an Introduction and Notes by Francis Macdonald Cornford (New York, 1945), IX, § 1 (*II. 380*), 73. It is difficult to see a connection between formal perfection and mundane purpose. Nonetheless, Karl Popper attacked Plato for developing his social thought around this connection, thereby initiating the regrettable history of utopianism in Western experience. Popper's case against Plato is mostly inferential; its terms match Aristotle's position as he directly and unambiguously stated it. K. R. Popper, *The Open Society and Its Enemies, Vol. I, The Spell of Plato*, 5th ed. rev. (Princeton, 1966), 73–81. Aristotle is not to be blamed for the utopian implications of Platonic idealism. Aristotle, not Plato, deserves Popper's blame for historicism, a brand of teleological thinking surviving naturalism, to which Popper has been notoriously hostile, and not dismissal as a mere disciple of Plato's. Ibid., 70.

[7] *The Politics of Aristotle*, trans. by Ernest Barker (New York, 1962), I, i, § 1 (*1252a*), 1.

[8] Ibid., I, ii, § 5 (*1252b*), 4; translator's emphasis.

[9] Ibid., I, ii, § 8 (*1252b*), 4–5, deleting editor's footnote and interpolations. Again: "a polis is constituted by the association of families and villages in a perfect and self-sufficing existence; and such an existence, on our definition, consists in a life of true felicity and goodness." III, ix, § 14 (*1280b–1281a*), 120. Felicity here is not *hedone*, or mere pleasure, but *eudaimonia*, which is "the energy and practice of goodness, to a degree of perfection, and in a mode which is absolute and not relative." VII, xiii, § 5 (*1332a*), 312, allegedly but not literally quoting the *Nicomachean Ethics* (trans. n. 2, 312). Cf. Locke: "as therefore the highest perfection of intellectual nature lies in a careful and constant pursuit of true and solid happiness, so the care of ourselves, that we mistake not imaginary for real happiness, is the necessary foundation of our *liberty*." John Locke, *An Essay concerning Human Understanding*, ed. with an Introduction by John Yolton (London, 1961), II, xxi, § 51, I: 219–20; emphasis in original.

Perfection then is a property specific to the *polis*, and the general good its one and only purpose as an association. Where a *polis* exists, there also must exist a *politeia*, which is the arrangement of offices to effectuate rule for public good.[10]

Aristotle held that there are three virtuous forms of rule and three that are vicious, corresponding in each category to rule by one, few, and many. Virtuous forms of rule are "directed to the advantage of the whole body of citizens." Those that are vicious benefit only the one, the few, or the many who do rule.[11] By serving the general good, though differently, the three right forms of rule give expression to the inherent perfection of the *polis*. In practice, forms of rule are good or bad "in relation to circumstances."[12] They can be improved or degraded by various techniques, including mixing elements of the different forms.[13] Whatever the circumstances, the *im*perfections, of rule, the *polis* is either perfectly what it is, or it cannot be said to exist at all.

Aristotle's treatment of *polis* and *politeia* in the *Politics* mirrors the discrimination between final and efficient causes to be found in his other writings.[14] The perfection of the *polis* implies a final cause giving purpose

---

See also Arendt's discussion of "public happiness." Though well known in the period of the American founding, the term is conspicuously incomplete in Jefferson's famous variation on Locke's "life, liberty and property." Nevertheless, Arendt concluded that "the Declaration of Independence, though it blurs the distinction between public and private happiness, at least still intends us to hear the term "pursuit of happiness" in its two-fold meaning: private welfare as well as the right to public happiness, the pursuit of well-being as well as being a 'participator in public affairs.'" Hannah Arendt, *On Revolution* (New York, 1963), 122–31, quoting 129.

[10] *The Politics of Aristotle*, III, vi (*1278a–1279a*), 110–13. The term *politeia* refers not simply to a prescribed arrangement of offices, or form of rule, narrowly construed, but also the prescribed ends, or principles, linking any such arrangement to an association's "way of life" and thus, at some cost to the distinction between *polis* and *politeia*, the way of life itself. Ibid., IV, i, § 10 (*1289a*), 156; IV, xi, § 1 (*1295a*), 180. No one English term captures what Aristotle had in mind. "Form of government" and "constitution" are most frequently used, though the former is too limited and the latter too distinctively modern—a matter considered below.

[11] Ibid., III, vii (*1279a–b*), 113–15, quoting § 5 (*1279b*), 115.

[12] Ibid., IV, xi, § 21 (*1296b*), 183–84.

[13] Ibid., IV, ix (*1294a–b*), 176–78.

[14] Aristotle's order of exposition in the *Politics* may well reflect his well-known

to all that is animate. Evaluation of the conditions of rule moves the discussion on to efficient causes—activities enabling or preventing the realization of public good. Connecting the two realms is the idea of sufficiency. A sufficiency of causes yields finality; self-sufficiency or independence is the operational measure of the conditions of rule good enough for the perfection of the *polis*. Appropriately the *Politics* also considers material conditions affecting self-sufficiency, as the text returns near the end to its initial concern with the *polis*.

In Aristotle's world of purpose, perfection is an exclusive attribute of the *polis* because the *polis* is the one association whose purpose is the general good. Yet "all associations are instituted for the purpose of attaining some good."[15] Aims differ; one association's good need not be good for another. "For good appears to be one thing in one pursuit or art and another in another: it is different in medicine from what it is in strategy, and so on with the rest of the arts."[16] Aristotle nevertheless saw good in our many pursuits because the multiplicity of ends pursued are means to a final or perfect good. Whenever ends are also means, the final good has yet to be achieved. Instead we have successive approximations of the final good: the achievement of immediate ends permits us to pursue more general ends, which, when achieved, permit us to move on to yet more general, or higher, ends. In describing this process, Aristotle spoke of finality or perfection comparatively: "a thing pursued as an end in itself is more final than one pursued as a means to something else."[17] The final good must then be "most final," or, in Latin renditions of this passage, "*perfectissimum.*"[18]

---

classification of causes. Richard McKeon, "Aristotle's Conception of Moral and Political Philosophy," *Ethics*, LI (1941), 281–87; Alan Gewirth, *Marsilius of Padua and Medieval Political Philosophy* (New York, 1951), 33–37. McKeon argued this for the four causes—final, formal, material, and efficient—in Aristotle's scheme. The last three are less easily separated from each other than seen apart from the first; later commentary conventionally treats the categories of final and efficient causes in opposition, with the latter's triumph marking the arrival of modern thinking. Cf. McKeon, 289–90; Gewirth, 34–35.

[15] *The Politics of Aristotle*, I, i, § 1 (*1252a*), p. 1.

[16] *The Nicomachean Ethics*, trans. H. Rackham (London, 1926), I, vii, § 1 (*1097a*), 26.

[17] Ibid., I, vii, § 4 (*1097a*), 26 (Greek), 27 (trans.).

[18] Ibid., I, vii, § 4 (*1097a*), 26–27; *Aristoteles latinus, XXVI 1–3, Ethica nicomachea,*

Means are not just particular ends, to be assessed merely for the good they contain. They must also be assessed in terms of virtue as a character trait. Like good, virtue is relative to the circumstances of its practice. "Justice is perfect virtue because it is the practice of perfect virtue; and perfect in a special degree, because its possessor can practise his virtue toward others and not merely by himself."[19] The term "degree" misleadingly suggests a finely graded continuum in the public practice of virtue.[20] Aristotle's teleological orientation presupposes developmental stages which are subject to comparison with a final stage, whether known or inferred.[21] Justice is virtue at its most perfect, just as the good life is goodness at its most perfect. In both instances, the last stage of perfection is possible only in the *polis*. In relating individual pursuits and the practice of virtue to public life, Aristotle gave his doctrine of perfection a paradoxical turn. To speak of perfection in the superlative simultaneously insists on the special, absolute character of perfection and encourages thinking about it comparatively.

II. AFTER ARISTOTLE

Recognizing the implications of holding *polis* and *politeia* apart, Classical writers generally gave their attention to the latter. We can see this choice in the language they used. Translations aside, Polybius never used the

---

2nd fascicle ed. by R. A. Gauthier (Leiden and Brussels, 1972), 75.

[19]Ibid., V, i, § 15 (*1129b*), 259. In another widely used translation, this passage reads: "justice *is* perfect virtue because it *practises* perfect virtue. But it is perfect in a special way." *The Ethics of Aristotle*, trans. by J. A. K. Thomson (Baltimore, 1955), 141; translator's emphases.

[20]The same results from speaking of felicity as "the practice of goodness, to a degree of perfection." Cited above, n. 9. A different translation—"happiness is the complete activity and employment of virtue"—leaves a different impression. *The Politics*, trans. by H. Rackham (London, 1932), 597, with Greek on facing page.

[21]Thanks to Valerie French for clarifying this point, which finds support in Aristotle's treatment of changes, or *metabolai*, in the form of Athenian rule. James Day and Mortimer Chambers, *Aristotle's History of Athenian Democracy* (Berkeley and Los Angeles, 1962), 66–71.

Greek term for "perfect" in describing the "political system" of Rome. He merely offered the opinion that it would be impossible to find a better one.[22] Speaking as Scipio, Cicero noted that any one of Aristotle's three forms of government, "though not perfect or in my opinion the best [*non perfectum illud quidem neque mea sententia optimum*], is tolerable, though one of them may be superior to another."[23] "The form which is a combination of all of them," he considered to be "superior to any single one of them."[24] Thereafter we find many comparatives and superlatives, but nothing of perfection.

For both Polybius and Cicero, the Roman Republic achieved its superiority by combining forms of rule. Both sought to identify optimal conditions of rule from cases, not principles or purposes. Even when Cicero spoke of an "ideal form of rule"—"a model supplied by nature"—the adjective in question is "*optimus*," not "*perfectus*."[25] The latter term, with its distinctive connotations of larger purpose and finality, suits the *polis* (in Latin, *civitas*, used interchangeably with *respublica* understood generically) as an association for the general good and arena for the practice of virtue. Those connotations ill suit *politeia* (in Latin, *status*, one form of which is *respublica* understood specifically) as an endlessly contested array of powers and privileges. Yet those very connotations assured a place for the language of perfection once the medieval world had recovered Aristotle's teachings.

For medieval Christianity, evaluation of forms of rule was a largely secular and therefore secondary matter. Far more important was the challenge of Aristotle's teachings to Christianity's Augustinian heritage. With the earthly city no more than a way station for sinners, consideration of the good life was beside the point. Attracted by Aristotle's purposeful conception of the world and the systematic character of his

---

[22]*The Histories*, with trans. by W. R. Paton (London, 1923), III, vi, § 18, 308 (Greek), 309 (trans.).

[23]*De re publica, De legibus*, with trans. by Clinton Walker Keyes (London, 1928), The Republic, I, xxvi, 66 (Latin), 67 (trans.). Much (mis)quoted from antiquity (cf. Chapter 2, n. 29) but long lost, this work was recovered only in the nineteenth century.

[24]Ibid., I, xxxv, 83.

[25]Ibid., II, xxxviv, 178–79. *Optimus status* is rendered there as "ideal constitution."

teachings, medieval thinkers could hardly avoid a consideration of the good life. Nor could they avoid doing so in Aristotle's terms. Thus in the *Summa theologica*, we find Aquinas defining the individual as a part of "that perfect whole which is the community [*communitatis perfectae*]"— the perfect community, on Aristotle's authority, being the *civitas*.[26] When Aquinas turned to the forms of rule, which he did briefly in the *Summa* and more fully in the essay *De regimine principium*, his language followed Aristotle's, even if his conclusions did not. As disclosed by "study of the divine order of providence," monarchy is the best [*optimum*] form of rule in human society, tyranny the worst [*pessimum*].[27]

Even if medieval thinkers were attracted to Aristotle's purposeful conception of the world, they found his worldly conception of purpose troubling. Their response was an attempt at reconciliation—"a reconciliation between the Aristotelian vision of the self-sufficiency of civic life and the more other-worldly preoccupations characteristic of Augustinian Christianity."[28] The problem of reconciling Aristotle and Augustine directed attention to the nature of the divine order. If that order were seen inclusively, with all that God has created finding a place therein, then the problem is solved by defining it away.

Plato had opened the way for this solution with the claim that the world cannot have been made "in the likeness of any Idea that is merely partial." Rather, "it is the perfect image of the whole of which all animals—both individuals and species—are parts."[29] From this claim follows a "principle of plenitude," a cosmic determinism, in which all

[26]St. Thomas Aquinas, *Summa theologica*, I–II, Q. 90, a. 2, in *Aquinas: Selected Political Writings*, ed. by A. P. D'Entrèves, trans. by J. G. Dawson (Oxford, 1948), 102–79, at 110 (Latin), 111 (trans.).

[27]*Summa*, I–I, Q. 103, a. 3: ibid., 106–07; *De regimine principium* (On Princely Government), I, i–iii: ibid., 2–83, at 2–19, quoting p. 15. Claims that Aquinas supported a mixed constitution arise from his concern that a monarchy may degenerate into tyranny. Inasmuch as "perfect virtue" is found in few persons, some limitations on the monarch are warranted. *Summa*, II–I, Q. 105: ibid., 149–51.

[28]Quentin Skinner, *The Foundations of Modern Political Thought, Vol. One: The Renaissance* (Cambridge, 1978), 50. See also A. P. D'Entrèves, "Introduction," in *Aquinas: Selected Political Writings*, ix–xiii.

[29]*Timaeus*, § 4 (*30*), quoted in Arthur O. Lovejoy, *The Great Chain of Being: A Study of the History of an Idea* (Cambridge, Mass., 1936), 50.

has its place.[30] A second way to see the divine order inclusively, of bringing heaven to earth, employs a different principle: "the principle of continuity." Aristotle himself provided the means for this solution in his systematic biology. "In spite of Aristotle's recognition of the multiplicity of possible systems of natural classification, it was he who chiefly suggested to naturalists and philosophers of later times the idea of arranging (at least) all animals in a single graded *scala naturae* according to their degree of 'perfection.'"[31]

Perfect animals have the final form of their species, and species are grouped into kinds (genera) by comparing those "parts" of animals that are "different in form."[32] Among these are differences in their means of reproduction, which, Aristotle believed, depend on a single, continuous variable.[33] Genera by genera, animals vary in their body heat. Aristotle's empirical claims led him to propose that "nature orders generation in regular gradation."[34] Genera differ for reasons that go beyond differences in form. Even if generation is continuously graded, genera are not because of their many differences. Instead, genera occupy the equivalent of developmental stages seen within species, yet without prospect of development. They are ranked.

The force of this proposition depends less on its empirical support than its generalizing effect. All that lives, indeed all of nature, can be graded on an ascending scale. Any living thing is perfect if it is a fully developed member of its species. Every species is therefore a perfected representation of its individual members and associated with species of

[30]The "principle of plenitude" is Lovejoy's designation for what Leibniz, who was its greatest exponent, occasionally called the "principle of perfection." According to Lovejoy, "perfection" and "fullness" are antitheses. "The principle of plenitude is rather the principle of the necessity of imperfection in all its possible degrees." Ibid, 339–40 n. 36. See further 31–55.

[31]The "principle of continuity" is also Lovejoy's coinage. Ibid., 55–59, quoting 58.

[32]"History of Animals" (*Historia animalium*), II, i (*497b*), in *The Complete Works of Aristotle: The Revised Oxford Translation*, ed. by Jonathan Barnes (Princeton, 1984), 792. On the importance of Aristotle's work in biology for his political thought, see Day and Chambers, *Aristotle's History*, 39–54.

[33]"Generation of Animals" (*De generatione animalium*), II, i (*731b–735b*), in *The Complete Works*, 1135–41.

[34]Ibid. (*733a*), 1138.

the same kind. The kinds themselves, as genera, are ordered by degrees of perfection. Aristotle said so himself: hotter animals are more perfect.[35]

The medieval conception of a divinely inspired, comprehensive and graduated natural order presupposes the principle of plenitude, which was taken to imply the continuity of all things. In tandem the principles of plenitude and continuity reinforced the underlying essentialism of Aristotle's scheme and coincided with the Platonist tendencies in Christian thought. Holding God as final perfection, Christians could devote themselves to more immediate, secular concerns without danger to their place in "the great chain of being." If a natural order such as this suited medieval needs, it also suited the world that emerged from the Middle Ages. Indeed it was taken on faith by medieval churchmen, early modern scientists and Enlightenment philosophers, thus dominating Western thought down to the time of the American founding.[36] When significant challenges to this way of thinking first appeared in the mid-eighteenth century, it was the principle of plenitude—the principle that all events are necessary and therefore good—which lent itself to caricature and dismissal, and not the more modest principle that all beings are connected.[37]

The principle of plenitude grants perfection exclusively to the cosmic whole, denying the possibility of human improvement or any other mundane purpose to social existence. The principle of continuity

[35]Ibid. (*733b*). Humanity, however, is a kind apart, and evidently more perfect, not because human beings are hotter than other animals, but as a consequence of many differences between humankind and other animals. For example, "man alone can learn to make equal use of both hands." "History of Animals," II, i (*497b*), 780.

[36]Lovejoy, *The Great Chain of Being*, 59. On the importance of this conception— "at once an expression of personal faith and a description of the material universe"— for Jefferson and his generation, see Daniel J. Boorstin, *The Lost World of Thomas Jefferson*, (Chicago, 1948) 30–40, quoting 35.

[37]Recall the concluding lines of *Candide ou optimisme* (1759), which is a notorious attack on Leibniz and other devotees of plenitude: "*Pangloss disait quelquefois à Candide: tous les événements sont enchaînés dans le meilleur des mondes possibles. . . .* [all events form a chain in this best of all possible worlds. . . .] *Cela est bien dit, répondit Candide, mais it faut cultiver notre jardin.*" *Les oeuvres completes de Voltaire* (Oxford, 1980), 48:260. According to Boorstin, "the American philosophers significantly used the less metaphysical 'chain of *beings*' more commonly than 'chain of being.'" *The Lost World of Thomas Jefferson*, 255 n. 7, his emphasis.

avoids this result, but only by including social arrangements in the
cosmic design. Aristotle himself held that families, villages and the *polis*
all have generic identity and occupy an ascending relation. Aristotle's
medieval and early modern followers took the same view, to the extent
of affirming the perfection of the *polis* or its equivalent.[38] A paradox
results. If the ascending series of social arrangements is but one segment
of a far greater chain, then the *polis* cannot have an exclusive claim on
perfection, as Aristotle insisted. While no one acknowledged this difficulty, it was implicitly resolved against the Aristotle of the *Politics* and in
favor of the idea—for which Aristotle's biology is largely responsible—
that perfection is a matter of degree.

Starting with Aquinas, the idea of degrees of perfection took on a
life of its own. God is perfection in the highest degree.[39] Love of God is
also perfection, fully achieved only in heaven. Removing obstacles to
the love of God is a "third perfection," but one that admits to degrees of
execution.[40] The door is opened to "states of perfection" attending
ecclesiastical offices, themselves graded. Bishops outrank members of
orders who outrank parish priests, who in turn outrank their parishio-
ners.[41] First among bishops, the Pope is presumably the most perfect of

[38]Aquinas, of course, as cited above (n. 26); Marsilius of Padua, *The Defender of
Peace* [*Defensor pacis*, 1324], trans. by Alan Gewirth (New York, 1956), I, iv, § 1, 12,
citing Aristotle; Franciscus de Victoria, *De jure belli*, 425, in *De Indis et de jure belli
relectiones* [1557], trans. by John Pawley Bate, rev. text by Herbert Francis Wright
(Washington, 1917), 169 (trans.), 277 (text); Francisco Suarez, *De legibus, ac Deo
legislatore* [1612], I, vi, § 19–21, and II, 12, § 2, in *Selections of Three Works of Francisco
Suárez, S. J.*, Vol. Two, *The Translation* by Gladys L. Williams, Ammi Brown, John
Waldron (Oxford, 1944), 85–88, 125, citing Aquinas and Aristotle; Hugo Grotius, *De
jure belli ac pacis libri tres*, Vol. One, *Reproduction of the Edition of 1646* (Washington,
1913), and Vol. Two, *The Translation*, Book I, I, xiv, § 1, 6, and 44, respectively, with
"*coetus perfectus*" translated "complete association" and later (Book I, III, vii, §1, 52 and
103) "perfect association," followed in the same paragraph by "*statum perfectae civitates*"
and reference to Aristotle.

[39]Indeed one of Aquinas' famous five proofs for the existence of God depends on
"the principle that comparisons of perfections describes degrees of approximation to a
superlative." David Sanford, "Degrees of Perfection, Argument for the Existence of
God," in Paul Edwards, ed., *Encyclopedia of Philosophy* (New York, 1967), 2:326.

[40]*Summa theologica*, II–II, Q. 184, quoted in R. Newton Flew, *The Idea of Perfection
in Christian Theology: An Historical Study of the Christian Ideal for the Present Life* (Oxford,
1934), 236.

[41]Flew, 236–38.

all the human kind. By inference the ascending series of associations extends beyond the *polis*, in the form of the Church's hierarchical order and, no less plausibly, in the organization of secular authority.[42]

A single logic of perfection leaves no room for competing hierarchies, as the long struggle between the Latin Church and the Holy Roman Empire duly testified.[43] The empire emerged from this struggle a spent victor, unable to control the exuberant cities and principalities within its reach. Gradations persisted, but their measurement changed. The qualitative language of perfection gave way to that simplest of quantitative criteria: size. Ordered by size, the many autonomous political associations within and beyond the Empire exhibited differences in kind, each kind discernible by reference to an optimal form of rule.[44] Attention turned once more to *politeia*.

Machiavelli—"that greater Columbus"—is the decisive figure in this shift.[45] Machiavelli's discussion of the forms of rule, his debt to Polybius, and his admiration of the Roman Republic as a mixed form are well known. What commentators have not noticed is the way Machiavelli used the language of perfection. Machiavelli's medieval predecessors saw perfection as relative, but only in the sense of taking on different manifestations in a fixed set of relations. Machiavelli also saw

[42]The latter inference was Dante's in arguing that "a monarch or Emperor is necessary for the well-being of the world." "Monarchy" (*Monarchia*), I, v, in *Monarchy and Three Political Letters*, trans. by Donald Nicholl (London, 1954), 11. While Dante acknowledged metaphysical degrees of perfection, his defense of monarchy as a form of rule is conducted entirely in the language of optimality (notwithstanding a translator who rendered "*ad optimam dispositionem mundi necesse est Monarchiam*" "monarchy is necessary for perfect world-order." Ibid., I, xi, 18; *Le opere di Dante Alighieri*, Edizione nazionale a cura della Società Dantesca Italiana (1965), 5 (*Monarchia*): 157.

[43]Skinner, 3–22, has conveniently reprised this struggle from the perspective of the Italian city republics, which of course were the extant incarnation of the *polis*, neither clearly subsumed by nor at the top of either hierarchy.

[44]Bartolus of Sassoferrato, a leading jurist of the 14th century, graded cities, nations and the Empire by size ("*gradu magnitudinis*") in "*De regimine civitates.*" Bartolus's Latin is quoted in R. W. Carlyle and A. J. Carlyle, *A History of Mediaeval Political Theory in the West, Vol. 6, Political Theory from 1300 to 1600* (Edinburgh, 1950), 78–79 n. 2.

[45]"It was Machiavelli, that greater Columbus, who had discovered the continent on which Hobbes could erect his structure"—a structure relating asocial bearers of rights to the conditions of rule. Leo Strauss, *Natural Right and History* (Chicago, 1953), 177.

perfection as relative, but in the sense of being contingent on an unlikely combination of events. Some republics never overcome their turbulent histories; others begin well and become better. Though lacking a "perfect form of rule [*ordine perfetto*]," they may nevertheless become perfect—"*per occorrenzia degli accidenti diventare perfette.*" Rome is a case in point. Its mixed form of rule strengthened by challenge, Rome became "*una republica perfetta.*"[46]

Machiavelli treated *republica* and *ordine* as interchangeably capable of perfection. In doing so, he subordinated the identity of any political association—the city republic of his own time no less than the Roman Republic—to its form of rule. By violating Aristotle's parallel construction of *polis* and *politeia* as differently caused and discursively separate, Machiavelli effectively linked improvements in public life, however achieved, to the position of particular political associations in the great chain of being. Improvements in them individually could yield an improved position for them all collectively. While Machiavelli would hardly have expected a general improvement in the conditions of rule, many of his successors were more sanguine in disposition. With Machiavelli's help, the idea of progress began its gradual ascent. Coincidentally, Machiavelli's conflation of *polis* and *politeia* eventually subverted the idea of a great chain, with its implication of essential entities and static relations.[47]

---

[46]Niccolò Machiavelli, *Discorsi supra la prima deca di Tito Livo* (Milano, 1984), I, ii, 64–68, quoting 64–65, 68.

[47]Lovejoy suggested that the idea survived as long as it did by being temporalized. The chain became a ladder, which rational beings might ascend over the course of time. (*The Great Chain of Being*, 242–87.) Social betterment would result, as it would if nature's design were latent, its realization dependent on the strivings of rational beings. Kant held that the "history of mankind could be viewed as the realization of a hidden plan of nature to bring about an internally—and for this purpose also externally—perfect constitution; since this is the only state in which nature can develop all faculties of mankind." Kant meant individual societies by the term "internally," and among societies by "externally." ("Idea for a Universal History with Cosmopolitan Intent," in *The Philosophy of Kant: Immanuel Kant's Moral and Political Writings*, ed., with an Introduction, by Carl J. Friedrich [New York, 1949], 127; emphasis deleted.) Kant's use of the term "constitution"—"*Verfassung*"—blurs the distinction between *polis* and *politeia*; on constitution as device for maintaining this distinction, see the next section of this chapter.

After Machiavelli, many writers employed the language of perfection. In one conspicuous line of development, perfection is dissociated from political life and its forms. Locke's state of nature is "a *State of perfect Freedom.*"[48] Yet "we are not by our selves sufficient to furnish our selves with competent store of things, needful for such a Life, as our Nature doth desire." Therefore, Locke concluded, "to supply those Defects and Imperfections which are in us, as living singly and solely by our selves, we are naturally induced to seek Communion and Fellowship with others."[49]

If political societies are created to remedy individual imperfections, then societal perfection is at most an incidental consequence of political arrangements and activities.[50] Rousseau could not even accept the premise of this argument. In his judgment, humanity's misfortunes arise not from our individual imperfections but from our "faculty of self-improvement"—"*le faculté de se perfectionner.*"[51] Self-improvement means

[48]John Locke, *Two Treatises on Government*, ed. by Peter Laslett (Cambridge, 1963), Second Treatise, II, § 4, 287; Locke's emphasis.

[49]Ibid., II, § 15, 295, "fairly accurately" (editor's note) quoting Richard Hooker, *Of the Lawes of Ecclesiasticall Politie* (1593), I, x. Cf. Samuel Johnson's entry on "perfection" in his *Dictionary of the English Language* (London, 1755, facsimile reprint, 1968), n. p., which quotes Hooker to different effect:

> Man doth seek a *triple* perfection, first a sensual, consisting in those things which very life itself requireth, either as necessary supplements or as ornaments thereof; then an intellectual, consisting in those things which none underneath man is capable of; lastly a spiritual and divine, consisting in those things whereunto we are led by supernatural means here, but cannot here attain. (Johnson's emphasis)

To the second "branch" belongs "the law of moral and civil perfection," meaning natural law. *Of the Laws of the Ecclesiastical Polity*, Preface, Book I, Book VIII, ed. by Arthur Stephen McGrade (Cambridge, 1989), I, xi, 103. Ch. xi, 100–07, deals extensively with perfection, with references to Aristotle, "Hooker's major non-Biblical source." Editor's note, 228.

[50]In passing, Locke described the attributes of "a perfect *Democracy*," without holding up this arrangement as an ideal or advanced form of rule. *Two Treatises on Government*, Second Treatise, X, § 132, 373; Locke's emphasis. Consider also Paine's claim: "the more perfect civilization is, the less occasion has it for government, because the more does it regulate its own affairs, and govern itself." *Rights of Man*, II [1792], 165.

[51]Jean-Jacques Rousseau, *A Discourse on Inequality*, trans. by Maurice Cranston (Harmondsworth, 1984), 88; *Du contrat social et autres oeuvres politique* (Paris, 1975), ed. Jean Ehrard, 25–122, at 48. "It would be sad for us to be forced to admit that this

society, and society is our downfall. Arguing in the same vein, Godwin came to a different conclusion. Since perfectibility and perfection stand in "express opposition," we should individually seek our improvement and society will take care of itself.[52] Either way, human perfectibility came into its own as an Enlightenment theme.[53] Asserting the sovereignty of the individual—and, by extension, the state—challenged the conceptual primacy of civic life. What Vattel called "the republic of Europe," an unstable balance of sovereign powers, displaced the Classical republican ideal of civic perfection.

Other writers after Machiavelli used the language of perfection specifically for discussion of political arrangements. Harrington claimed that "the perfection of government lieth upon such a libration [balancing] in the frame of it, that no man or men . . . can have the power to disturb it with sedition."[54] According to Pufendorf, "there is as rich a field of corruptions and vices in many commonwealths as in individuals, so that to be afflicted with the very fewest may be considered as almost equivalent to perfection."[55] Wolff held that "every nation [*gens*] ought to perfect itself and its form of rule [*statum*]."[56] In an essay known to have influenced Madison, Hume asked: "as one form of government must be allowed more perfect than another, independent of the manners and humours of particular men; why may we not enquire what is the most

distinguishing and almost unlimited faculty of man is the source of all his misfortunes"—sad but, for Rousseau, necessary.

[52]William Godwin, *Enquiry concerning Political Justice* (3rd ed., 1796), Vol. I, 93, quoted in John Passmore, *The Perfectibility of Man* (New York, 1970), 158.

[53]Ibid., 149–238; J. B. Bury, *The Idea of Progress: An Inquiry into Its Growth and Origin* (New York, 1932), passim; Martin Foss, *The Idea of Perfection in the Western World* (Princeton, 1946), 58–102.

[54] *The Commonwealth of Oceana*, in J. G. A. Pocock, ed., *The Political Works of James Harrington* (Cambridge, 1977), 179.

[55]*De jure naturae et gentium, Vol. Two, The Translation*, VII, v, § 10, 1033. Pufendorf occasionally used "perfect" in conjunction with "regular," speaking for example of "*civitatis perfectae & regularis.*" *Vol. One, The Photographic Reproduction of the Edition of 1688*, VII, v, § 13, 711. "Regular" is a key term in Pufendorf's analysis of political arrangements; see the next chapter.

[56]Christian Wolff, *Jus gentium methodo scientifica pertractatum, Vol. One, The Photographic Reproduction of the Edition of 1764*, and *Vol. Two, The Translation* by Joseph H. Drake (Oxford, 1934), § 35, 13 (Latin), 25 (trans., *status* there rendered "form of

perfect of all?"[57] On the evidence, it is hardly surprising that Adams would think about "more perfect" systems of mixed rule. Nor is it a surprise that the founders would revive Aristotle's idea that perfection is a property of the polity itself, and not its form of rule, as their hopes for the continuing improvement of the European diplomatic system were frustrated.

III. CHANGES IN KIND

The Constitution names as its first purpose the formation of a more perfect *union*. The frame of reference is not the institutional design that follows, but the union as a political association sufficient unto itself. While the latter is a republic, this is no ground for claiming it to be "more perfect"—more perfect than what? But the new union is incomparably different from its predecessor, a mere confederacy. Instead the union's degree of perfection comes from its place in the great chain of being, ahead of the old confederation, and beneath no other association on the earth. Both the Aristotelian sense of the words themselves and the tradition they express are perfectly clear.

To judge from *The Federalist*, the claim to have formed a more perfect union provoked little comment during debates over the ratifica-

---

government"). Vattel explained the nation's duty of perfecting itself without reference to political arrangements.

> *To preserve and perfect one's existence* is the sum of all duties to self.
>
> A Nation is *preserved* if the political association which forms it endures. If this association comes to an end the Nation or the State no longer exists, though the individuals composing it still live.
>
> A nation is *perfected* if it is made capable of obtaining the end of civil society; and a Nation is in a *perfect state* when it wants nothing necessary to arrive at that end.

E. de Vattel, *The Law of Nations or the Principles of Natural Law Applied to the Conduct and to the Affairs of Nations and of Sovereigns, Vol. Three, Translation of the Edition of 1758* by Charles G. Fenwick (Washington, 1916), I, ii, § 14, 13; see also Introduction, § 12, 6.

[57]David Hume, "Idea of a Perfect Commonwealth," *Essays: Moral, Political, and Literary* (Indianapolis, 1985), ed. Eugene F. Miller, II, xvi, 513.

tion of the Constitution. No one doubted the standing of the union as a *polis*, after all, only the particulars of its *politeia*. Nevertheless, the possibility of perfection came up in the latter context. In *Federalist* No. 9, Hamilton considered the practicality of devising "a more perfect structure" of government than the ancients had been able to imagine. Institutional innovations embodied in the Constitution were either "wholly new discoveries or have made their principal progress toward perfection in modern times."[58] Hamilton's view that improvements in the form of rule constituted ever closer approximations of perfection, or progress, was a commonplace of the day. If this is evidence against the great chain of being as a controlling metaphor in Western thought, then the claim to have formed a more perfect union is, as we have seen, striking evidence of the continued importance of the great chain. Discursive incongruities suggest a time of transition.

In *Federalist* No. 37, Madison also addressed the possibility of perfection in terms suggesting a time of transition. Madison's thoughts simultaneously recall Aristotle's systematic biology while anticipating both the subjective awareness and skepticism of our own time.

> The most sagacious and laborious naturalists have never yet succeeded, in tracing with certainty, the line which separates the district of vegetable life from the neighboring region of unorganized matter, or which marks the termination of the former and the commencement of the animal empire. A still greater obscurity lies in the distinctive characters, by which the objects in each of these great departments have been arranged and assorted. When we pass from the works of nature, in which all the delineations are perfectly accurate, and appear to be otherwise only from the imperfection of the eye which surveys them, to the institutions of man . . . , we must perceive the necessity of moderating still farther our expectations and hopes from the efforts of human sagacity.[59]

Madison's concern in writing these words was tactical. To put the

---

[58] *The Federalist*, ed., with an Introduction and Notes, by Jacob E. Cooke (Middletown, Conn., 1961), 51. To the same effect is Madison's judgment about the American people prior to the Constitutional Convention. "If their works betray imperfections, we wonder at the fewness of them." *Federalist* No. 14, 89.

[59] Ibid., 235. Madison further explained: "besides the obscurity arising from the complexity of objects, and the imperfections of the human faculties, the medium through which the conceptions of men are conveyed to each other, adds a fresh embarrassment." 236. So much for self-evident truths.

Constitution, as a product of political give and take, in a favorable light, he was obliged to argue against the "artificial structure and regular symmetry" that "an ingenious theorist" might have given it.[60] In questioning the practicality of achieving perfection, he cast doubt on its possibility.

More precisely, Madison cast doubt on the possibility of perfection in public life. Perfection as a personal quest has a long history in Christianity, with particular resonance, after the Reformation, for Pietists, Quakers and Methodists.[61] The Romantic movement codified what radical Protestants had long believed (and Rousseau and Godwin had intimated): self-realization is one thing, social improvement another.[62] In the latter case, lingering references to perfection follow in the tradition of Machiavelli but lack conviction.[63] When the point of reference is the Constitution itself, conviction is not lacking. It is misplaced.

So we may interpret the debate over the "original intent" of the Constitution's authors.[64] But the quest for a perfect Constitution mis-

[60]Ibid., 237. Also attributing the Constitution's minor imperfections to compromises among its framers, Hamilton remarked in passing: "I never expect to see a perfect work from imperfect man." *Federalist* No. 85, 591.

[61]Flew, *The Idea of Perfection in Christian Theology*, chs. XVI, XVII, XIX. For Aquinas, the long history of Christian asceticism challenged the Aristotelian conception that perfection requires human association and forced him to acknowledge that hermits and saints already have "a nature more perfect than that of men in general." *Commentum in libros politicorum seu de rebus civilibus*, I, i, quoted by D'Entrèves, "Introduction," xvii–xviii.

[62]Richard Rorty, *Contingency, Irony, and Solidarity* (Cambridge, 1989), xiii–xiv, 30, 97.

[63]John Stuart Mill notwithstanding:

> the merit which any set of political institutions can possess . . . consists partly of the degree in which they promote the general advancement of the community . . .; and partly of the degree of perfection with which they organize the moral, intellectual and active worth already existing, so as to operate with the greatest effect on public affairs.

Considerations on Representative Government, ed. with an Introduction by Currin V. Shields (New York, 1958), 27–28.

[64]"All Americans seem to agree . . . that our Constitution is perfect; that when properly interpreted, the Constitution requires that our society conform to the best principles of human governance." Mark A. Graber, "Our (Im)Perfect Constitution," *Review of Politics*, 51 (1989), 86.

construes its purpose. The Constitution is an instrument, a means to an end. Instruments need not be perfect to be effective, just good enough. Made over by the Constitution, the union *was* more perfect. The Constitution brought the United States to a new level, or stage of perfection in the scheme of things—and not just any scheme, but God's design of a great chain for all things. Institutions made for the union are not a discretionary improvement in political arrangements but a necessary response to a change in this scheme, a shift in the very conditions of rule.

As Gerald Stourzh has noted, "the *topos* of the *metabole politeion*"— the question of shifts or stages in the conditions of rule—was central to early modern political thought, its discussion, like so much else, shaped by Aristotle's.[65] Notwithstanding the primacy Aristotle gave to the *polis*, changes in political arrangements, or *politeia*, affect its character; efficient causes sum to final cause. Thus, "when the constitution [*politeia*] suffers a change in kind, and becomes a different constitution, the polis will cease to be the same polis, and will also change its identity."[66] Obviously small changes in *politeia* do not change the identity of the *polis*. A change "in kind" is required, but how much change, under what circumstances, is a change in kind? Was not the new union a change in kind, given the degree of change under the Constitution?

Without some means to regulate the causal relation of *polis* and *politeia*, these questions are difficult to answer. Aristotle's *Politics* points to the existence of a regulatory mechanism in the activities of the "*politeuma*," the body of citizens in any *polis*, but denies this body ontological standing. On the one hand, the body of citizens has supreme authority; on the other, citizenship is a matter of *politeia*.[67] As a result, Aristotle could say that the *polis* is the body of citizens, that body is the *politeia* itself, and, in a full-blown conflation, *politeia* "is the way of life of

[65]Gerald Stourzh, "*Constitution*: Changing Meanings of the Term from the Early Seventeenth to the Late Eighteenth Century," in Terence Ball and J. G. A. Pocock, eds., *Conceptual Change and the Constitution* (Lawrence, Kans., 1988), 36. Also recall n. 21, above.

[66]*The Politics of Aristotle*, III, iii, § 7 (*1276b*), 99.

[67]Ibid., III, vi, § 1 (*1278b*), 110; III, i, §§ 6–12 (*1275a–b*), 93–95.

a citizen-body."[68] Early modern thinkers resolved this impasse by changing the terms of reference. Replacing citizens, whose daily activities constitute public life, are the people, whose occasional exercises of sovereignty constitute the conditions of public life and secure the body politic's distinctive character.

As with any living body, the body politic has a "constitution," an ensemble of faculties disposing it to function successfully in ever changing circumstances. Stourzh has shown that it was "constitution," and not *politeia*, which emerged early in the seventeenth century as a new category of political practice.[69] Constitution in this sense is both descriptive, in acknowledging the primacy of the *polis* and affirming its character, and prescriptive, in making practices supporting the *polis* conceptually prior and legally superior to the practices identified with *politeia*. The sovereign people can change the constitution of the body politic as they wish, within the limits imposed by the nature and purpose of political association. These are changes in kind, acknowledged as such.

By the mid-eighteenth century all this was well understood. Consider Vattel's formulation, which, like his famous treatise generally, is clear if unoriginal. "The fundamental law which determines the manner in which the public authority is to be exercised is what forms the *constitution of the State*. In it can be seen the organization by means of which the Nation acts as a political body; how and by whom the people are to be governed, and the rights and duties of those who govern."[70] Furthermore, "it is unquestionable that a Nation which finds its very constitution unsuited to it has the right to change it." Vattel proposed that the nation, though a "whole people," may act through "a majority of votes"; otherwise action would be impossible.[71] Not considered is the

[68]Ibid., III, i, § 12 (*1275b*), 95; III, vi, § 1 (*1278b*), 110; IV, xi, § 3 (*1295a*), 180. See also n. 10, above.

[69]Gerald Stourzh, *Fundamental Laws and Individual Rights in the Eighteenth Century Constitution* (Bicentennial Essay No. 5, Claremont Institute for the Study of Statesmanship and Political Philosophy, 1984), 3–6; Stourzh, *"Constitution,"* 38–43.

[70]Vattel, *The Law of Nations*, I, iii, § 27, 17; emphasis in original. On the sense of "fundamental" in relation to "law" and "constitution" in Anglo-American thought, see Stourzh, *Fundamental Laws*, and Wood, *The Creation of the American Republic*, 273–82, for the post-revolutionary period.

[71]Vattel, *The Law of Nations*, I, iii, § 33, 18.

occasion for such a vote, although a convention of the people, or their representatives, would obviously suffice.

The process of Constitution-making in 1787 and 1788—from convening a representative assembly to ratifying its work—required Americans to fill the blanks in Vattel's formulation. For the people's representatives even to meet in Philadelphia implied a commitment to change in kind. Madison claimed as much in *Federalist* No. 40. "The States would never have appointed a Convention with so much solemnity, nor described its objects with so much latitude, if some *substantial* reform had not been in contemplation."[72] Changes in kind are exceptional undertakings with large consequences, and they demand exceptional care in execution.

Once a constitution is adopted, it must be preserved. It is vulnerable to incremental changes in existing political arrangements—none of them exceptional and all implemented through the normal operation of those arrangements. The solution, Madison indicated in *Federalist* No. 53, is to accord the Constitution a formal status appropriate to its function. "The important distinction so well understood in America between a Constitution established by the people and unalterable by the government, and a law established by the government, and alterable by the government seems to have been little understood and less observed in any other country."

Madison was quick to point out the contrast with Great Britain, where "the authority of parliament is transcendent and uncontroulable, as well with regard to the constitution, as the ordinary objects of legislative provision."[73] The British Constitution fails to provide a mechanism for the people to effect changes in kind. While Parliament is the appropriate vehicle for changes in matters of *politeia*, it is vulnerable to all the whimsical and unwitting outcomes that formal constitution-making avoids. Under the Constitution of 1787 the powers of Congress are far less than Parliament's, though greater than the Constitution's critics had wished. As Edmund Morgan has commented, the English, after their "cautious revolution" of 1688–89, "reinstated popular sover-

[72] *The Federalist*, 261; his emphasis.
[73] *The Federalist*, 360–61.

eignty as the reigning fiction of government, with the unreformed Parliament as its beneficiary."[74] The Americans, after their own, "incautious revolution," proceeded with cautious originality to dissociate Congress from the body politic and the possibility of changes in kind.[75]

Madison's "Constitution established by the people and unalterable by the government" is a "compact," which the founders understood in the most deliberate and formal sense of the term.[76] By means of a compact, the founders equipped the body politic with a constitution appropriate to its function, which is to mediate between *polis* and *politeia*. Merging form and function, compact and constitution, they solved the nettlesome problem of providing for controlled change. Nevertheless, as Madison emphasized, the Constitution is the people's doing, not the founders'.[77] If anyone's intent matters, it is the people's and not the founders'.[78] For purposes of interpretation the text itself is far

---

[74]Edmund S. Morgan, *Inventing the People: The Rise of Popular Sovereignty in England and America* (New York, 1988), 121.

[75]The quotation is from a chapter title of Morgan's, ibid., 239.

[76]Donald S. Lutz, *The Origins of American Constitutionalism* (Baton Rouge, 1988), 16–22. For Calvinists, giving compacts the particular form of a covenant, or agreement secured by God, assures requisite formality. For the more secular-minded, equating compacts with the social contract has this effect. According to the Preamble of the Massachusetts Constitution of 1780, "the body-politic is formed by a voluntary association of individuals: It is a social compact, by which the whole people covenants with each citizen, and each citizen with the whole people, that all shall be governed by certain laws for the common good." "A CONSTITUTION OR FRAME OF GOVERNMENT, *Agreed upon by the Delegates of the People of the* STATE OF MASSACHUSETTS-BAY . . . *1780*," in Oscar Handlin and Mary Handlin, eds., *The Popular Sources of Political Authority: Documents on the Massachusetts Convention of 1780* (Cambridge, Mass., 1966), 441; see also Wood, *The Creation of the American Republic*, 282–91. For Madison, states are "parties to the constitutional compact," with states defined as "the people composing those political societies [having territory and governments], in their highest sovereign capacity." "The Report of 1800," Jan. 7, 1800, in J. C. A. Stagg et al., eds., *The Papers of James Madison*, 19 volumes to date (Chicago and Charlottesville, 1962–), 17:309.

[77]"The authority of constitutions over governments, and of the sovereignty of the people over constitutions, are truths which are at all times necessary to be kept in mind." "The Report of 1800," 312. Also see *Federalist* No. 39, *The Federalist*, 250–53, analyzed below, Chapter 3.

[78]According to Madison:

more important than Madison's, or anyone else's, opinion, but hardly because the text is perfect. Just as natural law has its source (*fons*) in nature, popular sovereignty is a "fountain of power." The Constitution gives expression, as does human reason itself, for all its imperfections, to nature's design.[79]

> The legitimate meaning of the Instrument must be derived from the text itself; or if a key is to be sought elsewhere, it must be not in the opinions or intentions of the Body which planned & proposed the Constitution, but in the sense attached to it by the people in their respective State Conventions, where it rec'd all the authority which it possesses.

James Madison to Thomas Ritchie, Sept. 15, 1821, quoted by Michael Kammen, *A Machine That Would Go of Itself: The Constitution in American Culture* (New York, 1986), 88.

[79]Grotius, *De jure belli ac pacis, Vol. One* and *Vol. Two*, Prolegomena, §§ 8, 12: n. p. (Latin), 12, 14 (trans.). The figure of nature as the fountain of law and justice goes back at least to Cicero, Laws, I, v–vi, 314–19.

"As the people are the only legitimate fountain of power," Madison wrote in *Federalist* No. 49, "it is from them that the constitutional charter, under which the several branches of government hold their power, is derived." *The Federalist*, 339. On the "fountain of power" as a rhetorical figure in political discourse of the founding period, see Michael Kammen, *Sovereignty and Liberty: Constitutional Discourse in American Culture* (Madison, Wisc., 1988), 11–32. Cf. "The Declaration of the Rights of Man and of Citizens," by the French National Assembly [1789], III, which proclaimed that "the nation is essentially the source of all sovereignty." In commenting on this article, and Burke's claim that "in England, a King is the fountain," Paine distinguished "the *fountain* and the *spout*." The latter he associated with the king, the former with the people and their representatives. Paine, *Rights of Man*, I, 89. The Declaration is at 110–12.

Chapter Two

"The Compound Republic of America"

I. WHOLE AND PARTS

Madison's description of America under the Constitution as a "compound republic" approaches "more perfect union" in historical resonance. Again Adams's reading of Polybius confirms the Classical provenience of "compound" as a term of political art: "it is manifest that the best form of government is that which is *compounded of all three*," as in Aristotle's three forms of rule.[1] Compounding yields the mixed constitution so favored by Adams. Madison's understanding of the compound republic is different, and so is the frame of reference provided in *Federalist* No. 51.

> In a single republic, all the power surrendered by the people, is submitted to the administration of a single government; and usurpations are guarded

[1] *A Defence of the Constitutions of Government of the United States of America*, in Charles Francis Adams, ed., *The Works of John Adams*, Vol. 4 (Boston, 1851; reprinted New York, 1971), 435, quoting Spelman's translation of Polybius; emphasis in Adams's rendition.

against by a division of the government into distinct and separate departments. In the compound republic of America, the power surrendered by the people, is first divided between two distinct governments, and then the portion allotted to each, subdivided among separate and distinct departments. Hence a double security arises to the rights of the people. The different governments will controul each other; at the same time that each will be controuled by itself.[2]

In Madison's conception, a properly constructed republic is indeed a mixed form of rule in which popular sovereignty is honored but the perils of democracy avoided. Mixing is not just some happy combination of elements melded by time and circumstance. For the founders, division and balance were active principles in the composition of single republics. Bringing together a number of such republics for the larger good raised other issues. The historic method of association, through formal agreement, or *foedus*, had been tried and found wanting under the Articles of Confederation. The Constitution represented an alternative method, not one of aggregation through agreement, but of composition and division.

What makes the compound republic distinctive are both the units of composition and the principle of division. In a single republic, these units are functional parts, organs of governance representing whomever and divided however. In a compound republic, the units of composition are state-republics, each of which is composed of its own functional parts. The constituent republics need not be divided from each other (they already are); nor are they to be merged (in which event they would be replaced by a single republic). Instead a newly created political arrangement, itself taking the form of a republic, would occupy a level above the several separate republics. The new level depends on, but is divided from, the aggregate of republics occupying the level beneath, while the latter benefit in aggregate from a new arrangement which depends on no one of them individually. As Madison suggested, the two levels control each other for general advantage. Taken together, the two levels yield a compound of republics. Because the two levels cannot be taken apart, the compound of republics must itself be a compound republic.

[2] *The Federalist*, ed., with an Introduction and Notes, by Jacob E. Cooke (Middletown, Conn., 1961), 350–51.

What to call the arrangement of the new level—the republic above the state-republics—remains a question. Madison and his associates settled for "federal republic" and "federal Constitution" to distinguish the new *polis* and its *politeia* both from the several states with their own republican constitutions and from the earlier association of those same states under the Articles of Confederation.[3] Yet the usage of the time made the terms "confederate" and "federal" effectively synonymous. In *Federalist* No. 9, Hamilton's English for Montesquieu's *"république fédérative"* is "CONFEDERATE REPUBLIC," which Montesquieu defined as "a kind of assemblage of societies [*une société de sociétés*], that constitute a new one, capable of increasing by means of new associations, till they arrive at such a degree of power, as to be able to provide for the security of the whole united body."[4]

Montesquieu's formulation offered Hamilton a happy combination of authority and ambiguity. Montesquieu surely meant "federative" to be understood as Locke had used it: the power to protect against external threat, as distinct from the power to execute laws.[5] Locke held that, though distinct, these powers "are hardly to be separated" or placed "in the hands of distinct persons."[6] Montesquieu held otherwise, at least in the case of certain historic associations, or "perpetual republics," which allocated "a degree" of federative power to the assemblage as a whole. What form that power might take, what relation the whole might have to its parts, Montesquieu did not say.[7]

[3]Ibid., though "federal system" appears to refer to both levels of the compound republic, and not just the "federal" level.

[4]Ibid., 53; *De l'esprit des loix*, II, ix, §§ 3–4, in *Oeuvres complètes de Montesquieu* (Paris 1958, reproducing ed. of 1758), I, 172; *The Spirit of the Laws*, ed. by David Wallace Carrithers (Berkeley and Los Angeles, 1976, reprinting first English ed., 1750, trans. by Thomas Nugent), 183.

[5]John Locke, *Two Treatises of Government*, ed. by Peter Laslett (Cambridge, 1963), Second Treatise, XII, 382–84. Among the means of achieving security against outsiders is power to treat, which the term "federative" refers to literally.

[6]Ibid., § 148, 384.

[7]In striking contrast is Vattel's discussion of confederate republics.

> Finally, a number of sovereign and independent States may unite to form a perpetual confederation, without individually ceasing to be perfect States. Together they will form a confederate republic. Their joint resolutions will not

When in *Federalist* No. 9 Hamilton invoked Montesquieu's authority on the properties of a confederate republic, he concluded that it was an "association of two or more States into one State."[8] After hardening the already ambiguous relation of one and many into a flat contradiction, Hamilton disingenuously claimed that because the states continued as separate organizations, they "would still be, in fact and in theory, an association of States, or confederacy." This they would be despite their "perfect subordination" to what Hamilton interchangeably called general or federal authority.[9] Gone is even a pretense of discrimination between federative and executive powers. Instead we find manipulation of terms to the point of obfuscation: Federal still means confederal (nothing has changed) but it means something more (because the confederal arrangement, though exactly what Montesquieu had in mind, was not enough). Hamilton, Madison, and the "Federalists" had it both ways, using the word "federal" as Antifederalists did while devising, as J. G. A. Pocock has remarked, "an utterly new sense of the word."[10]

By contrast the characterization of the whole system as a compound republic involves no new sense of the term "compound," notwithstanding the difference between Adams's and Madison's conceptions. Both find warrant in an Aristotelian understanding of the relation of parts and wholes. According to Aristotle, wholes are compounded from parts which are themselves wholes. In the process such parts may, but need not and often do not, lose their original identities as wholes. Insofar as parts retain their identities, the whole remains a compound but, being a whole, is available as a part in the composition of some yet greater

---

impair the sovereignty of individual members, although its exercise may be somewhat restrained by reason of voluntary agreements.

E. de Vattel, *The Law of Nations or the Principles of Natural Law Applied to the Conduct and to the Affairs of Nations and of Sovereigns Vol. Three, Translation of the Edition of 1758* by Charles G. Fenwick (Washington, 1916), I, i, § 10, 12.

[8]*The Federalist*, 53–55, quoting 55.

[9]Ibid.

[10]J. G. A. Pocock, "States, Republics, and Empires: The American Founding in Early Modern Perspective," in Terence Ball and Pocock, eds., *Conceptual Change and the Constitution* (Lawrence, Kans., 1988), 69. See generally Pocock's superb discussion, 60–61, 66–73.

whole. Perspective decides: When seen from below, wholes are compounds. When seen from above, compounds are wholes. When seen from outside, wholes/parts in the form of compounds occupy positions in an ascending order of relations.

In the *Politics*, Aristotle applied this understanding of wholes and parts to *polis* and *politeia* as separate dimensions of political life. An inclusive political association, the polity "exists by nature," while forms of rule are human constructions "which differ from one another in kind."[11] Forms of rule vary, but not infinitely. Their differences are limited by the possible relations of a polity's parts. The polity provides a frame of reference for composition. In Aristotle's careful formulation, a "polis . . . belongs to the order of 'compounds' in the same way as all other things which form a single 'whole,' but a whole composed, none the less, of a number of different parts."[12]

As we saw earlier, families compose villages, and villages compose the polity. Families also compose classes, which, given differences in wealth, are three in number. Differences in vocation, merit and birth yield lesser partitions within classes. "Sometimes all these parts share in the control of the constitution [*politeia*]; sometimes only a few share; sometimes a number of them share."[13] The arrangement of parts corre-

[11] *The Politics of Aristotle*, trans. by Ernest Barker (New York, 1962), I, ii, § 8 (*1252b*), 5; IV, iii, § 5 (*1290a*), 161. Recall the discussion of "changes in kind," ch. 1. The term "polity" refers in these pages to any autonomous political entity, which for Aristotle could only be an inclusive political association, or *polis*. It is not a transliteration of "*politeia*" or, as in Barker's translation of *The Politics*, the term for *politeia* when Aristotle was referring specifically to virtuous political arrangements. Ibid., 87n.; III, vii, § 3 (*1279a*), 114.

[12] Ibid., III, i, § 2 (*1274b*), 92. For additional discussion of Aristotle's doctrine of composition, see ibid., trans. n., 95–96. We find Aquinas faithfully repeating it.

> Now nature proceeds in its operations from the simple to the complex [*ex simplicibus ad composita*]; and among things which result from natural agency that which is more complex is the more perfect [*quod est maximime compositum est perfectum*] and constitutes the integration and purpose of the others. One can at once see this in respect of any whole and its parts.

St. Thomas Aquinas, *Commentum in libros politicorum seu de rebus civilibus* (Commentary on the Politics of Aristotle), I, i, in *Aquinas: Selected Political Writings*, ed. by A. P. D'Entrèves, trans. by J. G. Dawson (Oxford, 1948), 194 (Latin), 195 (trans.).

[13] Ibid., IV, iii, § 4 (*1290a*), 161.

sponds to an arrangement of offices; parts translate into forms. A given form of rule follows from the dominant position of its corresponding part, within which some lesser part may also dominate. Or parts may balance and a mixed form result.

In Aristotle's system, there are two sets of ascending relations operating in tandem. One stems from individuals, composed of heads, hands, hearts and other parts and composing families. Families compose villages which in their turn compose polities. The other stems from the fact that important social attributes both distinguish individuals and encourage them to form associations with particular ends, then classes, and finally arrangements of rule. If forms have their own ascending order of relations, they must be parts/wholes in their own right. With ontological parity thus implied, it is not clear why Aristotle's two chains of ascending relations should be held apart. Classes would certainly seem to fit between villages and polities, and vocational and other local associations between families and villages. That classes are both components of the polity and determinants of that polity's form of rule is a generalizable feature of a single chain. At any given level, parts always have diverse characteristics and the whole will have its own form.

Nothing prevents extrapolation of the single chain in either direction, to the limits of the imagination. Aristotle stopped with the *polis* because he saw nothing that might qualify as a higher level of organization. He was aware of course that two or more polities could agree to form alliances and engage in other collaborative undertakings. Such agreements among neighboring polities would yield a confederacy, which is neither a new polity replacing the old ones nor a new kind of arrangement operating above the level of polities. Aristotle offered two reasons for this conclusion. First, a *polis* is "composed of different *kinds* of men, for similars cannot bring it into existence."[14] Aggregating similar parts is not compounding, because something more but nothing new results. Second, the *polis* is already sufficient for the good life, and nothing new is needed.[15] Arrangements that provide more of the good life only make the *polis* better at being perfect.

[14]Ibid., II, i, § 3 (*1261a*), 41.
[15]Ibid., III, ix, §§ 5–8 (*1280a–b*), 118–19.

II. THE THEORY OF CORPORATIONS

In a medieval context, Aristotle's case for the polity as the highest level of social life was doubly defective. On the one hand, the small size of the polity argued against, rather than for, its sufficiency in providing the good life, especially in the instance of security. As Hobbes was to demonstrate conclusively, using alliances and confederation to achieve security only raises the general level of insecurity.[16] On the other hand, the abundance of vocationally defined associations, or guilds, actively participating in city politics, made clear that the *polis*—in Latin, *civitas*—was hardly alone in affording the good life.[17]

Rather than abandon Aristotle's obviously useful principle of ascending relations, his medieval followers added a second principle, which Aristotle had anticipated by relating forms of rule to the polity's parts. This principle was developed in commentaries on Roman law and is now known as the theory of corporations. A corporation is a legal entity, a person with rights and duties, in the simplest case composed of natural, living persons with rights and duties of their own. In more complex cases, corporations are composed of corporate persons, in turn composed of natural persons. However composed, any corporation must consist of natural persons; their presence is a constant. Guilds are corporations which happen to be organized around vocationally defined activities. Consisting of artisans, guilds may be composed of "companies" having a corporate character of their own. The *civitas* is also a corporation, necessarily consisting of natural persons whom it organizes territorially. Nevertheless, the *civitas* is composed of corporations, be they precincts, guilds or both.

No corporation is sole custodian of the good life. Put another way, any social arrangement compounding different activities and contribut-

---

[16]Thomas Hobbes, *Leviathan*, ed. by C. B. Macpherson (Harmondsworth, 1968), I, xiii, 183.

[17]On guilds in that time, see Antony Black, *Guilds and Civil Society in European Political Thought from the Twelfth Century to the Present* (Ithaca, 1984), 3–75.

ing some definite and distinctive element to the good life of its participants can be perfect in just the degree its legal standing affords. Where
does legal standing come from? Insofar as the corporation is a legal
fiction, "it depends for its existence on the constitutive will of another
(the person who makes or institutes it.)"[18] Legal standing for corporate
personality comes from above. Insofar as the corporation is an embodiment of the collective will of its members, who have rights and duties of
their own, corporate personality comes from below.

To see these views in conflict is, as J. P. Canning has argued, a
contrivance of modern scholarship.[19] Indeed we can find in Aristotle an
alternative way of conceptualizing the situation. "In *all* cases where
there is a compound, constituted of more than one part but forming one
common entity—whether the parts be continuous or discrete—a ruling
element and a ruled can be traced."[20] Corporations of the same kind and
whatever stands above them together constitute a compound, within
which the superior rules. Ruling must thus be consistent with the
integrity of the compound, which means that the corporate character
of the parts cannot be denied. Furthermore, the ruling element in
the compound is itself subject to rule as a corporate part of some higher
compound. All compounds are locked, not just linked, in relations of
rule. Even as the theory of corporations enabled medieval thinkers to

---

[18]J. P. Canning, "The Corporation in the Political Thought of the Italian Jurists of
the Thirteenth and Fourteenth Centuries," *History of Political Thought*, I (1980), 16.
Canning's discussion informs this one. See also Otto Gierke, *Associations and the Law:
The Classical and Early Christian Stages*, ed. and trans. by George Heiman with an
interpretative introduction to Gierke's thought (Toronto, 1977), and Gierke, *Natural
Law and the Theory of Society 1500 to 1800*, trans. by Ernest Barker (Boston, 1957),
respectively consisting of Sections 2 and 3, and 11 of Gierke's *Das deutsche
Genossenschaftsrecht*, 3 (1881); Brian Tierney, *Religion, Law, and the Growth of Constitu-
tional Thought 1150–1650* (Cambridge, 1982), 19–28; Black, *Guilds and Civil Society*, 76–
95; Harold J. Berman, *Law and Revolution: The Formation of the Western Legal Tradition*
(Cambridge, Mass., 1983), 215–21; Canning, "Law, Sovereignty and Corporation
Theory, 1300–1450," in J. H. Burns, ed., *The Cambridge History of Medieval Political
Thought c. 350–c. 1450* (Cambridge, 1988), 454–76.

[19]It more especially comes from Otto Gierke's magisterial presence in the study of
corporations in medieval thought. Canning, "The Corporation," 15–18.

[20]*The Politics of Aristotle*, I, v, § 3 (*1254a*), 12; emphasis in trans., translator's
interpolations deleted.

escape the limitations of Aristotle's thought and countenance a variety of social arrangements for public good, it bolstered the Aristotelian foundations of the great chain of being.

The theory of corporations powerfully influenced early modern political thought. In the general scheme of ascendant relations, recognition of corporate personality at every level translates into rights and duties as the legal content of relations of rule. Natural persons have rights and duties; so do all the corporate entities of which they are members and all the entities of which those corporations are members. Popular sovereignty is insured; corporations composed of natural persons represent those persons while functioning independently of them. In turn those corporations find themselves represented, again by virtue of their legal standing, in the corporate entities they compose. Legal standing, rights and duties, and virtual representation are all consequences of one's station in the natural order of things, whether one is a natural or a corporate person.

Understood in corporate terms, the great chain of being provides a frame of reference for divergent tendencies in early modern political thought exemplified by the work of Bodin and Althusius.[21] Bodin claimed that sovereignty, or "the absolute and supreme power of a republic," incontestably resides with the ruler. In response Althusius insisted that sovereignty is held by the people, who conditionally grant the ruler the necessary power to rule for the public good.[22] Both writers make their claims in the context of layered corporations.[23] For Bodin, families, colleges (functionally differentiated associations), communities and republics all have corporate identity and stand in ascending relation.

[21]Jean Bodin, *The Six Bookes of a Commonweale*, reproducing the English translation of 1606 by Richard Knolles, ed. by Kenneth D. McRae (Cambridge, Mass., 1962); *The Politics of Johannes Althusius*, abridged translation of 3rd ed. (1614) by Frederick S. Carney (Boston, 1964).

[22]The quoted passage is a literal translation of Bodin's French. Knolles' translation reads: "Maiestie or Soueraigntie is the most high, absolute, and perpetuall power the citizens and subiects in a Commonweale." Bodin, *The Six Bookes*, A77; I, viii, 84. "*Majestas*," which is conventional Latin for "sovereignty" and the term Althusius used, suggests the awesome yet still comparative dignity of high station.

[23]Bodin, *The Six Bookes*, III, vii, 361–86; *The Politics of Johannes Althusius*, II–IX, 22–73. See Black, *Guilds and Civil Society*, 129–42, for a convenient summary.

Sovereignty resides exclusively in the republic, with the powers of lesser entities lawfully determined by the sovereign. In Althusius we find virtually the same series—families, colleges, cities, provinces and finally universal public associations, whether kingdoms or republics. The universal public association "is a polity in the fullest sense," which rules other corporate entities. Nevertheless the power to rule, or sovereignty, never belongs to individuals. Instead it belongs to "the entire associated body of the realm." Rulers are agents of the polity who take on "the function of governing, but not the plenitude of power."[24]

Bodin's conception of sovereignty would seem on its face to eliminate the need for an ascending arrangement of corporate entities. However a republic is constituted, its legitimacy comes from acknowledgement by other republics. Sovereign equality is the result. Bodin insured his fame by providing others with the conceptual grounds for abandoning a way of thinking he continued to espouse. By contrast, Althusius consigned himself to centuries of obscurity because he *succeeded* in reconciling the corporate way of thinking with a conception of sovereignty which had all the radical potential of Bodin's conception. To have done for the nineteenth century nation-state what Bodin did for absolutist monarchies, Althusius need only have conflated people and polity as Bodin did ruler and polity.

Althusius was able to reconcile his conception of sovereignty with the corporate framework by distinguishing between the polity's relation to natural and to corporate persons. The first is a condition of rule, of and for the people. "For as the whole body is related to the individual citizens, and can rule, restrain, and direct each member, so the people rules each citizen."[25] The second relation is that of a compound, as a whole achieving good beyond the good its parts continue to achieve. "The members of a realm . . . are not, I say, individual men, families, or collegia. . . . Instead, members are many cities, provinces and regions agreeing among themselves on a single body constituted by mutual union and communication."[26]

---

[24] *The Politics of Althusius*, 61, 65, 66.
[25] Ibid., 65.
[26] Ibid., 61.

Even this formulation violates the strict ordering of ascending relations by placing cities and provinces on the same level.[27] The circumstances of the Holy Roman Empire would have made a strict ordering unduly scholastic. Nevertheless the clear implication is that the people function as a whole but not as a corporate entity in their own right. Instead sovereignty emanates from beneath the corporate framework and realizes its effects in successively higher levels of political organization. By contrast, Bodin effectively substituted sovereignty for sufficiency as the defining attribute of the highest corporate level of political life, with effects realized in successively lower levels of organization. If sovereignty has a source above the highest corporate level, it can only be divine. From Bodin it is an easy step to the divine right to rule as popular sovereignty's inverse equivalent. Bodin's top-down conception of sovereignty also means that subordinate corporate levels are always vulnerable to the sovereign ruler. The corporate framework has no conceptual integrity of its own.

Althusius's scheme works against this result by discriminating between sovereign people and compound polity. He also strengthened his bottom-up conception with the language he used to describe the corporate framework. Althusius began his exposition by defining politics as "the art of associating men for the purpose of establishing, cultivating, and conserving social life among them."[28] For Althusius, association (his Latin is *consociatio*) meant much more than mere aggregation.[29] The point of association is symbiosis, a living together, beyond expediency, for the good and self-sufficient life.

---

[27]It also implies that families and colleges differ from cities, provinces and republics. The difference is between private and public associations. The theory of corporations derived from Roman private law and came to be applied to public life. In Gierke's interpretation, Althusius's project was to resolve "all public law into private law." Otto Gierke, *The Development of Political Theory*, 1880 ed. trans. by Bernard Freyd (New York, 1932), 266. Support for the great chain of being required no less, although traces of an older way of thinking remain.

[28]*The Politics of Althusius*, 12.

[29]Cicero made this point more clearly than Althusius did, in a passage the latter quoted incompletely. "A people is not just a collection [*coetus*] of everyone brought together [*congregatus*] in any sort of way, but of a number of individuals associated [*sociatus*] by agreement [*consensu*] on rights and the good." *De re publica, De legibus,* with

The subject matter of politics is therefore association in which the symbiotes [*symbiotici*] pledge themselves to each other, explicit and tacit agreement [*pacto*], to mutual communication of whatever is useful and necessary for the harmonious exercise of social life.[30]

Althusius typically referred to the polity as a "universal symbiotic association." As such it is "a mixed society," a compound consisting of "people united in one body by the agreement of many symbiotic associations."[31] The body is the whole, the associations the parts, which are themselves wholes. Agreement makes the larger whole—the people united—without sacrificing the identity of corporate members as the price of agreement. Althusius was not proposing a contract theory for the origins of political society, in which the contractors alienate their rights for the common good.[32] Agreement is ongoing; political arrangements are constitutive consequences of "the mutual communication of whatever is useful and necessary."[33]

Yet agreement is not merely occasional and instrumental, its result an alliance of convenience. Reference to communication as much as to agreement tells us this. So does Althusius's use of *pactum*, not *foedus*.[34]

---

trans. by Clinton Walker Keyes (London, 1923), The Republic I, xxv, 64; translation provided. In Althusius's rendition, the first part is dropped, while the second part substitutes the past participle of *consociato* for *sociatio*. *Politica methodice digesta of Johannes Althusius*, reprinted from 3rd ed. of 1614, with an Introduction by Carl Joachim Friedrich (Cambridge, Mass., 1932), I, § 7, 16.

[30]Ibid., I, § 2, 16; *The Politics of Althusius*, 12.

[31]*The Politics of Althusius*, 61.

[32]Consider Hobbes's formulation. "The Greatest of humane Powers, is that which is compounded of the powers of most men, united by consent, in one person, Naturall or Civill, that has the use of all their Powers depending on his will; such as is the Power of a Common-wealth. . . ." *Leviathan*, I, x, 150. Hobbes's use of "compound" affords an Aristotelian veneer to reasoning wholly at odds with Aristotle's or Althusius's. For Hobbes, the sovereign's powers result from subtraction (their surrender from below) and addition (in the sovereign's hands) rather than multiplication.

[33]Quoted above and cited, n. 30; see also *The Politics of Johannes Althusius*, 61.

[34]"*Foedus*" is related to "*fides*," or "faith," and refers in the first instance to "formal agreement between states or peoples." P. G. W. Clare, ed., *Oxford Latin Dictionary* (Oxford, 1982), 717. Indo-European in origin, the concept has always suggested a discretionary element when applied to clan relations. B. W. Liest, "The Fides Commandment," in Albert Kocourek and John H. Wigmore, eds., *Evolution of Law: Select Readings on the Origins and Development of Legal Institutions*, Vol. II, *Primitive and Ancient Legal Institutions* (Boston, 1915), 492. A large literature to the contrary, "*foedus*"

Contemporary efforts to construe Althusius as an early federal theorist are seriously misleading if the term "federation" is taken to refer to an alliance among otherwise autonomous partners.[35] In Althusius's time, "federation" meant just this, and it continued to until the time of the American founding. Althusius's scheme demands a different vocabulary, Aristotelian in temper, which indeed he provided. By calling him a consociationalist, we simultaneously give him the credit he is due and mark the eclipse of his ideas in modern political theory.

III. AFTER ALTHUSIUS

After Althusius, we hear much about the Holy Roman Empire as a *respublica composita*. There was little else it could plausibly be. Pufendorf would soon deny even this possibility with an analysis so powerful and systematic that it effectively discredited any alternative. His conclusion is famous: the Empire was a monstrosity.[36]

---

bears no evident relation to "covenant." "*Pactum*" is related to "*pax*," and refers to "an agreement or compact" securing or imposing peace. *Oxford Latin Dictionary*, 1280–81. The difference between "*foedus*" and "*pactum*" is very much the difference between a defensive alliance and a collective security system, the former responding to the vagaries of external threat, the latter to the inevitability of internal disturbances to the peace. Also see Ch. 1, n. 76, above.

[35]In rehabilitating Althusius and his consociational scheme, Gierke was first to identify him as a federal theorist. *The Development of Political Theory*, 265–69; *Natural Law and the Theory of Society*, 70–76. See also Heinz H. F. Eulau, "Theories of Federalism under the Holy Roman Empire," *American Political Science Review*, 35 (1941), 643–64; Thomas Roeglin, "Medieval Constitutionalist or Modern Federalist?" and Patrick Riley, "Three Seventeenth Century German Theorists of Federalism: Althusius, Hugo and Leibniz," both in Daniel J. Elazar, ed., *Federalism as Grand Design: Political Philosophers and the Federal Principle* (Lanham, Md., 1987), 15–48 and 49–83. Using the term "federal" as now understood for a way of thinking which stood in opposition to federalism as then understood would seem to be an instance of reading history backwards, with unnecessary confusion ensuing. Cf. S. Rufus Davis's entertaining commentary in *The Federal Principle: A Journey through Time in Quest of a Meaning* (Berkeley and Los Angeles, 1978), 51–53.

[36]See Murray Forsyth, *Unions of States: The Theory and Practice of Confederation*

Much influenced by Hobbes, Pufendorf accepted a strict conception of sovereignty as indivisible. This meant that sovereignty must be exercised or delegated by a single person, whether a natural person, as Bodin presumed, or a corporate person.[37] Pufendorf also took advantage of Hobbes's distinction between regular and irregular systems. "By SYSTEMES," Hobbes understood "any numbers of men joyned in one Interest. . . . *Regular* are those where one man, or Assembly of men, is constituted Representative of the whole number. All other are *Irregular*."[38] Applying this conceptual apparatus to polities [*civitates*], Pufendorf held that there are but three regular forms of rule based on the location of supreme power: a single person, a council of the few, and the people as a whole.[39]

Regular polities can be defective. Yet vicious or morbid forms do not yield new species of republics, "for such vices change neither the nature of power itself nor its proper subject."[40] When defects are so great that they "cannot be explained away as any mere disease," most students choose to "call such republics mixed, as if they were compounded of simple forms that have turned in on themselves and modified their

---

(New York, 1981), 80, for Pufendorf's development of this theme in several tracts appearing before his major treatise cited below. See generally Forsyth's sensible treatment of Bodin, Althusius and Pufendorf, 72–85.

[37]Pufendorf argued,

> Yet in moral compound bodies [*in corporibus moralibus compositis*] something can be attributed to the body which cannot be attributed to all the members . . . ; and, therefore, the whole [*universitas*] is an actual moral person distinct from the individual members, to which a special will, as well as actions and rights, can be attributed, which do not fall to the individuals.

Samuel Pufendorf, *De jure naturae et gentium libri octo*, Vol. One, *The Photographic Reproduction of the Edition of 1688*, and *Vol. Two, The Translation* by C. H. Oldfather and W. A. Oldfather (Oxford, 1934), VII, v, § 5, 703 and 1027 respectively. See also Gierke, *Natural Law and the Theory of Society*, 118–21.

[38]*Leviathan*, II, xxii, 274; Hobbes's emphases.

[39]*De jure naturae*, VII, v, § 3, 701 (Latin), 1024 (trans.). The paraphrasing here is closer to Pufendorf's Latin than is the Oldfathers' translation.

[40]Ibid., VII, v, § 11, 708 and 1035. Pufendorf used "*civitas*" and "*respublica*" more or less interchangeably.

elements."[41] Pufendorf's attack on the concept of a mixed republic follows Aristotle in recognizing that forms must be parts if they are to constitute a new whole in mixed form. Specifically, monarchy, aristocracy and democracy are corporate entities or estates formally represented in the new polity. Yet, given the nature of sovereignty, two conditions beset such polities. Either they are weakly united and "open to internal disorders," or they tacitly and awkwardly vest supreme power in a permanent body. In the latter case the result is "an aristocracy, but one very ill-adapted to transact business."[42] In either case, such polities are irregular to the point of being fatally flawed.

Pufendorf held that weakly united polities depend on a pact [*pactum*], whereas regular republics require a bond [*vinculo*] decisively locating sovereignty at the higher corporate level.[43] The former thus resemble a defective form of a system of polities, the regular form of which is a confederation. When Pufendorf turned to regular systems, he noted that the parts, the constituent polities, "are bound to each other by a perpetual treaty [*foedere perpetuo*]."[44] Such treaties have limited objectives and confer limited powers to any permanent council they may create. The final location of sovereignty depends on a treaty's specific terms but is never indeterminate. Indeed, it is subject to a simple operational test: "whenever affairs are decided on the principle of a majority of votes, so that the opposition is also obligated, it constitutes a departure from the regular form of systems, and the establishment of an irregular body, or of a single polity."[45]

Pufendorf's analysis effectively eliminates Althusian pacts from a role in composition. Pacts fall between instrumental treaties of alliance (*foedera*) and affectively motivated unions (*vinculi*). The first yields "*systemata ex pluribus perfectis civitatibus composita*," the second "*civitas ex*

---

[41]Ibid., VII, v, § 12, 710 and 1037.

[42]Ibid., VII, v, § 13, 711 and 1039.

[43]Ibid. "*Vinculum*" literally means "fetter" or "shackle." More figuratively it refers to "a force or impulse uniting people, a link, bond (esp. of friendship, kinship and sim.)." *Oxford Latin Dictionary*, 2065–66.

[44]*De jure naturae*, VII, v, §18, 717 and 1046.

[45]Ibid., VII, v, § 20, 720 and 1051, "*civitatem*" there rendered "state."

pluribus corporibus subordinatis . . . composita."[46] Nothing in between is
stable or normal; any so-called *respublica composita* is therefore dismissed.

"After Pufendorf had once rejected the notion of a 'composite
State,'" Otto Gierke observed, "it became the orthodox, and we may
almost say the unquestioned, view . . . that a State which stood above
other States was an impossibility."[47] Yet Gierke also noted a gradual
recovery of *respublica composita* as an admissible category, at least for
Germans confronted with the anomalous but enduring Empire.[48] In an
American context, Pufendorf's analysis never threatened the conceptual
credibility of either the mixed constitution, which Adams favored, or
the compound republic. The founders saved the former idea by using
the doctrine of the separation of powers, which is concerned only with
forms, to sever the archaic equivalence of forms and estates. They saved
the latter idea by ignoring the vast literature addressed to the peculiar
circumstances of the Holy Roman Empire and, more importantly,
engaging in the least possible discussion of sovereignty.[49] The terms of
any such discussion, as set by Bodin, Hobbes and Pufendorf, could only
cast doubt on a system of ascending corporate relations, in which
majesty and the power to rule, along with almost everything else,
increases by degrees. Montesquieu was safe. His discussion of the
separation of powers and the properties of confederations gave the
founders just what they needed from European political thought and no
more.

Most accounts of the Constitutional Convention emphasize the
struggle over representation between delegates from large states who
favored proportional representation in the proposed national legislature

[46]"systems composed of many perfect polities"; "a polity composed of many
subordinate bodies." Ibid., VII, v, §§ 2, 16, 701, 716.

[47]*Natural Law and the Theory of Society*, 196.

[48]Ibid., 197–98; Eulau, "Theories of Federalism," 659–62.

[49]Cf. Michael P. Zuckert, "A System without Precedent: Federalism in the
American Constitution," in Leonard W. Levy and Dennis J. Mahoney, eds., *The
Framing and Ratification of the Constitution* (New York, 1987), 149:

> the Articles of Confederation may have been sovereignty-obsessed, but . . . the
> founders slid past it [the issue of sovereignty] with remarkable ease. The
> Constitutional Convention had few discussions that centered on the issue, and
> none of the rancor that characterized it in the era just before the Civil War.

and small-state delegates who sought to preserve the Confederation's provision for equal state voting; the hybrid, compound scheme sent out to the state conventions is seen as the unanticipated consequence of the interaction of the two camps. All such accounts neglect what delegates commonly accepted, namely, the corporate coexistence of towns and municipalities, counties, states, and the states associated in the form of a republic. The delegates' only alternative would be to substitute administrative districts for corporate entities and ruler's agents for government at several levels. That alternative—"*municipia* in the people's empire"— was all too close to European experience and would soon see systematic, self-conscious application under Napoleon.[50]

Rationalized rule from one or several sovereign centers was also the likely outcome of an unmitigated victory for either camp at the Constitutional Convention. If one layer fully gave way to the other, the scheme of ascending layers would itself collapse. Neither camp could afford the luxury of winning. Both could fall back on a compound republic novel less in conception than in particular features hammered out in Philadelphia. Historians and political theorists who emphasize the novelty of these arrangements fail to appreciate the founders' predilection for an old-fashioned way of thinking in which political arrangements, however novel, must always take into account the purposive, corporate character of social life.[51] As with Aristotle, so with the American founding: first the *polis*, then *politeia*.

[50]Pocock, "States, Republics and Empires," 71. See also Ostrom's passing reference to "two concepts in governance" as "design principles"—*Genossenschaft* (comradeship or association) *versus Herrschaft* (lordship or hierarchical rule)—which we may take as aligning with the alternatives presented here. *The Political Theory of the Compound Republic: Designing the American Experiment*, 2nd ed. (Lincoln, Neb., 1987), 8. Others writing on the American founding seem to be unaware of these two traditions in social thought, the latter of which culminates in Weber's immensely influential legal and political sociology. Nicholas Greenwood Onuf, *World of Our Making: Rules and Rule in Social Theory and International Relations* (Columbia, S.C., 1989), 197–205.

[51]Instructive recent examples are Lance Banning, "The Practicable Sphere of a Republic: James Madison, the Constitutional Convention, and the Emergence of Revolutionary Federalism," in Richard Beeman et al., *Beyond Confederation: Origins of the Constitution and American National Identity* (Chapel Hill, 1987), 162–87, and Michael P. Zuckert, "Federalism and the Founding: Toward a Reinterpretation of the Consti-

IV. ASSOCIATION, CONSOCIATION

The political arrangements identified with a compound republic depend on a teleological vision in which purposive association is at the center of human experience and social meaning. Paradoxically, such a vision faded in the United States with the proliferation of political and civil associations, which Tocqueville brought to attention and later came to be called pluralism.[52] Apparently fulfilling Aristotle's vision of purposeful activity, these associations have always been corporate entities, normally equipped with constitutions specifying conditions of membership, offices and powers, activities, and sources of revenue. Law may facilitate their incorporation, and government regulates their activities. Nevertheless instruments of incorporation, whether internal to the association or legally expedited, do not normally specify the relations among associations. Instead their relations are understood in *liberal* terms, as analogous to relations among self-interested, autonomous individuals. The very term "corporation" has come to be synonymous with business enterprises which are both legally incorporated and prohibited from coordinating their activities.

Pluralism enlists corporate entities in liberalism's service. By sheltering these entities without fixing them in place, the compound republic freed them to serve a wide array of private interests. The compound republic was both an acknowledgment of the great chain of being—within which every possible association's purpose and extent determines its exact place—and its replacement. Once the compound republic no

---

tutional Convention," *Review of Politics*, 48 (1986), 166–210. Both essays focus on the way powers assigned to each level were bargained out during the Convention; the two levels themselves are treated as constants bounding the Convention's bargaining space. Although Zuckert was more explicit about levels as such, his use of "compound" is limited to given levels (182), making it indistinguishable from Banning's "mixed regime" (165). Nowhere are the corporate character and relation of the two levels acknowledged.

[52]Alexis de Tocqueville, *Democracy in America*, ed. by Phillips Bradley, 2 vols. (New York, 1954), 1:197–205; 2:114–28.

longer needed to order associations, they, like individuals, could pursue particular interests without reference to higher purpose. No wonder then that teleological vision inspiring the compound republic declined in proportion to the republic's success.

After World War II, American political theorists argued that pluralism was necessary to representative democracy. They celebrated the profusion of associations dedicated to the pursuit of stated interests, the competition among these groups for influence and rewards, and their ever-changing coalitions and bargains. The structure of society inevitably assumed a prominent place in the study of pluralism.[53] Committed to positivism and behavioralism, students of American politics joined sociologists in the "chopping up of political man" as member of sundry associations.[54] The state disappeared in favor of "the political system," itself an empty abstraction best suited only for taxonomic purposes.[55] The term "pluralism" functioned as an all-purpose description of American society, liberal ideology and academic vocation.

When political scientists investigated political arrangements elsewhere—most notably, in "plural societies" such as Belgium, the Netherlands, Switzerland, and Austria—they found an abundance of associations and strong regional cleavages.[56] Arend Lijphart, with a bow to

[53]Illustratively: *"polyarchy requires a considerable degree of social pluralism—that is, a diversity of social organization with a large measure of autonomy with respect to one another."* Robert A. Dahl and Charles E. Lindblom, *Politics, Economics, and Welfare: Planning and Politico-Economic Systems Resolved into Basic Social Processes* (New York, 1953), 302–9, quoting 302; their emphasis. See also William Kornhauser, *The Politics of Mass Society* (Glencoe, Ill., 1959), and C. Wright Mills's critique of "romantic pluralism" and its preoccupation with balance in *The Power Elite* (New York, 1959), 242–68.

[54]Sheldon S. Wolin, *Politics and Vision: Continuity and Vision in Western Political Thought* (Boston, 1960), 429–34, quoting 430. For a monumental example appearing the year of Wolin's critical assessment, see Seymour Martin Lipset, *Political Man: The Social Bases of Politics* (New York, 1960).

[55]David Easton, *The Political System: An Inquiry into the State of Political Science* (New York, 1953). Entries for "forms of government" and the "public good" do not appear in the index of this influential inquiry into the nature of politics.

[56]A *"plural society* is a society divided by . . . 'segmental cleavages.'" Arend Lijphart, *Democracy in Plural Societies: A Comparative Exploration* (New Haven, 1977), 4, quoting Harry Eckstein. The seminal discussion of "plural society" is J. S. Furnivall's. "Some Problems of Tropical Economy," in Rita Hinden, ed., *Fabian Colonial Essays* (London, 1945), 167–71. Hans Daalder culled other terms from the relevant literature:

Althusius, called these "fragmented but stable" regimes "consociational democracies."[57] But the metaphor is misleading: each "fragment" is a fully realized political association. To avoid stalemate and immobilism, Europe's consociational polities tend toward government by coalitions of parties representing major ethnic groups. Elections diminish in importance, majoritarian rule is a formality. Each party has a veto, which necessitates minimal agendas, devolution to subsidiary bodies and quiet accommodation behind ideological smokescreens. If complete stasis is to be avoided, elites must rule complicitly. An "elite cartel" requires a degree of cultural compatibility and personal trust among its participants, which separates them from the bulk of people whom they purport to represent.

Under the circumstances, the term "consociational democracy" is certainly a euphemism and perhaps an oxymoron. Lijphart concluded that "the elitism of consociational democracy should not be compared

---

"'vertical pluralism,' 'segmented pluralism,' 'social fragmentation,' 'ideological compartmentalization,' or . . . a Dutch metaphor . . . , *verzuiling*—literally meaning pillarization." "The Consociational Democracy Theme," *World Politics*, 26 (1974), 606.

[57]Arend Lijphart, "Consociational Democracy," *World Politics*, 21 (1969), 211. Also see Lijphart, *Democracy in Plural Societies*, and Daalder, "The Consociational Democracy Theme," for support of otherwise undocumented statements about consociational democracy in the pages to follow.

The direct source of the term "consociation," is David E. Apter, who identified "consociational systems" as one of three types of modernizing polities.

> *Technically, consociation is a joining together of constituent units which do not lose their identity when merging in some form of union.* Consociational forms may range from a relatively loose confederation of groups and states to federal arrangements with a recognized structure.

The Political Kingdom in Uganda: A Study in Bureaucratic Nationalism (Princeton, 1961), 24 (Apter's emphasis). Apter offered no authority for his "technical" definition, but his debt to an Aristotelian tradition of thought exemplified by Althusius is clear. The consociational form is "pyramidal," not hierarchical; there is no chain of command. "Power is dispersed and shared between the constituent units and a central agency. Legitimacy inheres in a representative principle"—presumably some principle for the representation of groups in governance—"and is shared by the whole collectivity." However represented, the people are sovereign. "Collective or corporate leadership is characteristic" (p. 24).

with a naive theoretical ideal of equal power and participation by all citizens but with the degree of elite predominance that is the norm in democratic regimes of all kinds." The telling criticism of consociational democracy is "not its undemocratic character but its potential failure to bring about and maintain political stability."[58]

Why has "consociational engineering," as Lijphart called it, proven so difficult, and stability, not to mention meaningful representation, so elusive? Lijphart's answer weighs "the problem of elite control of the segments" and "the problem of arriving at intersegmental elite agreements."[59] Lijphart felt that an important factor in the relative success of European consociational democracies is their small size, which means that "elites are more likely to know each other personally and to meet often."[60] As will be seen in the next chapter, this is exactly Aristotle's defense of the *polis* as necessarily small. Yet for Lijphart, unlike Aristotle, the nature and purpose of the consociational polity—political association, union of segments, layered construction—are inconsequential to its stability. Madison by contrast proceeded from Aristotelian premises, even as he demonstrated—contra Aristotle—that the compound republic could solve the related problems of size and factionalism at one and the same time.

"Consociational democracy" is a close contemporary equivalent to "compound republic." In both cases, an arrangement of rule organized on some representative formula must be understood as following from acceptance of a compositional scheme. All such schemes involve corporate entities (segments, regions) organized into layers. Thanks to the American experience, these schemes are referred to as "federal" or "confederal," depending on the distribution of powers among layers. Nevertheless, Lijphart had little to say about federalism, beyond admitting "parallels with consociational theory."[61] For anyone exploring such parallels, contemporary thinking about federalism offers little guidance.

[58]Lijphart, *Democracy in Plural Societies*, 50.
[59]Ibid., 234.
[60]Ibid., 64.
[61]Ibid., 42. Similarly Apter's acknowledgment of the relevance of federalism goes no further than the passage quoted above in n. 57.

Chapter Three

"Extent and Proper Structure"

I. READING MADISON

Of all *The Federalist* essays, none is more famous than Madison's No. 10, which concludes by exhorting us to "behold a Republican remedy for the diseases most incident to Republican Government." What is this remedy? Briefly stated, it is to be found in "the extent and proper structure of the Union."[1] The rhetorical power of this passage is undiminished by its familiarity. Nevertheless, its language suggests a conceptual difficulty. The problem and its remedy are both said to be republican—they inhere in republican government, which is a form of rule or *politeia*. Yet Madison found this remedy in the union, which is a purposive association in the sense of the *polis*. Although the words "compound republic" promote the same confusion, our examination of them reveals a concern first for the purpose of political life and then for its conditions. Inspection of *Federalist* No. 10 points to the reverse: the conditions of rule dominate the discussion; the purpose and character of the new union are all but forgotten.

Federalist No. 10 begins with mention of "a well-constructed Union,"

---

[1] *The Federalist*, ed., with an Introduction and Notes, by Jacob E. Cooke (Middletown, Conn., 1961), 65.

and moves directly into a consideration of the threat of factionalism in "popular governments." Madison's analysis of factionalism leads to a critique of democracy, defined as "a Society, consisting of a small number of citizens, who assemble and administer the Government in person," and endorsement of the republican form, by which Madison meant "a Government in which a scheme of representation takes place." Representation permits rule by some few—"a small number of citizens elected by the rest"—over "the greater number of citizens, and greater sphere of country." If republics escape the "in person" criterion of democratic rule, then there is no immediately discernible limit on the number of their citizens or their territorial extent. Indeed Madison argued an inverse relation between the size of a republic and the likelihood of disruptive factionalism. Bigger is better: "it clearly appears, that the same advantage, which a Republic has over a Democracy, in controling the effects of faction, is enjoyed by a large over a small Republic—is enjoyed by the Union over the States composing it."[2] Form of rule comes first, and then comes association for added advantage.

Madison returned to the character of republican rule in *Federalist* No. 14, there expostulating on "the great principle of representation," which modern Europe discovered but America was first to implement. Madison acknowledged a physical limit on the size of republics, which is an extrapolation of the limit on democracies. Representatives must be able to meet as their duties require; under the Articles of Confederation, "representatives of the States have been almost continually assembled." On this evidence, the union would hardly have reached its limit. The relation of size and form of rule firmly established, Madison turned briefly to the division of responsibility between the "general government" and the "subordinate governments" of the states. The former's

---

[2]Ibid., 56–64. Hume anticipated Madison's argument in his essay, "Idea of a Perfect Commonwealth," *Essays: Moral, Political and Literary*, ed. Eugene F. Miller (Indianapolis, 1985), II, xvi, 527. "Though it is more difficult to form a republican government in an extensive country than in a city; there is more facility, when once it is formed, of preserving it steady and uniform, without tumult and faction." See Douglass Adair's seminal treatment: "'That Politics May Be Reduced to a Science': David Hume, James Madison, and the Tenth *Federalist*," *Huntington Library Quarterly*, 20 (1957), 343–60.

"jurisdiction is limited to certain enumerated objects, which concern all the members of the republic," while the latter "extend their care to all those other objects, which can be separately provided for." Only then did Madison resume discussion of the advantages of an "extended republic," all resulting from union. These advantages obtain, not just for individuals, but even more clearly and substantially for states as such: new states may be added to the union, transportation and communication will improve, distant frontiers will be easier to protect.[3]

The structure of Madison's argument seems to substantiate a deep-seated change "in the ways Anglo-Americans thought about private 'interest' and the public good."[4] No longer was civic participation—the good and purposeful life—synonymous with the public good. Instead the purpose of politics was to arrange for the public good, conceived now as a condition in which many interests flourish and none clash unduly. Among possible political arrangements, representative institutions best served that purpose; economies of scale further suggested an arrangement of representative institutions at two levels, one responsive to the play of general interests, the other responsive to more local interests. Scholars of the founding era are struck by "the pervasiveness of representation."[5] Questions of representation dominated the Constitutional Convention; answers wrung from the delegates after intensive debate decisively shaped the way even the most reflective among them, like Madison, understood their creation.[6]

Madison's treatment of factionalism and representation in *Federalist*

---

[3] *The Federalist*, 83–89. Not to be confused with "extended republic" is "extended polity," which Jack P. Greene introduced "as an analytic category to apply to the far—flung association of separate entities represented by the early modern overseas European empires." *Peripheries and Center: Constitutional Development in the Extended Polities of the British Empire and the United States, 1607–1788* (Athens, Ga., 1986), ix.

[4] Cathy D. Matson and Peter S. Onuf, *A Union of Interests: Political and Economic Thought in Revolutionary America* (Lawrence, Kans., 1990), 3. See also Peter Onuf, "James Madison's Extended Republic," *Texas Tech Law Review*, 21 (1990), 2375–87.

[5] Gordon S. Wood, *The Creation of the American Republic, 1776–1787* (Chapel Hill, 1969), 596.

[6] Lance Banning, "The Practicable Sphere of a Republic: James Madison, the Constitutional Convention, and the Emergence of Revolutionary Federalism," in Richard Beeman et al., *Beyond Confederation: Origins of the Constitution and American National Identity* (Chapel Hill, 1987), 178.

Nos. 10 and 14 has led scholars to give priority to the extended *republic* and to neglect the *compound* republic.[7] We need to remember, however, that Madison's concern is the Constitution itself. His conception of the Constitution presupposes a necessary connection between questions of governance, or *politeia*, and the structure of the union, the *polis*. The usual reading of *Federalist* Nos. 10 and 14 obscures the connection between the union and its republican form and reverses their logical sequence. Without union, there can be no extension or, indeed, no republic.

Thus there is more to Madison's argument than interests and their representation. As a practical issue, disparity in the size of states led necessarily to the conceptual and political centrality of representation in the design of political arrangements. The size of the union was also a practical issue, but one substantially, if incidentally, disposed of when the problem of large and small states was solved by forming the union into a compound republic instead of an alliance. Representative institutions hammered out in Philadelphia necessitated the compound republic and clarified its character. In effect, size—here, differences in the scale of people's interests and activities—served as a criterion for assigning the responsibilities of rule to different levels of the compound republic. Once devised, if only as an expedient, the compound republic captured the extended republic and established it above the less extensive republics through the principle of representation.

For Madison's purposes in *Federalist* Nos. 10 and 14, the priority of *polis* over *politeia* went without saying, or at least required no more than the rhetorical invocation of "a well-constructed Union." Hamilton spared Madison the need to say more because of his detailed treatment of the character of the union in *Federalist* No. 9, published the day before No. 10 appeared. Terence Ball called these two numbers "a one-two punch" and treated them as a suite.[8] Taken together they significantly alter the structure of Madison's argument.

---

[7]Thus Robert A. Dahl could formally recapitulate the "Madisonian argument" and never mention the union. *A Preface to Democratic Theory* (Chicago, 1963), 32–33. Vincent Ostrom also noticed this feature of Dahl's influential book. *The Political Theory of the Compound Republic: Designing the American Experiment* (Lincoln, Neb., 1987), 2.

[8]Terence Ball, *Transforming Political Discourse: Political Theory and Critical Conceptual History* (Oxford, 1988), 56–67, quoting 57.

Hamilton began *Federalist* No. 9, just as Madison did the next number, by referring to the Union as an antidote to faction. There is one, symptomatic difference. Hamilton's union is "firm," Madison's "well-constructed." Hamilton proceeded then to a discussion, not of democracy, but of the "petty Republics" of antiquity. Their infamous tendency for disorder had led to recent improvements in the republican form of rule. Among these improvements Hamilton listed "the representation of the people in the legislature by deputies of their own election." In the spirit of "amelioration," Hamilton argued that extension, the creation of "one great confederacy," would secure and improve "popular systems of civil government."[9]

Hamilton invoked the time-tested principle of extending rule through confederation in order to rebut the case against the Constitution offered in Montesquieu's name. Hamilton's adversaries had "with great assiduity cited and circulated the observations of Montesquieu on the necessity of a contracted territory for a republican government."[10] After the telling comment that several of the existing states already exceeded the limited size Montesquieu had in mind, Hamilton turned Montesquieu against the Constitution's foes.

> So far are the suggestions of Montesquieu from standing in opposition to a general Union of the States, that he explicitly treats of a CONFEDERATE REPUBLIC as the expedient for extending the sphere of popular government and reconciling the advantages of monarchy with those of republicanism.

There follows a long quotation from Montesquieu, which Hamilton took to reprise "the principal arguments in favour of the Union," as well as demonstrate "the tendency of the Union to repress domestic faction

---

[9] *The Federalist*, 50–52.

[10] Ibid., 52. According to Montesquieu,

> it is natural to a republic to have only a small territory; otherwise it cannot long subsist. . . . In a large republic the public good is sacrificed to a thousand views. . . . In a small one, the interest of the public is easier perceived, better understood, and more within the reach of every citizen.

Montesquieu, *The Spirit of the Laws*, ed. by David Wallace Carrithers (Berkeley and Los Angeles, 1976, reprinting first English ed., 1750, trans. by Thomas Nugent), VIII, xvi, §§ 1–2, 176.

and insurrection." Only then did Hamilton consider representation, but *not* of the people. Rather, states directly represented in the Senate kept for themselves "certain exclusive and very important portions of sovereign power."[11] Representation thus contributes to a "firm" union in which the levels of association are carefully defined and supported. If *Federalist* Nos. 9 and 10 are taken together, the union comes first, then comes the form of rule. *Federalist* No. 14 starts with the form of rule and ends with the union; balance and symmetry are maintained in what must be seen as a unified treatment of the size issue.

The impression that Madison gave priority to political arrangements in his consideration of the extended republic, and to the principle of representation in solving the size problem, owes much to his forceful contrast of "democracy" and "republic." What Hamilton called the "petty Republics" of antiquity Madison dismissed as members "of the democratic species."[12] As noted, Madison held representation to be a republic's deciding feature; by definition, then, no republic can have existed in antiquity. Why would Madison have taken a position as artificial, even silly, as this? Ball has suggested that Madison's Antifederalist adversaries forced him to defend the republican character of the new arrangements; this he did in a "conceptual counterattack," by radically redefining the concept of republic.[13] A less dramatic interpretation only requires Madison to have understood the political advantage of implying that his adversaries were democrats, no more trustworthy than democracies, because they opposed the Constitution's "Republican remedy" for the crisis of the union. In any event, Madison found himself in the peculiar position of seeming to dismiss all previous discussion of the size issue as applicable only to democracies.

[11]Ibid., 52–55. Contrast this with Hamilton's position at the Constitutional Convention: "the general power . . . must swallow up the State powers, otherwise it will be swallowed up by them. . . . Two sovereignties cannot co-exist within the same limits." Hamilton's speech of June 18, 1787, in Max Farrand, ed, *The Records of the Federal Convention of 1787*, 4 vols. (New Haven, 1911–87), 1:287. See also above, Chapter 2, on Hamilton's interpretation of Montesquieu.

[12]*The Federalist*, 84.

[13]Ball, *Transforming Political Discourse*, 76.

II. SIZE OF THE UNION

The great Classical authority on the question of size, as with so much else, is Aristotle's *Politics*. That treatise begins with a discussion of the *polis*, devotes its bulk to matters of *politeia*, returns at the end to the *polis*, its relation to the character and education of citizens, and to material circumstances. As for the last of these, there are two factors to consider: population and territory, and not just the quantity, but the "capacity," of each. Capacity refers to the performance of function. The function of the population is for its members to engage in the many activities appropriate both to their own ends and the purpose of their association, which is to be self-sufficient as a whole. These activities take place within a territory that must provide people with the means for their activities and their collective sufficiency.[14]

In considering capacity, Aristotle first considered the "human material." Too small a population prevents self-sufficiency. Polities may exceed that minimum so long as they continue to fulfill their function, which they can only do when political arrangements also function as they should. Here Aristotle found a clear and simple limit on the maximum size of polities. Where the population is "overlarge," citizens cannot "know one another's characters," and political arrangements suffer.[15] This was Madison's point of departure. If a polity could be no larger than that permitting the citizens to know each other, then the best form of rule is democracy, or direct rule by all citizens. But democracies are turbulent; greater size necessitates representation (or monarchy), which eliminates this tendency.

Aristotle never made the equation between a *polis*—an association whose members know one another's character—and democratic rule. Small size hardly prevents rule by one or a few or necessarily recommends against these arrangements, so long as self-sufficiency and the

---

[14]*The Politics of Aristotle*, trans. by Ernest Barker (New York, 1962), VII, iv, §§ 1–5 (1325b–1326a), 290.

[15]Ibid., VII, iv, §§ 11–13 (1326b), 291–92.

good life prevail. As Aristotle noted, if arrangements call for some citizens to govern and others to be governed, then the function of the former is to "issue commands and give decisions," while the latter's function includes "the distribution of offices." By implication the former act on behalf of the latter—"representing" them in governance—and may be removed from office for failing to do so.[16]

Nothing Aristotle said about polities precludes political arrangements relying on the principle of representation. Furthermore, such arrangements raise the upper limit on the number of citizens in a successful polity. Citizens need not know all other citizens; they need only know about the character of those citizens who would represent them. Representatives for their part need know the character of their own number and anyone they choose to represent themselves at yet a higher level. To be true to Aristotle, no representative assembly should exceed the number of citizens in a simple *polis*, and it may, but need not, be democratic in arrangement.

Madison pursued just this line of reasoning in *Federalist* No. 55, concluding, however, that even the *polis* was too large. "Had every Athenian citizen been a Socrates; every Athenian assembly would still have been a mob."[17] In *Federalist* No. 14 Madison said nothing about the size of representative assemblies. His only concern was the distance over which representatives were obliged to travel that they might meet in person. This is a question of territory, not population, which Aristotle next addressed in relation to the *polis* and its material circumstances.

At the lower limit, Aristotle required enough territory to allow self-

[16]"Although the ancient Greeks had a number of institutions and practices to which we would apply the word 'representation,' they had no corresponding word or concept." Hanna Fenichel Pitkin, "Representation," in Terence Ball, James Farr, Russell L. Hanson, eds., *Political Innovation and Conceptual Change* (Cambridge, 1989), 133. Cf. Madison's balanced judgment in *Federalist* No. 52: "the scheme of representation, as a substitute for a meeting of the citizens in person, being at most but very imperfectly known to ancient polity; it is in more modern times only, that we are to expect instructive examples." *The Federalist*, 355.

[17]*The Federalist*, 374; Madison resumed this line of reasoning in *Federalist* No. 58. Both numbers deal with features of the representative institutions proposed under the Constitution. See also Ostrom's cogent presentation of Madison's "size principle." *The Political Theory of a Compound Republic*, 92–97.

sufficiency. The upper limit depends on a number of conditions: the lay of the land, access to the sea, availability of resources, ease of defense, and location of the leading city, from both a commercial and a military point of view. Each of these conditions bears on the others, and all of them are affected by the activities of residents, not to mention the political arrangements they undertake. Obviously Greek city republics would occupy less territory than the American states, given differences in physical geography, level of technology and socio-political experience.

Madison specifically repudiated a Classical understanding of what a republic is and how large it may be. Nevertheless, Madison's treatment of the size issue adapts Aristotle's reasoning to the circumstances of the new union. Because Aristotle treated size as a property of the *polis*, it hardly matters what Madison said in this context about particular political arrangements. In any event, extending the republic through union gave the union primacy over those arrangements. If, as Madison held, extension is a "Republican remedy," it is also, for Madison no less than for Aristotle, a property of composition. The extended republic *is* a compound republic.[18]

Federalist Nos. 9, 10, and 14 even follow the expository structure of *The Politics*. First is purposeful association, then political arrangements, and finally association again, this time in reference to the material circumstances shaping the character of association. If the last paragraphs of *Federalist* No. 14, dealing with the advantages of union, do not seem substantial enough to complete the parallel, then Madison's *Federalist* No. 39 is surely conclusive. This number begins what is promised as "a candid survey of the plan of government." Union is not the point; rather it is "whether the general aspect and form of the government be strictly republican." This time Madison's "proof" of the system's "republican complextion" reaches beyond the application of the representative principle to its foundation, which is the principle of popular sover-

---

[18]Cf. Vincent Ostrom, *The Meaning of American Federalism: Constituting a Self-Governing Society* (San Francisco, 1991), 82: "allusions to an extended republic presuppose a compound republic: an association of republics within a republic where all are bound by rules of constitutional law." Note 28, below, comments on Ostrom's conception of a compound republic.

eignty.[19] Madison then suggested rhetorically, on behalf of his opponents, that a republican form did not suffice; the Constitution's drafters "ought, with equal care, to have preserved the *federal* form, which regards the Union as a *Confederacy* of sovereign States."[20] Madison's exposition suddenly, though hardly unexpectedly, turns on itself to honor the priority of *polis* over *politeia*.

The rest of *Federalist* No. 39 is devoted the character of the new Union, although the language Madison used ill-suits the purpose. Still speaking for the Constitution's critics, Madison went on to describe the new union as "a *consolidation* of the States." Consolidation would indeed be a "broad and radical innovation," and one might well ask by what authority was it undertaken. Madison asked this question first to deny that the new union was anything so radical as a consolidation of the states in the form of a national government and, second, to find authority for what was proposed in the exercise of popular sovereignty. Thus, "the Constitution is to be founded on the assent and the ratification of the people of America." Yet the people act "not as individuals composing one entire nation; but as composing the distinct and independent States to which they respectively belong." Popular ratification, though "given by deputies elected for the special purpose," takes place state by state. "The act, therefore, establishing the Constitution, will not be a *national* but a *federal* act."[21]

If the act of establishing the Constitution is (con)federal, then Madison is correct in concluding that each state must be "a sovereign body independent of all others, and only to be bound by its own

---

[19]*The Federalist*, 250–53. The term "popular sovereignty" never appears in *The Federalist*. Michael Kammen, *Sovereignty and Liberty: Constitutional Discourse in American Culture* (Madison, Wisc., 1988), 22. Madison did say in *Federalist* No. 39,

> if we resort for a criterion, to the different principles on which different forms of government are established, we may define a republic to be, or at least may bestow that name on, a government which derives all its powers directly or indirectly from the great body of the people; and is administered by persons holding their offices during pleasure, for a limited period, or during good behaviour.

The Federalist, 251.

[20]Ibid., 253; Madison's emphasis.

[21]Ibid., 254; again Madison's emphasis.

voluntary act." How then can the people be sovereign? That the people hold "supreme authority in each State" is true as far as it goes; popular sovereignty means that the people have supreme authority in any political association. The availability of states as instruments of the people's will hardly makes them sovereign. Clearly the act of establishing the Constitution is neither national nor federal (unless the latter term is used inventively and subversively, as it is in *Federalist* No. 9 but not here). Rather the ratification process entails "a conceptual breakthrough": by implementing popular sovereignty, ratification in, but not by, states solved "the dilemma posed by governmental sovereignty."[22] Establishing the Constitution was a deliberate act of composition, its consequences consociational in the Althusian sense.

Madison continued in the same vein to examine the scope and operation of government under the Constitution, and the procedure for amending the Constitution. In each instance he identified the proportion of confederal and national attributes and concluded that the Constitution offers a fine balance of both—a compromise acceptable to all. In the spirit of the Great Compromise on representation, Madison's Constitution effects a compromise on the character of the union by splitting the difference between consolidation and confederation. Yet Madison understood the union—"new modelled" in its "structure"—to be qualitatively different from either a single, consolidated state or a

[22]John M. Murrin, "1787: The Invention of American Federalism," in David E. Narrett and Joyce S. Goldberg, eds., *Essays on Liberty and Federalism: The Shaping of the U. S. Constitution* (College Station, Tex., 1988), 36.

[23]Quoting *Federalist* No. 14, *The Federalist*, 89. Madison had summarized his position in *Federalist* No. 39 by saying, "the proposed Constitution therefore is in strictness neither a national nor a federal Constitution; but a *composition* of both." Ibid., 257, emphasis added. Here Madison used the term "composition" synonymously with "mixture," and not in the sense indicated by "compound republic." Thus Madison's summary concludes by reiterating the mix of federal and national elements in the foundation and amendment procedure of the Constitution, and in the sources, operation, and extent of governmental powers. Nevertheless, his use of "composition" may reflect an awareness that the union, as opposed to the Constitution, was an alternative to compromise precisely because it was a composition. The usual interpretation finds novelty in the Constitution as compromise and not the union as composition. See for example, Martin Diamond's influential essay, "What the Framers Meant by Federalism," in Robert A. Goldwyn, ed., *A Nation of States* (Chicago, 1963), 26–27.

confederation of states.[23] The conceptually implausible fiction that sovereignty is divisible shrouds what is radical about the Constitution: it took popular sovereignty—a fiction also, but one that was powerful and ideologically resonant for most Americans[24]—and put it to work. By ratifying the Constitution, the sovereign people created a compound republic, its ascending levels "a chain of connection with the people," as James Wilson proclaimed during Pennsylvania's ratification convention.[25]

"The doctrine of popular sovereignty provided Federalists with a neat solution to the problem of freedom and power: the 'people' never relinquished their power at all."[26] In their constitutive acts, people cannot alienate what is inalienable by its nature. Hobbes notwithstanding, people cannot alienate their rights to liberty and happiness. Collectively, the people do not alienate their sovereignty when they assert their power for "public happiness."[27] Sovereignty is not the issue for the

[24]Edmund S. Morgan, *Inventing the People: The Rise of Popular Sovereignty in England and America* (New York, 1988). Morgan's claim that the fiction of popular sovereignty was largely an English invention of the mid-seventeenth century underestimates its importance in the medieval church and later for Calvinists generally. Otto Gierke, *The Development of Political Theory*, 1880 ed. trans. by Bernard Freyd (New York, 1932), 143–240; Quentin Skinner, *The Foundations of Modern Political Thought, Vol. Two, The Age of the Reformation* (Cambridge, 1978), 332–48; Brian Tierney, *Religion, Law, and the Growth of Constitutional Thought 1150–1650* (Cambridge, 1982), 54–79.

[25]Wilson's speech, December 11, 1787, in John P. Kaminski et al., eds., *The Documentary History of the Ratification of the Constitution*, 10 vols. to date (Madison, Wisc., 1976–), 2:580.

[26]Peter S. Onuf, *The Origins of the Federal Republic: Jurisdictional Controversies in the United States, 1775–1787* (Philadelphia, 1983), 207. Gerald Stourzh has usefully distinguished the "*dissociation* of legislative and sovereign power in the colonial period" from the "institutionalization of the constituent power of the people in the era of constitution building 1776–1788." *Fundamental Laws and Individual Rights in the 18th Century Constitution* (Bicentennial Essay No. 5, Claremont Institute for the Study of Statesmanship and Political Philosophy, 1984), 18–21, quoting 18; his emphasis.

[27]Madison implied as much in *Federalist* No. 45.

The public good, the real welfare of the great body of the people is the supreme object to be pursued; and that no form of Government whatever, has any other value, than as it may be fitted for the attainment of this object. Were the plan of the Convention [the proposed Constitution] adverse to the public happiness, my voice would be, reject the plan. Were the Union itself inconsistent with the

compound republic, for there is none to distribute between corporate levels. The distribution of powers between levels is an issue, but, like all distributive issues, it can be solved through bargaining and agreement. Agreement on a compound republic transformed the insoluble dilemma of dividing sovereignty into an issue that the delegates at Philadelphia, after arduous deliberation, could solve. Madison acknowledged this outcome with admirable succinctness in *Federalist* No. 46: "the Foederal and State governments are in fact but different agents and trustees of the people, instituted with different powers, and designated for different purposes."[28]

Popular sovereignty made the compound republic possible, the sheer size of the states taken together made it expedient, and differences in the size of the states made it politically necessary. The creation of a compound republic made extension a property of the union, which itself took the form of a republic composed of republics. Only insofar as extension related to population, and then only as a matter of quantity, not capacity, are representative institutions the frame of reference. Otherwise extension referred to population and territory generally, as a matter of capacity, and legally, as a matter of jurisdiction. Madison

---

public happiness, it would be, abolish the Union. In like manner as far as the sovereignty of the States cannot be reconciled to the happiness of the people, the voice of the citizen must be, let the former be sacrificed to the latter.

The Federalist, 309. On "public happiness," see also Chapter 1, n. 9.

[28]Ibid., 315. See also Ostrom, *The Political Theory of the Compound Republic*, 108–12, and *The Meaning of American Federalism*, 89–92, on the Constitution as a formula for distributing powers among "multiple units of government." While Ostrom properly recognized the union as Madison's republican remedy (*Political Theory*, 103–7; *Meaning*, 82) and noted the irrelevance of a Hobbesian conception of sovereignty (*Political Theory*, 22–23; *Meaning*, 94–95), he denied the compound republic its corporate character on the mistaken belief—fostered by his reading of Hamilton's *Federalist* No. 15—that corporate organization precludes a direct relation between the people and all levels of political association (*Political Theory*, 36–41; *Meaning*, 87–89). Hamilton wrote, "the great and radical vice in the construction of the existing Confederation is the principle of LEGISLATION for STATES or GOVERNMENTS, in their CORPORATE or COLLECTIVE CAPACITIES, and as contradistinguished from the INDIVIDUALS of which they consist." *The Federalist*, 93. Eliminating this vice does not eliminate a corporate relation between levels; the point of the Constitution is precisely to avoid a "national" remedy for a republican vice.

hinted at the operational significance of jurisdiction in *Federalist* No. 14, when he described the distribution of powers between the general and subordinate governments of the union. Jurisdictional principles familiar to the founders specified the scope of law by reference to land first, then persons, and finally the character and purpose of particular activities. Jurisdiction provided extension with a spatial frame of reference; territory as quantity, not capacity, took precedence.

Extending the compound republic meant bringing land, people and activities within its scope. States were defined by their territorial extent, and controversies between states were jurisdictional by definition. Migration to unoccupied lands took place either within states or precipitated jurisdictional adjustments leading to new states.[29] Jurisdictional concerns shaped the federal government's relations to other countries— relations already framed by a system of rules, "the law of nations," based on territorial jurisdiction. An expanding collection of states, jurisdictionally linked to each other and the federal government, admirably suited the pursuit of interest and the development of a liberal political economy.

Reading history with Madison's help, the union came first, and then its extension, expedited by representative institutions and responsive to material circumstances. Thus did it become a "union of interests." That some interests were clearly and increasingly sectional introduced cracks in the compound republic's interlocking arrangements—cracks between levels and regions. Reading history backwards makes them obvious, yet they were already a factor at Philadelphia, though concealed by the Great Compromise on representation. "It is interesting," but not at all surprising as a political matter, "that Madison ignored sectionalism in his supposedly prescient tenth *Federalist*."[30]

[29]Few historians have understood the importance of jurisdictional controversies in paving the way for the compound republic or of jurisdictional principles in its early development See, however, Onuf, *Origins of the Federal Republic*, and Peter S. Onuf, *Statehood and Union: A History of the Northwest Ordinance* (Bloomington, Ind., 1987).

[30]Onuf, *The Origins of the Federal Republic*, 172

III. LIMITS AND LEVELS

Does the compound republic have limits? As new states entered the union, improvements in transportation and communication, which Madison foresaw, permitted Congress to draw members from ever greater distances. While increases in population forced the members of Congress to represent ever larger numbers of people, especially when the House of Representatives was kept small enough that members could still know each other's character, those same improvements also permitted the people to judge the character of those who would represent them. Certainly the process of adding states faced a territorial limit, but one that receded for decades and then took decades longer to reach. Well before that time, the compound republic began a different process of extension, the character and limits of which are poorly understood even today.

Almost imperceptibly the compound republic developed new levels in its ascending series of political association. Emerging at the top, an institution apart, is the presidency. Long freed from corporate relation to the states and increasingly from coordinate relation to Congress, buttressed instead by a "plebiscitary relationship" with the public, the President has acquired a large, exceedingly visible staff.[31] As a level of association, the presidency is organized like a popular monarchy, preoccupied with large questions of state and status no less than royal courts were in the seventeenth and eighteenth centuries.

Congressional willingness to authorize a vast range of activities beyond its supervisory capacity entailed the delegation of its authority to an ever larger number of functionally differentiated administrative and regulatory agencies. Many of these agencies are autonomous under law, their senior officers appointed for long terms and professional staff · protected by tenure. Other agencies are nominally responsible to the

---

[31] Quoting Theodore J. Lowi, *The End of Liberalism: The Second Republic of the United States*, 2nd ed. (New York, 1979), 146; Lowi's book details developments summarily presented here.

President through Cabinet officers but autonomous in practice. As a whole they resist episodic attempts by Congress and the President to control or even contain their activities. In effect they constitute a level of association situated beneath the presidency. While this level is too disorganized to be called a republic, its parts too fractious to count as a confederacy, it has extended irresistibly to provide the country's liberal political economy and constituent interests a comprehensive infrastructure of support.

The Constitution of 1787 made the federal republic and its representative institutions the highest level in the compound republic. After two centuries of growth in the country's capacity, as Aristotle understood the term, and a comparable growth in governmental capacity, what remains of the federal republic is now two levels from the top. Between the federal republic and the states another functional level of association shows signs of emerging. Regional transportation authorities best illustrate its institutional character. Between states and the next territorially defined level—counties, cities and towns—and even that level and the next—precincts and neighborhoods—may be detected incipient functional levels populated with planning commissions and the like. In idealized form, the compound republic today is a fully extended chain consisting of alternating territorial and functional levels. The territorial levels are more typically republican in form (although the highest level is subject to monarchical, the lowest to democratic, tendencies), and the functional levels, formally less constrained, are the points at which the compound republic continues its lateral extension.

Idealized representations are just that. The political geography of the United States is so deformed that its alternating territorial and functional layers are hard to recognize and the composite, a "marble cake," even harder to visualize.[32] In response political scientists grant their overwhelming attention to *politeia*, and even then make behavior their primary concern while treating institutions either as constants or dependent variables. In this context the study of American federalism is a marginal specialty, its concern for the *polis* distinctly unfashionable.

---

[32]The metaphor is Morton Grodzins's. "Centralization and Decentralization in the American Federal System," in Goldwyn, ed. *A Nation of States*, 3–4.

Even if political science were to rediscover the *polis*, obstacles remain. Students of federalism must overcome their preoccupation with locating and dividing sovereignty, and thus their belief that the Constitution splits the difference between a confederacy and a unitary state—between many sovereignties and one. Sovereignty is indivisible; after Bodin, Hobbes and Pufendorf, no other position is tenable. The only choice is to jettison the concept of sovereignty. Functional growth among independent states prompted a school of international thought, called Functionalism, to do just that.[33] Functionalists were struck by the willingness of states' leaders to adopt multilateral treaties creating narrowly defined international organizations, such as the Universal Postal Union in 1874. In aggregate these treaties seem to distribute powers between two levels—the level of states in association and the level of states individually—according to the degree to which any publicly assigned set of tasks is technical, that is, not political in character.

Highly technical functions go to the higher level, where they are efficiently discharged by nonpolitical specialists, because states' leaders recognize that more is gained collectively than they lose individually. Leaders retain highly political functions for themselves, but they define what is political more narrowly as they benefit from the activities of widening range of technically oriented organizations above them. Because these organizations serve the public good without coordination among themselves or intervention from member states, politics does not reappear at the higher level, and states will continue to adopt treaties transferring bits and pieces of their powers until their sovereignty has effectively disappeared.

Functionalists were not always clear on what happens to sovereignty. The most famous of them, David Mitrany, offered this formulation:

> Sovereignty cannot be in fact transferred effectively through a formula, only through a function. By entrusting an authority with a certain task,

[33]See Ernst B. Haas, *Beyond the Nation-State: Functionalism and International Organization* (Stanford, 1964), 3–25; Charles Pentland, *International Theory and European Integration* (New York, 1973), 64–87. Haas referred to Functionalism in the upper case to distinguish it from functionalism in anthropology and sociology; the same convention is adopted here.

carrying with it command over the requisite powers and means, a slice of sovereignty is transferred from the old authority to the new.[34]

Formulas for dividing sovereignty are untenable. Mitrany's functional alternative is tenable only if sovereignty is dispensed with, not if it is transferred, for transfer by the "slice" is still a matter of division.[35] States' leaders will surely notice the reappearance of what they construe as their sovereignty at the higher level and reclaim it. Functionalism's prediction that sovereignty would disappear as new functional organizations were created failed the test of history. States' leaders saw the situation just as Mitrany described it, and rejected its implications.

The proliferation of functional activities *within* states has vastly exceeded comparable activities among states. Yet if such developments have led to a drastic redistribution of powers in the United States, they have met little resistance. Sovereignty was not an issue because new functional organizations formed a level below, rather than above the president as chief of state, and relations with other states were not immediately affected. In the American system, federalism and functionalism work together to organize and promote the exuberant growth of governmental agencies and activities.

[34]David Mitrany, *A Working Peace System*, Introduction by Hans J. Morgenthau (Chicago, 1966), 31.

[35]To write of "the pooling and sharing of sovereignty rather than the transfer of sovereignty to a higher level," as Robert O. Keohane and Stanley Hoffmann have in the context of the European Community, is no gain over Mitrany's formulation when "pooling of sovereignty" is defined as "the transfer of states' legal authority over internal and external affairs to the community as a whole, although not to supranational organs as such." What is the whole and what becomes of authority transferred to it? "Institutional Change in Europe in the 1980s," in Keohane and Hoffmann, eds., *The New European Community: Decisionmaking and Institutional Change* (Boulder, Colo., 1991), 13, 35 n. 11.

Part Two

A NEW WORLD ORDER

Optimistic American revolutionaries hoped to exploit and enhance tendencies toward stability, lawfulness and civility in the European system of states. The revolutionary impulse was not to turn away from the old world, or to turn it upside down. Instead American independence would contribute to the progress of European civilization by promoting a new system of alliances that would encourage free trade and restrain potential belligerents. The balance of power would provide a responsive context for enlightened diplomacy. Just as the European balance made American independence possible, an independent America would refine and improve the balance.

Revolutionary foreign policy epitomized Enlightenment faith in harmony and progress. Peace and prosperity would result from the expansion of mutually beneficial trade relations and diminishing opportunities for disruptive military conquests. British efforts to deprive Americans of their liberties had proved futile: a weak power exploited the balance of power to counter the preponderant force of a great power. Once the United States had secured its independence, it had no interest in war and every reason to cultivate relations with prospective trading partners throughout the world. The new states' republican constitutions reinforced their commitment to an enlightened statecraft that would guarantee peace and strengthen their union.

Yet Revolutionary hopes could not be sustained. Potential allies were more interested in strategic than commercial opportunities. The United States could only manipulate the balance of power if it could exercise power effectively. The irony of the Peace of Paris, ending the war in 1783, was that the victorious Americans lost their leverage: they no longer engaged or offset British power in ways that benefited Britain's rivals. To compound the irony, the weakness of the union—most apparent after 1783 in Congress's inability to formulate a national commercial policy—prevented American diplomats from negotiating the commercial treaties that would constitute a more civilized system of alliances. To be a progressive force in the society of nations, the United States would have to threaten credible sanctions—commercial and military—against wary or recalcitrant foreign powers. To exploit the balance of power, the United States would have to become a real power.

Postwar diplomatic frustrations also raised troubling questions about the organization of the American union under the Articles of Confederation. The Articles remained unratified throughout most of the war, and outstanding controversies among the states—most notably over control of Western lands—remained unresolved. In the first years after independence, however, Revolutionaries could look forward to growing harmony among the American states. After all, republics were constituted for peace and dedicated to securing the liberties and serving the interests of self-governing citizens. And if Europe were "a sort of republic," prospects for movement toward peace, stability and a regime of law were all the more favorable among the American republics. Yet such expectations proved unfounded. Even after the belated ratification of the Articles in 1781, the tendency of Congressional politics was centrifugal: as states sought to influence the direction of national policy or counter the influence of other states, their representatives became increasingly aware of distinct corporate and regional interests. Congress provided a forum for defining conflicting interests, but not reliable mechanisms for resolving them—or for promoting the national interest.

The crisis of congressional government called into question the

applicability of Vatellian precepts to the American states. In the absence
of superintending authority, reformers argued, republics were as prone
to conflict as other sovereign nations. The danger was most conspicuous
in Congress's faltering efforts to define a national commercial policy.
The fragility of peace and harmony *among* the American states became
apparent as American diplomats were frustrated in their efforts to
promote national interests and Enlightenment ideals.

As Vattelian internationalists, Revolutionary diplomats sought, but
failed, to negotiate treaties that would secure national independence,
foster trade and promote a more lawful world. Britain refused to
negotiate a commercial treaty with the erstwhile colonists that would
reopen lucrative West Indian markets. Meanwhile, Spain's refusal to
acknowledge American rights to the free use of the Mississippi precipitated sectional divisions that threatened the union. Constitutional reformers recognized that advantageous treaties, particularly with Britain
and Spain, were the *sine qua non* of union. They also knew that the
creation of a strong union was an essential precondition for success in
negotiating such treaties.

The move toward federal union followed from the failure of
confederal arrangements to guarantee harmony among the states and
Congress's resulting inability to conduct foreign policy. Reformers were
convinced that the Confederation, or any treaty organization lacking
plenary authority over the states' external relations, could not prevent
the American system from degenerating into a dangerous state of nature
where the threat of war was endemic. Turning from Enlightenment
faith in progress through conventional diplomatic means, the framers
sought to reconstitute the system along Classical republican lines. The
Vattelian system was predicated on the independence and sovereignty of
every state; the framers' predicated their federal republican system on
the people's sovereignty. The rights of the republican states of the
United States—and the liberties of republican citizens—could only be
secure when they all acknowledged a higher law, their own perfected
law of nations.

Federal Constitutional reform was paradoxically an affirmation and
a rejection of Revolutionary internationalism. Congress's powerless-
ness, its inability to figure in the European balance of power, jeopardized

American Revolutionary diplomacy and its Vatellian goals of independence, prosperity and law. Progress toward these goals depended on creating "a more perfect union," a compound republic fundamentally antithetical to Vattel's balance-of-power system. Now the European system of states would be the antitype, a negative model, for the American system. This sense of difference, first emphasized by Federalists in the campaign to ratify the Constitution, would deepen in subsequent years as the European system collapsed.

Chapter Four

The American State System

I. REVOLUTIONARY HOPES

American independence would change the world, Yale President Ezra Stiles told the Connecticut General Assembly in his 1783 election sermon. A new "commercial system," including the "maritime nations, on both sides" of the ocean, would guarantee "the *benevolence* as well as the *opulence* of nations, and advance the progress of Society to civil perfection." Meanwhile, by extending the defensive alignment of neutral powers first formed under Russia's leadership in 1780, a more inclusive "*armed neutrality* will disarm even war itself of hostilities against trade; will form a new chapter in the laws of nations, and preserve a free commerce among powers at war." Stiles predicted that a new system of trade relations would lift international society from its current "savage" condition to a higher plane of morality and civility. These happy results did not depend on republican revolutions in the old regimes of Europe. To the contrary, old regime statecraft would create a new world order. "All the European powers will henceforth, from national and commercial interests, naturally become an united and combined guaranty, for the free navigation of the Atlantick."[1]

[1]Ezra Stiles, *The United States Elevated to Glory and Honour,* 1783 Connecticut

The American Revolution was an epochal event for Stiles and many contemporaries on both sides of the Atlantic because it promised to accelerate historic tendencies toward stability, lawfulness and civility in the European system, of which the new United States would now be a part. Like many other prophets of progress in this period, Stiles celebrated the increasing scope of predictability and rationality in human affairs. Far from "turning the world upside down," the American Revolution promised to make the old world more manageable. The Americans would advance the cause of European civilization by active participation in its diplomatic system, not by promoting revolutions elsewhere or by conducting their republican experiments in splendid isolation. As a recognized member of the international community, the United States could begin to negotiate the alliances that would call Stiles's new commercial and diplomatic system into existence.

The Enlightenment critique of old regime corruption and despotism testified to a widespread faith in the possibilities of progress and improvement. Given the increasing administrative competence and power of the monarchical governments that constituted Europe, it is hardly surprising that these hopes should focus less on the revolutionary change in particular states than on the evolution of the system of states as a whole. The penchant of some philosophes for "enlightened despotism" reflected their expectation that international relations would become progressively more predictable and rational. Under the new dispensation, power itself would cease to be terrible. The eighteenth century idea of a "balance of power" epitomized this enlightened optimism.[2] One state's power was defined relative to others', and

Election Sermon, 2nd ed. (Worcester, 1785), 49–50, 84–85, 84. See the discussion in Edmund S. Morgan, *The Gentle Puritan: A Life of Ezra Stiles* (Chapel Hill, 1962), 444–61, esp. 453–55.

[2]Herbert Butterfield, "The Balance of Power," in Butterfield and Martin Wight, eds., *Diplomatic Investigations: Essays in the Theory of International Politics* (Cambridge, Mass., 1966), 132–48; M. S. Anderson, "Eighteenth Century Theories of the Balance of Power," in Ragnhild Hatton and M. S. Anderson, eds., *Studies in Diplomatic History* (London, 1970), 183–98. Also see citations provided in the Introduction, n. 9, above. James Hutson makes a compelling case for the pervasiveness of balance-of-power thinking in America in *John Adams and the Diplomacy of the American Revolution*

alliances compensated for inequalities that in any case tended to diminish as the diplomatic system became more complex and refined.

Far from rejecting this tradition of statecraft, many American Revolutionaries embraced it with characteristically boundless enthusiasm. Liberty-loving Americans may have been driven to revolution by their fear of unchecked British power, but they were confident that power could be restrained under their new state constitutions. Sanguine in their faith that British power was subject to limitation by other powers, if not by the fabled British "constitution," Revolutionary diplomatists did not hesitate to seek alliances abroad. "Realist" means—exploiting the balance of power and appealing to the self-interest of other nations—would serve progressive ends. It was incumbent on the Americans, explained former royal governor Thomas Pownall, a prominent British friend of the Revolution, to step forward "as an active Existing Agent" and assume the privileges and prerogatives of the "other Personal Sovereigns" who constituted world society.[3] Foreign powers, acting according to their own self-interest, would help the Americans secure their independence and then collaborate in the construction of a new world order.

Enlightenment liberals were not hostile to old regime statecraft when it was exercised under the light of reason and directed toward progressive ends. Their hopes for global peace and prosperity were predicated on the emergence of a more complex balance of power, not on the abolition of power politics. It was for this reason that Edmund Burke welcomed Revolutionary America into the European community. "A great revolution" has taken place, Burke wrote in 1782, "a revolution made not by chopping and changing of power in any of the existing states, but by the appearance of a new state, of a new species, in a new part of the globe."[4] By adding new states to the European system,

---

(Lexington, Ky., 1980), 1–32. But he fails to develop the implications of his assertion (p. 10) that for Revolutionaries the balance "was a progressive principle in international affairs."

[3] T[homas] Pownall, *A Memorial Addressed to the Sovereigns of America* (London, 1783), 129.

[4] Charles William (Earl Fitzwilliam) and Sir Richard Rourke, eds., *The Works and Correspondence of the Right Honourable Edmund Burke*, vols. 1-2, *Correspondence, 1744–*

the collapse of new world empires would provide increasing security for the states of the old world. Dismantling mercantilist systems would promote the balance of power while expanding the scope of peaceful, commercial relations. The refinement of the balance would in turn minimize the occasions for future wars and facilitate the development of a more civilized law of nations.

The successful conclusion of the Revolution and the emergence of the United States as an independent, sovereign power promised to transform the context of old world diplomacy. According to Burke, American independence "has made as great a change in all the relations, and balances, and gravitations of power, as the appearance of a new planet would in the system of the solar world."[5] The unequal competition for New World empire, culminating in recognition of Britain's preponderant power in the 1763 Peace of Paris, had precipitated a crisis for the European system. American independence not only rectified this extraordinary and unstable imbalance of power but promised to inaugurate a more highly developed and stable system. British liberals therefore could be complacent about the outcome of the Revolution. Notwith-

---

1797, 2nd ed. (London, 1852), 2:435. For similar language see [Edmund Jenings], *A Translation of the Memorial to the Sovereigns of Europe upon the Present State of Affairs, Between the Old and the New World, Into Common Sense and Intelligible English* (London, 1781), 2–3: "The Congress of the United States of North America is a new primary planet, which . . . must . . . shift the common centre of gravity of the whole system of the *European* world." Condorcet also expected the American Revolution to have a positive impact on the European balance. Condorcet, "The Influence of the American Revolution on Europe" [1786], trans. and ed. by Durand Echeverria, *William and Mary Quarterly*, 3rd ser., XXV (1968), 85–108. James Hutson may be right in arguing that this view was in fact mistaken: the Revolution "did not *immediately* change the balances or system of international relations" and "did not challenge the accepted method of conceptualizing international politics." Hutson, "The Treaty of Paris and the International State System," in Prosser Gifford, ed., *The Treaty of Paris in a Changing States System* (Lanham, Md., 1985), 13. But the point is that Burke and other sympathetic commentators *believed* that the American Revolution would have a progressive impact because it promised to transform the European balance. It was precisely for this reason that Pownall, Richard Price, and other pro-American writers were so concerned about the problems of union.

[5] *The Works and Correspondence of the Right Honourable Edmund Burke*, 2:435.

standing its military defeat, Britain was well situated to exploit the commercial opportunities that a more durable peace would bring.[6]

American Revolutionaries embraced the precepts of Vattelian internationalism, both in the conduct of foreign policy and in creating a "perpetual Union" under the Articles of Confederation. For Enlightenment optimists, the creation of the Confederation represented an opportunity to test the inherent tendencies toward balance and moderation in a rationally organized system of states. "It is but little above two hundred years since that enlarged system called the balance of power, took place," John Witherspoon of New Jersey told Congress in July 1776, "and I maintain, that it is a greater step from the former disunited and hostile situation of kingdoms and states, to their present condition, than it would be from their present condition to a state of more lasting and perfect union."[7] If Europe, despite its motley and unequal assortment of despotic regimes, was becoming more peaceful and civilized, American conditions should have accelerated and fulfilled these progressive tendencies. Reasonable republican statesmen, constitutionally responsible to their constituents, surely would be able to sustain peace and union among themselves and thereby secure American interests in the larger world. As republics, the American states supposedly had no incentive to make war on each other. In any case, the balance of power among them

---

[6]Thomas Day, Esq., *Reflections upon the Present State of England, and the Independence of America* (London, 1783), 1, 5, 44–45; Richard Champion, *Considerations on the Present Situation of Great Britain and the United States of America with a View to their Future Commercial Connexions* (London, 1784), 273. See below for discussion of the debate over British commercial policy toward the United States.

[7]John Witherspoon's Speech in Congress [July 30, 1776], Paul H. Smith, ed., *Letters of the Delegates to Congress, 1774–1789*, 17 vols. to date (Washington, D.C., 1976–), 4:586–87. According to [Jenings], *A Translation of the Memorial to the Sovereigns of Europe*, 21, the United States "is an empire the spirit of whose government extends from the centre to the extreme parts. Universal participation of council creates reciprocation of universal obedience." Richard Price believed that the Articles "make considerable advances towards" a union that could preserve "universal peace," but that Congress must have sufficient authority to enforce its decisions. Price, *Observations on the Importance of the American Revolution, and the Means of Making It a Benefit to the World*, 2nd ed. (London, 1785), reprinted in Bernard Leach, ed., *Richard Price and the Ethical Foundations of the American Revolution* (Durham, N. C., 1979), 187.

should have encouraged circumspect and conciliatory policies and discouraged violent conflict.

Yet the inadequacy of enlightened statecraft for preserving peace and promoting the public good soon became clear, both in the internal affairs of the union and in the states' relations with European powers. The balance of power among the American states was neither stable nor self-perfecting.[8] With the respective states increasingly conscious of— and acting on—what they considered their distinct corporate interests, the survival of the union itself became increasingly problematic. Nor did the faith of Vattel and other publicists in the development of an international legal regime based on a progressive balance of power seem warranted in America. The authority of the Confederation Congress, the guarantor of law and order among the American republics, diminished dramatically in the postwar period. And if Congress, the supposedly sacred and perpetual American treaty organization, was verging on collapse, the treaties American diplomats had negotiated or hoped to negotiate with foreign powers also were in jeopardy.

The Federalist founders of 1787 recognized that union would not be spontaneous, even among constitutional republics committed to the preservation of liberty and the rule of law. In order to survive, the American union had to be made "more perfect"; only an effective and inclusive federal polity, itself organized along republican lines, could secure a peaceful and lawful order among the states. This meant that, as nationalist reformers long had urged, the United States would be able to present a single, energetic face to the world at large. For statesmen who despaired of ever achieving the goals of Revolutionary diplomacy without reconstituting the American state system, federal constitutional reform thus represented a realistic accommodation to European power politics. This realism did not entail rejection of the federal union, or

---

[8]Debates over the Articles and later the Constitution focused on the relative claims of large and small states. See Peter S. Onuf, *The Origins of the Federal Republic: Jurisdictional Controversies in the United States, 1775–1787* (Philadelphia, 1983); idem, "Maryland: The New Republic in the New Nation," in Michael Allen Gillespie and Michael Lienesch, eds., *Ratifying the Constitution* (Lawrence, Kans., 1989), 171–200; idem, "New State Equality: The Ambiguous History of a Constitutional Principle," *Publius*, 18 (1988), 53–69.

abandonment of liberal policy goals. For Madison, Jefferson, and the emergent Republican opposition of the 1790s, a unified and energetic foreign policy was the essential precondition for strengthening the union, not obliterating the states. A strong union also would enable American diplomats to promote peace under a progressive international legal order and prosperity through the expansion of international trade.[9]

II. COMMERCE

Many Enlightenment thinkers embraced the central liberal assumption that the spread of commerce promotes the progress of civilization.[10] Thomas Paine was convinced that commerce "has had a considerable influence in tempering the human mind." The "want of the individual" had "first produced the idea of society"; as these "wants" became more extensive, the individual had to "seek from another country what before he sought from the next person" and a more inclusive notion of a world society, transcending national boundaries, thus emerged.[11] The Unitarian minister and liberal reformer Richard Price, a prominent English

[9]Frederick Marks, III, *Independence on Trial: Foreign Affairs and the Making of the Constitution* (Baton Rouge, 1973). On Republican foreign policy see Merrill D. Peterson, "Thomas Jefferson and Commercial Policy, 1783–1793," *William and Mary Quarterly*, 3rd ser., XXII (1965), 584–610, and Drew R. McCoy, "Republicanism and American Foreign Policy: James Madison and the Political Economy of Commercial Discrimination, 1789 to 1794," *William and Mary Quarterly*, 3rd ser., XXXI (1974), 633–46. For a valuable discussion of what union meant to the founders, particularly Madison, see Peter B. Knupfer, *The Union As It Is: Constitutional Unionism and Sectional Compromise, 1787–1861* (Chapel Hill, 1991), 23–55. For another view, emphasizing the "experimental" and provisional character of union during the founding era, see Paul C. Nagel, *One Nation Indivisible: The Union in American Thought, 1776–1861* (New York, 1964).

[10]Albert O. Hirschman, *The Passions and the Interests: Political Arguments for Capitalism before Its Triumph* (Princeton, 1977); Ralph Lerner, "Commerce and Character: The Anglo-American as a New-Model Man," *William and Mary Quarterly*, 3rd ser., XXVI (1979), 3-26.

[11]Thomas Paine, *A Letter Addressed to the Abbé Raynal, on the Affairs of North-America* (Philadelphia, 1782), 47, 46.

supporter of the American Revolution, agreed that foreign trade, "by creating an intercourse between distant kingdoms, . . . extends benevolence, removes local prejudices [and] leads every man to see himself more as a citizen of the world than [of] any particular state."[12]

Cosmopolitan proponents of commercial interdependence did not reject the Vattelian system of equal and independent sovereignties. Their quarrel was with a misguided, unenlightened conception of a state's true interests. As Price explained, an *excessive* "love of our country," a perverted patriotism that masked and justified "a love of domination; a desire of conquest, and a thirst for grandeur and glory" was one of the "most destructive, principles in human nature."[13] But the American Revolutionaries rose "above the atmosphere of local thoughts," wrote Paine, and thus could recognize "mankind, of whatever nation, or profession they may be, as the work of one Creator." Inspired by the "true idea of a great nation," the Revolutionaries sought to extend and promote "the principles of universal society."[14] They understood that their true interest lay in promoting a more peaceful, lawful and prosperous international system. This meant perfecting, not rejecting, the principle of national sovereignty, the fundamental premise of the Vattelian system.

The new world would show the way toward lasting peace. Price was hopeful that the time was "coming, when a conviction will prevail, of the folly as well as the iniquity of wars; and when the nations of the earth, happy under just governments, and no longer in danger from the passions of Kings, will find out better ways of settling their disputes."[15] If for Price, the enlightened Christian, such Vattelian hopes had a millennial dimension, he nonetheless shared the deistic Paine's faith in the progressive rationalization of diplomacy among increasingly "just" national sovereignties. Thomas Pownall also applauded the Americans' enlightened foreign policy. Measured against this new standard of "political

---

[12]Richard Price, *Observations on the Importance of the American Revolution*, 210.

[13]Richard Price, *A Discourse on the Love of Our Country. Delivered on November 4, 1789, in the Meeting-House in the Old Jewry* (London, 1789), 5; *Observations on the Importance of the American Revolution*, 210.

[14]Paine, *Letter Addressed to the Abbé Raynal*, 70.

[15]Price, *A Discourse on the Love of Our Country*, 29.

civilization," he concluded, the nations of Europe could "scarce be said to have emerged out of their Savage State."[16]

Friends of the Revolution expected American independence to change the world by inaugurating a new pattern of trade relationships. "By a free commerce," Pownall predicted, the Americans would "diffuse to the World at large the surplus portion of those good things which they must be continually creating in their own World."[17] The United States will "become a free port to all the nations of the world" and will "expect, insist on, and demand, in fair reciprocity, a free market in all those nations, with whom she trades."[18] Commercial alliances would promote the refinement and improvement of the balance of power system. In this new order enlightened statesmen would recognize the advantages of peace and predictability—and the increasingly unacceptable costs of war.

Before the Revolution, the "monopolizing systems" of the imperial powers subordinated trade to strategic considerations. But the European nations would now combine against any one of their number which sought to monopolize the new world's bounty. This new commercial competition would enrich and civilize the world. "Balance in the commercial world" depended on dismantling artificial barriers to free trade.[19] "Nations begin to be convinced of the futility of becoming great by conquest," wrote Pennsylvanian William Bingham in 1784, and are "more inclined to abandon the cruel system of war, in order effectually to enrich themselves by pursuing the peaceful line of commerce."[20]

Optimistic American Revolutionaries eagerly accepted the invitation to exploit and promote progressive tendencies in the European system. Though recognizing that the new nation was in conventional terms a weak power, they believed that it was well situated to encourage

[16]Pownall, *A Memorial Addressed to the Sovereigns of America*, 63.

[17]Ibid., 137–38.

[18][Jenings], *A Translation of the Memorial to the Sovereigns of Europe*, 27.

[19]Ibid., 41, 36.

[20][William Bingham], *A Letter from an American, Now Resident in London, to a Member of Parliament, on the Subject of the Restraining Proclamation; and Containing Strictures on Lord Sheffield's Pamphlet on the Commerce of the American States*, 2nd ed. (Philadelphia, 1784), 3.

and reward prospective trading partners which embraced liberal principles. The American war provided Britain's rivals with an opportunity to redress a dangerous imbalance of power and to set the terms of a durable peace. For liberal internationalists, a military balance, institutionalized in a comprehensive peace treaty, would clear the way for a new system of commercial relations. For the Americans, of course, the most compelling reason to negotiate treaties with the powers of Europe was to gain desperately needed support for their war effort. But American diplomats also hoped to prepare the way for a favorable postwar settlement. By insisting on commercial reciprocity when opening their ports to European allies, the new nation would secure its position as the "arbitress" of commerce, "the Mediatrix of Peace, and of the polite business of the world."[21]

The premise of Congress's model treaty of 1776, the prototype for subsequent commercial agreements, was that access to American markets was itself sufficient inducement for the European powers to support the American cause. American negotiators were to seek reciprocal trading privileges for the new nation's merchants—securing them all the commercial "Rights, Liberties, Priviledges, Immunities and Exemptions" enjoyed by the other power's nationals—or, failing this, most-favored nation status.[22] Equal, reciprocal terms were offered to all:

---

[21][Jenings] *A Translation of the Memorial to the Sovereigns of Europe*, 26.

[22]The Plan of Treaties, July 18, 1776, is in Worthington C. Ford, ed., *Journals of the Continental Congress*, 34 vols. (Washington, 1904–1937), 5:576–89. On the importance of the model treaty for the "new diplomacy" see Felix Gilbert, *To the Farewell Address: Ideas of Early American Foreign Policy* (Princeton, 1961). Gilbert's interpretation has been effectively challenged by James Hutson, who emphasized the "realism" of American foreign policy makers and discounted the influence of Enlightenment idealism. Hutson, "Treaty of Paris"; idem, "Intellectual Foundations of Early American Diplomacy," *Diplomatic History*, I (1977), 1–19; idem, "Early American Diplomacy: A Reappraisal," in Lawrence S. Kaplan, ed., *The American Revolution and "A Candid World"* (Kent, Ohio, 1977), 40–68; idem, *John Adams and the Diplomacy of the American Revolution*, 148–50. For a balanced assessment, see William C. Stinchcombe, "John Adams and the Model Treaty," in Kaplan, ed., *The American Revolution*, 69–84.

The crucial distinction between "free trade" and "commercial reciprocity" is made clear in the standard work on early American commercial policy, Vernon G. Setser, *The Commercial Reciprocity Policy of the United States, 1774–1829* (Philadelphia, 1937). John E. Crowley has characterized Revolutionary leaders as "neo-mercantilist."

thus the Franco-American Treaty of Amity and Commerce of 1778 *"exclude[s] no other power* from enjoying the same benefits by a like treaty." The cumulative effect of such treaties would be to dismantle the artificial barriers to free intercourse that promoted misunderstanding and conflict among nations. Commerce would no longer be "an exclusive scrambling rivalship," but would become "an equal communication, concentring the enjoyments of all regions and climates, and a consociation of all nations, in one communion of the blessings of Providence."[23]

Yet the fulfillment of the Revolutionaries' hopes depended on problematic contingencies. The European powers had to respond to the new diplomatic situation according to a rational and enlightened conception of their true interests—as the Americans defined them. Rationality, according to internationalists, was defined by accurately calculating a nation's advantages and opportunities within the balance-of-power system. But the United States' diplomatic standing, the power it plausibly could bring to bear on behalf of its essential interests, was in large measure a function of the war itself. As long as the Americans sustained the fight against Britain, strategic considerations might lead the other powers to grant commercial concessions. It was by no means clear, however, that in peacetime a weak, peripheral power had much to offer even when potential allies practiced the most enlightened diplomacy.

The dilemma for Americans was that progress toward a more civilized world was defined in terms of the progressive operation of the balance-of-power system. It was the balance of coercive power—that is, the continuing threat of war—that made the expansion of commercial relations possible and desirable.[24] Whether or not the American repub-

---

Neo-Mercantilism and the American Revolution: Political Economy and Anglo-American Trade, 1750–1790 (forthcoming). *Political* considerations were always, by definition, preeminent in Revolutionary American commercial diplomacy, and free trade— simply opening American ports without restriction—was never seen as a panacea. Nevertheless, given American goals, the term "neo-mercantilist" hardly seems appropriate.

[23][Jenings], *A Translation of the Memorial to the Sovereigns of Europe,* 34, 41, 40; U.S. State Department, *Treaties and Other International Agreements of the United States of America, 1776–1949,* 13 vols. (Washington, 1968–76), 7:763–76.

[24]For the Revolutionaries' recognition of the importance of coercive power, see

lics could act effectively in the balance system depended on their capacity for united action. European perceptions of the Confederation's durability therefore were crucial to the success of treaty negotiations. Through such treaties the balance of power could be refined and improved. In a Vattelian world, treaties constituted the crucial mechanism for elaborating and extending the law of nations.

III. TREATIES

The Revolutionaries' internationalist commitments converged with a powerful tendency in American constitutionalism toward natural law principles. The distinction between foreign and domestic spheres, and therefore between international and constitutional thought, was not clearly drawn in this period. The conflation of the two spheres, particularly pronounced in the case of the British Empire, is critical for understanding the Revolutionary American idea of treaties.[25]

As Americans sought foreign alliances in order to secure their independence, they invested treaties with the aura of higher law. Rejecting British imperial rule, Revolutionaries believed they could better secure their rights by redefining their place—through treaties—in the larger world. Vattel taught them that treaties could perform law-making functions. Treaty-as-law therefore stood opposed to the perversion of law in Parliamentary statutes depriving colonists of their rights. The conclusion that the British Empire, perhaps even Britain

---

the quotations collected by Hutson in *John Adams and the Diplomacy of the American Revolution*, 31–32.

[25]We are indebted to Gerald Stourzh, *Alexander Hamilton and Republican Government* (Stanford, 1970), 126–70. For suggestive comments on the importance of balance-of-power thinking in both international and constitutional thought see Hutson, *John Adams and the Diplomacy of the American Revolution*, 143; and Edward S. Corwin, "The Progress of Constitutional Theory between the Declaration of Independence and the Meeting of the Philadelphia Convention," *American Historical Review*, XXX (1925), 535.

itself, had no true constitution reinforced the Vattelian tendency to see the European system as "a sort of republic," constituted by treaties.

Frustrated in their quest for constitutional guarantees and federal union within the British empire, Americans naturally emphasized the law-making functions of treaties. With their enthusiasm for defining their fundamental rights in writing, the Revolutionaries juxtaposed the changeable and arbitrary character of imperial commercial policy with the fixity and liberality of treaty engagements.[26] The British empire collapsed because its foundations were rotten; British insistence on the unequal, subordinate position of the colonies precluded a lasting union. By contrast, treaties with foreign powers presupposed the equal standing, common interests, and mutual consent of the contracting parties. Treaties were the basic instruments through which the rights of nations were recognized and confirmed, the fundamental acts that created international society.

Radical imperial reformers had long sought a formal "treaty" or alliance that would protect the colonists from encroachments on their constitutional and commercial rights and privileges. John Adams thus invoked commercial treaties that bound "distinct states . . . in perpetual league and amity" as the best model for a reformed imperial constitution.[27] The point of such an agreement would be to create a durable,

---

[26]Gerald Stourzh, *Fundamental Laws and Individual Rights in the 18th Century Constitution*, Bicentennial Essay No. 5 (Claremont Institute for the Study of Statesmanship and Political Philosophy, 1984).

[27]"Novanglus" [John Adams], March 6, 1775, in Bernard Mason, ed., *The American Colonial Crisis* (New York, 1972), 207. See the discussions in Onuf, *The Origins of the Federal Republic*, 26; and idem, "Rights under the Articles of Confederation" (forthcoming). Given the colonists' willingness to accept imperial commercial regulation, a treaty was the obvious means of defining American rights within the British mercantile system. Before and after independence, John Crowley has shown, British pro-Americans who shared the colonists' mercantilist predilections warmly endorsed the idea of an Anglo-American commercial treaty. *Neo-Mercantilism and the American Revolution*, passim. For example, John Cartwright proposed a "General treaty between Great-Britain and the states of America" in his *American Independence the Interest and Glory of Great Britain* (Philadelphia, 1776; reprinting London ed., 1774), in Paul H. Smith, ed., *English Defenders of American Freedoms, 1774–1778* (Washington, 1972), 182. For further discussion of Cartwright's proposals see Robert E. Toohey, *Liberty and Empire: British Radical Solutions to the American Problem, 1774–1776* (Lexington, Ky., 1978), 36–52.

mutually advantageous relationship between the colonies and the mother country. The ambiguous, undefined character of existing arrangements fostered constitutional controversies that threatened to destroy the empire; only by drawing a clear line between British authority and colonial rights could the continuing allegiance of the king's American subjects be guaranteed.[28] Some formal agreement, a "treaty," was the logical instrument for redefining the imperial relationship on a constitutional basis.

Colonial reformers thought in terms of a "treaty" rather than a "constitution" for several reasons. "Constitution" was associated in a general way with the "rights of Englishmen," and more specifically with the institutional arrangements guaranteeing those rights: Americans thus argued that their colonial charters were "constitutions" that enabled them to enjoy the rights claimed by Englishmen at home.[29] These customary references, and the absence of any general agreement on the status of the empire as a political community, made it difficult to conceive of an "imperial constitution." Furthermore, until Americans began drafting their own state constitutions, the relationship between the general concept of "constitution" and specific written texts remained problematic. As the imperial crisis deepened, the possibility of any agreement over what "constitution" meant, much less over particular provisions, became increasingly remote. For legalistic and

[28] *Speeches of His Excellency Governor Hutchinson* (Boston, 1773), reprinted in John Philip Reid, ed., *The Briefs of the American Revolution* (New York, 1981), passim. The colonists' denial of Parliamentary pretensions to sovereignty emphasized the importance of allegiance to the crown in sustaining the imperial connection. An explicit, "constitutional" settlement of the imperial crisis would be like a treaty that depended on the king's prerogative to conduct foreign policy—Locke's "federative power"— not on his "sovereignty." For the monarchical turn in American thinking about the imperial relationship see Jack P. Greene, *Peripheries and Center: Constitutional Development in the Extended Polities of the British Empire and the United States, 1607–1788* (Athens, Ga., 1986), 132–44. See also the provocative discussion in Jerrilyn Greene Marston, *King and Congress: The Transfer of Political Legitimacy, 1774-1776* (Princeton, 1987), 13– 34, and passim.

[29] Greene, *Peripheries and Center*, 114–24, 132–44; Jack P. Greene, ed., *The Nature of Colony Constitutions: Two Pamphlets on the Wilkes Fund Controversy in South Carolina By Sir Egerton Leigh and Arthur Lee* (Columbia, S. C., 1970), 3–55; Peter S. Onuf, ed., *Maryland and the Empire, 1773: The Antilon-First Citizen Letters* (Baltimore, 1974), 3–39.

literal-minded Americans, treaties had the inestimable advantage of being explicit agreements grounded in the consent of the contracting parties.[30] The regulation of imperial trade by some kind of treaty therefore represented an equitable alternative to the unilateral determinations of the British Parliament.

The colonists declared their independence and sought alliances with France and other European powers because of the failure to establish a federal union *within* the British empire. Federal treaty connections with other independent nations would secure American rights under a developing law of nations. Far from being a defect, the *absence* of a superior authority that could command submission was the essential condition for a lawful international system. Fidelity to law in a society of sovereign states, all of which—like the United States—were more or less capable of vindicating their rights by force of arms, was a function of enlightened self-interest. Restrained by constitutional limitations yet liberated from the selfish and belligerent motives that drove old world monarchs to violate their engagements, America's republican rulers would prove true to their words. The Americans' good faith was guaranteed by their recognition that the real interests of nations were harmonious.

Optimistic Revolutionaries therefore expected treaties they negotiated to play a crucial role in launching a "new chapter in the laws of nations."[31] American enthusiasm for the idea that treaties should perform a legislative function was conspicuous in the provisions of the 1776 model treaty. By accepting its terms and thus becoming part of the new nation's commercial system, America's allies would simultaneously endorse universally applicable legal principles. The recognition of a progressive principle in a treaty set a pattern for subsequent agreements that would signify the common consent of humanity.

The American conception of law-making treaties was clearly revealed in Benjamin Franklin's 1782 project for an agreement on the

---

[30]On the importance of explicit texts for Revolutionary Americans see Robert A. Ferguson, "'We Do Ordain and Establish': The Constitution as Literary Text," *William and Mary Law Review*, 29 (1987), 3–25; Michael Warner, "Textuality and Legitimacy in the Printed Constitution," American Antiquarian Society, *Proceedings*, XCVII (1987), 59–84.

[31]Stiles, *The United States Elevated to Glory and Honour*, 85.

status of noncombatants. If alliances failed to eliminate warfare, they might at least limit its impact on neutrals and noncombatants. Franklin thus recommended that the definitive peace treaty with Britain include a proviso enabling "fishermen, all cultivators of the earth, and all artisans or manufacturers . . . peaceably [to] follow their respective employments" and merchants to continue exchanging "the necessaries, conveniences, and comforts of life" during any future war between the two nations. Although not included in the Peace of Paris, Franklin's article was incorporated in the treaty with Prussia in 1785.[32] Frederick the Great thus joined the United States in teaching "a good lesson to mankind," John Adams exulted.[33] By such means, concluded Thomas Jefferson, the law of nations progressed, "humanizing by degrees."[34] According to Stiles, "a generous and truly liberal system of national connexion . . . will almost annihilate war itself."[35]

When the colonists declared their independence, wrote Thomas Paine, "every corner of the mind [was] swept of its cobwebs," and "as the mind closed itself towards England, it opened itself towards the world." The treaties with France, creating an "alliance not of courts only but of countries," established the basic pattern of republican foreign policy. Further treaties would be the means of extending "friendship" and "free communication" and of eliminating "prejudice . . . all over the world." Rather than confronting each other like "individuals in a

[32]Franklin's proposed article is in Gerald Stourzh, *Benjamin Franklin and American Foreign Policy*, 2nd ed. (Chicago, 1969), 230, and discussed at 230–32. The Prussian Treaty is in *Treaties and Other International Agreements*, 8:78–87; Franklin's article (XXIII) is at 85–86. See also Jonathan R. Dull, "Benjamin Franklin and the Nature of American Diplomacy," *International History Review*, V (1983), 346–63.

[33]John Adams to Baron de Thulmeier, Feb. 13, 1785, cited in Stourzh, *Benjamin Franklin and American Foreign Policy*, 231.

[34]"Reasons in Support of the New Proposed Articles in the Treaties of Commerce," enclosed in American Commissioners [Adams, Franklin, and Jefferson] to De Thulemeier, Nov. 10, 1784, in Julian P. Boyd et al., eds., *The Papers of Thomas Jefferson*, 25 vols. to date (Princeton, 1950–), 7:491. See the discussion in Gilbert, *To the Farewell Address*, 70–72; Gregg L. Lint, "The American Revolution and the Law of Nations, 1776–1789," *Diplomatic History*, I (1977), 20–34; and Daniel G. Lang, *Foreign Policy in the Early Republic: The Law of Nations and the Balance of Power* (Baton Rouge, 1985).

[35]Stiles, *The United States Elevated to Glory and Honour*, 85.

state of nature," nations would gradually attain a higher level of civility and morality in their relations. Whatever their internal constitutions, Paine explained, the nations of the world "are relatively republics with each other." Due respect for the equality and integrity of the other members of this universal republic was "the first and true principle of alliancing."[36]

The Treaty of Paris in 1783 was a collective acknowledgement that the United States was "actually independent as any nation of Europe."[37] The new nation's standing in international society and its capacity to enter into binding agreements were confirmed. The Americans, given their frustrating experience in the empire, naturally predicated the vindication of their rights on just such conspicuous public confirmations. As enthusiastic Vattelians, they believed that a lawful world order was grounded in the voluntary acts of sovereign equals. In effect, they translated the imperatives of radical constitutionalism into the realm of foreign policy.

IV. CONFEDERATION

When Revolutionary Americans thought of their new states as independent sovereignties, they could—by identifying the American system with an idealized version of the European republic—assume that the natural tendency of enlightened statecraft was toward union. Congressional government, despite what would later be seen as its fatal constitutional defects, supposedly provided the institutional mechanism for defining and promoting common interests. Because a more perfect union was the goal, not the precondition, of Revolutionary republican statecraft, the failure to complete the Confederation until 1781 did not necessarily portend disaster. The desideratum was progress toward more harmony and interdependence: disputes that delayed final approval of the Articles could be considered tests of the new American diplomacy

---

[36]Paine, *A Letter Addressed to the Abbé Raynal*, 50–51, 52, 45, 52.
[37]Day, *Reflections upon the Present State of England*, 20.

and their resolution the means toward closer union. Congressmen therefore were not unduly exercised by the protracted process of drafting acceptable articles of Confederation and gaining the states' unanimous agreement. The lack of a formal mandate did not prevent Congress from conducting the war, or from providing a diplomatic forum for the American states.[38]

Given the organization of the Continental Congress, with each colony-state exercising an equal suffrage, and the tasks it confronted, the Revolutionaries tended to conceive the problem of union in diplomatic rather than constitutional terms. As representatives of their state legislatures, congressmen had to negotiate interstate agreements on how to prosecute the war while preparing the way for a comprehensive postwar settlement. Certainly lasting peace among the American republics depended on defining the precise terms of their alliance. Yet the very fact that the states were already making common cause against British tyranny was sufficient warrant of the devotion to liberty and enlightened self-interest that would secure "perpetual union."

The new United States inherited a daunting variety of conflicts over boundaries and public lands from the imperial regime.[39] The Revolutionaries naturally attributed these conflicts, and the chronic history of factionalism in the various colonies, to British corruption and despotism.[40] By the same logic, memorably expressed by Paine in *Common Sense*, the British connection had involved the colonies in "wars and quarrels" with foreign powers "who would otherwise seek our friendship, and against whom we have neither anger or complaint."[41] Yet

[38]On the adoption and development of the Articles see Jack N. Rakove, *The Beginnings of National Politics: An Interpretive History of the Continental Congress* (New York, 1979), esp. 135–91. See also Merrill Jensen, *The Articles of Confederation: An Interpretation of the Social-Constitutional History of the American Revolution, 1774–1781* (Madison, Wisc., 1940); Greene, *Peripheries and Center*, 153–80; and Peter S. Onuf, "The First Federal Constitution: The Articles of Confederation," in Leonard W. Levy and Dennis J. Mahoney, eds., *The Framing and Ratification of the Constitution* (New York, 1987), 82–97.

[39]Onuf, *Origins of the Federal Republic*; Marston, *King and Congress*, 231–50.

[40]Onuf, *Origins of the Federal Republic*, 9.

[41]Paine, *Common Sense* [1776], excerpted in Jack P. Greene, ed., *Colonies to Nations: A Documentary History of the American Revolution* (New York, 1967), 270–83, quoting 278.

Paine and his colleagues did *not* assume that such conflicts would spontaneously disappear with independence, or that the traditional rivals of Britain automatically would become the Americans' fast "friends." Instead, this legacy of rivalries and conflicts at home and abroad defined the new Congress's diplomatic agenda. The states would have to define their respective claims as well as their common interests in an explicit and comprehensive peace settlement. Meanwhile, American diplomats would have to persuade foreign powers to become allies, demonstrating that it was in their interest to recognize and cooperate with the United States.

The tortuous history of the Articles reflected a tension between diplomatic exigencies—the need to demonstrate that the states were capable of collective action, and therefore of negotiating and upholding engagements with European powers—and the natural tendency for the states to postpone a possibly disadvantageous peace settlement. The reluctance of several states to ratify testified to the general understanding that the proposed "treaty" of alliance created binding and irrevocable obligations. When the British campaign in the Chesapeake finally forced Maryland to endorse the Articles in 1781, the state assembly insisted that it did *not* thereby recognize the large states' western land claims.[42] An express disavowal was necessary because these controversial claims otherwise undoubtedly would be confirmed by the special courts authorized by Article IX. By dissociating ratification from a definitive territorial settlement, Marylanders limited the scope of Congress's effective authority. Yet, ironically, Maryland's policy exemplified the American faith in the efficacy of treaty obligations. Ratification had to be postponed, and then expressly qualified, because of the extensive authority it would give Congress—not because Congress would be powerless or constitutionally defective.

As long as American statesmen were preoccupied with promoting union through resolving interstate conflicts, delegating new powers to

[42]The "exclusive claim of any particular State" to the western lands was not binding on "this or any other State." Maryland ratification, dated Feb. 3, 1781, laid before Congress Feb. 12. *Journals of Congress*, 19:138–40. On French pressure to ratify see St. George L. Sioussat, "The Chevalier de la Luzerne and the Ratification of the Articles of Confederation by Maryland, 1780–1781," *Pennsylvania Magazine of History and Biography*, 60 (1936), 391–418.

Congress, and negotiating foreign alliances, the idea that *treaties* were *constitutional* was widely assumed. As an anonymous editor helpfully explained when publishing a collection of American state papers, "the Treaty [of Confederation] is the Constitution, or mode of Government, for the collective North-American Commonwealth." The editor's placement of the Article—after the state constitutions and the Declaration of Independence, but before the Franco-American treaties of 1778—is also suggestive. The Articles were the crucial link between the individual states and the larger world: raised on the solid foundation of republican government in the states, the "collective North-American Commonwealth" would take a leading role in promoting the progressive development of the European system.[43]

In the ratification debates of 1787–1788, Federalists disparaged the Articles by comparing them unfavorably to those state constitutions on which the proposed federal Constitution was modelled. But for Antifederalists—and even for earlier "nationalist" reformers who had sought to expand Congress's delegated powers—the comparison made little sense. The federal treaty was not constitutional because it resembled the state charters, but rather because it was constructed on the foundation they provided. The Revolutionaries did not neglect the problem of union when they drafted republican constitutions for the states: instituting republican governments in the states was the necessary precondition for union, and a Confederation the appropriate means for its progressive perfection. The Revolutionaries assumed that the American states, acting as distinct moral agents under republican constitutions, would seek to secure and expand harmonious relations and thereby strengthen the union. But the history of the Confederation challenged this faith, ultimately precipitating the reconstitution of the union.[44]

---

[43] *The Constitutions of the Several Independent States of America; The Declaration of Independence; The Articles of Confederation; The Treaties between His Most Christian Majesty and the United States of America* (Philadelphia; reprinted London, 1782), vii. The Articles were placed *before* the state constitutions in the 2nd ed. (London, 1783).

[44] On the reconception of "union" see Cathy D. Matson and Peter S. Onuf, *A Union of Interests: Political and Economic Thought in Revolutionary America* (Lawrence, Kans., 1990), 50–66, 82–100.

V. DIPLOMATIC FRUSTRATIONS

The Revolutionaries gained their independence by successfully exploiting the old world balance of power.[45] The French offered crucial financial and military assistance because they had an interest in curbing British power. Fearing that Anglo-American rapprochement would enable Britain to reassert its dominant position in the European system, they pressed the Americans to declare their independence and to establish a viable confederation.[46] Once victory was assured, however, the convergence of interest between the United States and the continental powers—belligerent or neutral—was no longer self-evident.[47] If the Americans hoped that commercial competition among the European powers would promote their interests, they also recognized the primary importance of re-establishing their trade with Britain—and the British West Indies—on a favorable basis. A commercial accord was in the interest of both Britain and its former colonies: French manufactures—and credit facilities—could not possibly satisfy American demand. The question was not whether Anglo-American trade would resume, but rather on what terms.

Negotiating a commercial treaty with Britain that would help create a more open and competitive trading system was the crucial test of postwar American diplomacy. The Americans could not offer the British exclusive privileges without abandoning fundamental diplomatic commitments, or violating agreements with other powers. John Adams, the American minister in London, therefore depended on a combination of appeals to enlightened self-interest and threats of commercial

[45]Hutson, *John Adams and the Diplomacy of the American Revolution*; Jonathan R. Dull, *A Diplomatic History of the American Revolution* (New Haven, 1985); Lawrence S. Kaplan, *Colonies into Nation: American Diplomacy 1763–1801* (New York, 1972), 73–181.

[46]Rakove, *The Beginnings of National Politics*, 93–94, 178–79; William C. Stinchcombe, *The American Revolution and the French Alliance* (Syracuse, 1969), 85–86, and passim.

[47]These divergent interests became conspicuous at the Paris peace negotiations. Richard B. Morris, *The Peacemakers: The Great Powers and American Independence* (New York, 1965).

retaliation: the British would forfeit the commercial advantages they presently enjoyed in American markets if the treaty project failed.[48] According to the precepts of enlightened statecraft, such threats should have provided sufficient incentive for reaching an accord. But Adams's success hinged on British perceptions of American power, specifically on Congress's ability to speak authoritatively for all the states. Even friendly British commentators warned that the weakness of the union jeopardized diplomatic initiatives they otherwise enthusiastically endorsed.[49]

Advocates of a commercial treaty with the former colonies argued that the end of the war offered Britain an historic opportunity to escape its diplomatic isolation and negotiate a new system of alliances. Efforts to suppress the independence movement had been unnatural and counter-productive.[50] The only legitimate basis for Anglo-American accord was common interest: restraints on trade raised artificial barriers to a mutually beneficial commerce. The colonists saw themselves as powerless to resist the supposedly disadvantageous terms imposed on them by impe-rial authorities, but now that they had secured their independence, a

[48]Charles R. Ritcheson, *Aftermath of Revolution: British Policy Toward the United States, 1783-1795* (Dallas, 1969), 18–45; John R. Howe, Jr., *The Changing Political Thought of John Adams* (Princeton, 1966), 124–29; Setser, *The Commercial Reciprocity Policy of the United States*, 74.

[49]Price, *Observations on the Importance of the American Revolution*, 187; [Pownall], *A Memorial Addressed to the Sovereigns of America*, 22–23, 129. See the discussion in Colin Bonwick, *English Radicals and the American Revolution* (Chapel Hill, 1977), 150–87. Passing on reports from his widespread correspondence, Tench Coxe told James Madison, Feb. 15, 1788, that the federal Constitution "is approved by all the warmest friends of America in England." John P. Kaminski et al., eds., *The Documentary History of the Ratification of the Constitution*, 10 vols. to date (Madison, 1976–), 16:122, 123n.

[50]The standard account of the failure of commercial negotiations is Vincent T. Harlow, *The Founding of the Second British Empire, 1763–1793*, 2 vols. (London, 1952–1964), 1:448–92. For provocative discussions of political economy in this period see Bernard Semmel, *The Rise of Free Trade Imperialism: Classical Political Economy, the Empire of Free Trade, and Imperialism* (Cambridge, 1970), 14–47; John E. Crowley, "Neo-Mercantilism and *The Wealth of Nations*: British Commercial Policy after the American Revolution," *The Historical Journal*, XXXIII (1990), 339–60; and idem, *Neo-Mercantilism and the American Revolution*. The contemporaneous political situation is described in John Cannon, *The Fox–North Coalition: Crisis of the Constitution, 1782–4* (Cambridge, 1969).

commercial treaty would restore and guarantee the natural community of interests that mercantilist policies had destroyed.

Britain's prosperity depended on the prosperity of its trading partners, including its erstwhile American subjects. "It is commerce alone which has raised us to our late envied pitch of greatness," Thomas Day argued, and "it is by commerce alone that we can hope to preserve some political importance."[51] Because the Americans were natural allies, Britain should resume trade with its former colonists on the most generous terms. "There is no country in the world so fit for England to trade with as the United States," wrote "An American": the American market would be able "to consume all the manufactures England ever can make, even should she be converted into one great workshop."[52] Meanwhile, American farmers played a crucial and lucrative role in supplying British West Indian markets. Notwithstanding the recent war, the Jamaican Brian Edwards explained in 1784, "interest" would "have its natural bias on the mind of America." If a commercial treaty established a "mutual and satisfactory intercourse . . . upon the liberal principles of equity and reciprocity," the former colonists would prove "our best friends and customers in peace, and in war our firmest allies." Otherwise, the new nation would be driven into France's arms, and the "enlivening gleam of returning conciliation and *foederal union*" would thus be "obscured."[53]

[51]Day, *Reflections on the Present State of England*, 45. On the advantages of a more liberal trading system see the arguments in Josiah Tucker, *Cui Bono? Or, an Inquiry, What Benefits Can Arise either to the English or the Americans, the French, Spaniards, or Dutch, from . . . the Present War? Being a Series of Letters, Addressed to Monsieur Necker*, 2nd ed. (Gloucester, 1782), 16, 32, 46. Though notoriously hostile to the American Revolutionaries, Tucker had long advocated recognizing the new nation's independence. For his importance as a seminal free-trader see Semmel, *The Rise of Free Trade Imperialism*, 14–24; and Crowley, *Neo-Mercantilism and the American Revolution*, ch. 1.

[52][An American], *Remarks on Lord Sheffield's Observations on the Commerce of the American States* (London, 1784), 30, 45.

[53]Brian Edwards, Esq., *Thoughts on the Late Proceedings of Government, Respecting the Trade of the West Indies Islands with the United States of North America*, 2nd ed. (London, 1784), 3, 53 (Appendix, "Humble Address of the Grand Inquest of the County of Middlesex" to Gov. Archibald Campbell of Jamaica); our emphasis. See also [Bingham], *Letter from an American*, 24–25, on the likelihood that British discrimination would strengthen the American union.

Proponents of closer Anglo-American ties made their case by invoking traditional balance-of-power precepts. The challenge was to promote British prosperity and power within a more complex European system, recognizing that the former colonies were now in a position to manipulate the balance to their advantage. The Americans' success at coalition-building in the Revolution was a powerful argument for Anglo-American accord, and the Peace of Paris constituted a public acknowledgement that the Americans were capable of upholding treaty obligations and therefore of participating responsibly in international society. Being forced to recognize the colonies' independence might be humiliating to the British, but should not prevent enlightened statesmen from seeking an American alliance that would serve the national interest.

Yet it was precisely on this question of competence that Anglo-American accord foundered. As John Crowley has shown, British opponents of an American treaty who shaped the Pitt ministry's policies were no less liberal than "liberal" pro-Americans who sought to revive old colonial trade patterns.[54] But the anti-Americans did not think it was necessary, or even possible, to negotiate with the United States. Because Congress was powerless to enforce treaty obligations on the states, Lord Sheffield wrote, commercial negotiations were pointless.[55] George Chalmers agreed that any engagement with the United States would be chimerical. As long as the "jealousies of the United States prevented the establishment of a competent power," it was "illusory and idle" to deal with Congress, a mere "body of men" who "can neither impose taxes, nor regulate trade." None of the conditions that made international agreements possible—or desirable—could be said to exist. The Americans had nothing to offer in exchange for access to the British West Indies: with or without a treaty, British manufacturers would continue to dominate American markets. Even if it were competent to act—a highly dubious premise—Congress was barred by the most-favored-nation clause of the 1778 Franco-American alliance from granting exclusive commercial privileges to any other power. British

[54]Crowley, "Neo-Mercantilism and *The Wealth of Nations.*"
[55]Earl of Sheffield (John B. Holroyd), *Observations on the Commerce of the American States* (London, 1783), 102–7. On the importance of this pamphlet for British American policy see Harlow, *The Founding of the Second British Empire*, 454–56.

hardliners thus concluded that there could be no incentive to establish political ties with the Americans that would transform the West Indian colonies into a "free port" and thus complete the dismemberment of the empire.[56]

Sheffield and his colleagues were willing to concede commercial privileges to the Americans—for instance in the direct trade between Britain and the United States—where they clearly served British interests. They opposed any treaty concessions on the West India trade, however, because they were convinced that British naval power depended on protecting British shipping from American competition.[57] Embracing the hardliners' logic, the British government enacted a series of discriminatory measures against American traders, beginning with the July 2, 1783, Order-in-Council stipulating that American provisions could only be carried to the British islands in British vessels.[58] Why, hardliners asked, should Britain forfeit an essential strategic interest, thus jeopardizing its position in the European system without any offsetting gain? Yet this anti-American policy was not predicated on inveterate hostility toward a more liberal commercial regime: in 1786, the Pitt ministry proceeded to negotiate a remarkably liberal commercial treaty with France.[59] The decisive difference in these negotiations was the recognition that France was a power to be reckoned with in the European system. "Natural allies" or not, the Americans were incapable of negotiating or upholding treaty obligations.

The frustrations of postwar diplomacy raised troubling questions about the place of the United States in the European system. For Americans, British reluctance to negotiate a commercial treaty was as galling as the unilateral limitations on the West Indies trade set forth in successive orders-in-council. British diplomats evidently did not con-

[56]George Chalmers, *Opinions on Interesting Subjects of Public Law and Commercial Policy; Arising from American Independence* (London, 1784), 161, 166, 152.

[57]Crowley, "Neo-Mercantilism and *The Wealth of Nations*," 347–48.

[58]For a brief discussion of the orders, and American responses, see Matson and Onuf, *A Union of Interests*, 44–45.

[59]John Ehrman, *The British Government and Commercial Negotiations with Europe, 1783–1793* (Cambridge, 1962), 28–69; Semmel, *The Rise of Free Trade Imperialism*, 38–44.

sider the United States a truly independent power whose friendship could ever be of any consequence. Yet many American statesmen were convinced that a commercial accord was essential to the completion of the peace, and that failure to negotiate a treaty would reduce the new nation to a neo-colonial status and jeopardize its independence.[60] They agreed with British critics that America's weak bargaining position resulted from Congress's constitutional inability to impose credible sanctions. "Unless the United States can act as a nation and be regarded as such by foreign powers," a congressional committee warned in April 1784, "our foreign commerce must decline and eventually be annihilated." It was therefore essential that Congress "be vested with powers competent to the protection of commerce."[61]

Revolutionary Americans hoped the United States would take a leading role in constructing a new transatlantic order. Commercial treaties were supposed to extend free trade and dismantle the "monopolizing systems" of Britain and other imperial powers. But was the Confederation Congress capable of negotiating and enforcing treaties? Skeptics on both sides of the Atlantic doubted that Congress could even preserve peace among the American states.[62] Pervasive concerns about its competence thus raised fundamental questions about the Revolutionary American conception of union. Astute observers at home and abroad concluded that the failure to deal with union as a constitutional problem undercut American efforts to act effectively in the larger world. A misplaced faith in the growing interdependence and harmony of their own sovereign republics jeopardized the goals of Revolutionary foreign policy.

---

[60]See citations and discussion in Peter S. Onuf and Nicholas G. Onuf, "American Constitutionalism and the Emergence of a Liberal World Order," in George Athan Billias, ed., *American Constitutionalism Abroad: Selected Essays in American Constitutional History* (Westport, 1990), 70–71.

[61]Committee report of April 22, 1784. *Journals of Congress*, 26:369–71.

[62]Sheffield, *Observations on the Commerce of the American States*, 103, 105. For further discussion and citations see Ritcheson, *Aftermath of Revolution*, 33–42.

Chapter Five

Foreign Affairs and Federal Union

I. CRISIS OF UNION

As an improved, rationalized, and republicanized version of the European state system, the American system should have developed toward union, with a growing number of interstate accords on controversial issues and with Congress exercising an expanding array of delegated powers. But the tendencies of the American system were clearly centrifugal, particularly after the war was won. The most sensitive and disturbing indicator of the progress of union was the poor success of American diplomats in negotiating favorable treaties abroad.[1] American statesmen were unable to define, much less defend or promote, the common interests of all the states, even when they were obviously threatened by foreign powers.

Foreign policy frustrations reflected and exacerbated sectional ten-

---

[1]Frederick Marks, III, *Independence on Trial: Foreign Affairs and the Making of the Constitution* (Baton Rouge, 1973); Jack N. Rakove, *The Beginnings of National Politics: An Interpretive History of the Continental Congress* (New York, 1979), 342–52; Drew R. McCoy, *The Elusive Republic: Political Economy in Jeffersonian America* (Chapel Hill, 1980), 76–104; Cathy D. Matson and Peter S. Onuf, *A Union of Interests: Political and Economic Thought in Revolutionary America* (Lawrence, Kans., 1990), 67–81.

sions. While hopes for an Anglo-American commercial treaty disappeared, a proposed pact with Spain—under which the Americans were
supposed to disclaim the exercise of their "rights" to the free navigation
of the Mississippi for twenty-five years in exchange for commercial
concessions—unleashed a firestorm of protest in states with an interest in
frontier development.[2] The southern state delegations in Congress
exercised a sectional veto against the treaty project, leading many
thoughtful Americans to conclude that the union itself could not—and
perhaps should not—survive.[3]

The belated ratification of an inadequate Confederation reinforced
powerful centrifugal tendencies in postwar American politics. Many
commentators concluded that common danger of British tyranny had
been the only effective bond of union.[4] With that danger removed, the
states were bound to act more and more like petty European powers,
suspicious of their neighbors' intentions and intent on promoting their
own interests. Constitutional reformers thus attributed the unenlightened
and selfish policies that jeopardized the Confederation to the "phantom
of *State* sovereignty."[5] Far from being the foundation of union, they
concluded, the independence of the respective states was its leading
liability. Reformers thus rejected the Vattelian premise that the independence of the states was the essential precondition for union, or that
an alliance of equals was its appropriate form. Here was the crucial
conceptual change: reformers now emphasized the defective character
of a confederal treaty that encouraged the states to exercise dangerous
powers and pursue mutually destructive policies.

[2]Matson and Onuf, *A Union of Interests*, 64–66; Thomas P. Slaughter, *The Whiskey
Rebellion: Frontier Epilogue to the American Revolution* (New York, 1986), 36–45.

[3]Matson and Onuf, *A Union of Interests*, 83–86; editorial note, in John P. Kaminski
et al., eds., *The Documentary History of the Ratification of the Constitution*, 10 vols. to date
(Madison, Wisc., 1976–), 13:54–57, 149–52.

[4]Charles James Fox predicted that the states' "usual animosities and jealousies will
return with an elastic force" after the war. Quoted in "Sketches of the Present Times
in North America," *The Times* (London), Feb. 2, 1786. For extended commentary on
the "approaching dissolution of the Union," see Eugene R. Sheridan and John M.
Murrin, eds., *Congress at Princeton: Being the Letters of Charles Thomson to Hannah
Thomson, June-October 1783* (Princeton, 1985), quoting letter of Oct. 21, 83.

[5]Rufus King's speech, June 30, in Max Farrand, ed., *The Records of the Federal
Convention of 1787*, 4 vols. (New Haven, 1911–87), 1:489.

The future of the union depended on preventing sectional blocs—and even individual states—from subverting or obstructing Congress as it discharged its sovereign functions. This meant abandoning the Revolutionaries' idea that a treaty of confederation, premised on the independence and equality of signatory states, could sustain union. "A sanction is essential to the idea of law, as coercion is to that of Government," Madison wrote in his "Vices of the Political system of the U[nited] States" (April 1787):

> The [con]federal system being destitute of both, wants the great vital principles of a Political Cons[ti]tution. Under the form of such a Constitution, it is in fact nothing more than a treaty of amity of commerce and of alliance, between so many independent and Sovereign States. From what cause could so fatal an omission have happened in the articles of Confederation? from a mistaken confidence that the justice, the good faith, the honor, the sound policy, of the several legislative assemblies would render superfluous any appeal to the ordinary motives by which the laws secure the obedience of individuals.[6]

Madison and his coadjutors insisted that a federal government exercising sovereign powers over foreign affairs and interstate relations had to be established on a constitutional basis. Where Revolutionaries had defined union as the tendency and goal of republican statecraft in a confederation of free republics, reformers now proclaimed that an institutionalized, constitutional union was the essential precondition for fulfilling the Revolution's promise of liberty. When the union was thus perfected the United States could negotiate treaties with foreign powers that would be recognized as "the law of the land." But until such time, "what foreign power would trust us?"[7]

That the Federalists could denounce the Articles *because* they were no more than a treaty, and were so obviously less than a constitution,

---

[6]Madison, "Vices of the Political System," April-June 1787, in J. C. A. Stagg et al., eds., *The Papers of James Madison*, 19 vols. to date (Chicago and Charlottesville, 1962–), 9:351.

[7]"Marcus" III [James Iredell], *Norfolk and Portsmouth Journal*, March 5, 1788, in *The Documentary History of the Ratification of the Constitution*, 16:325. Under the Confederation, Congress unanimously resolved in March 1787, that treaties were "part of the law of the land, and are not only independent of such [state] Legislatures, but also binding and obligatory on them." Ibid., 326n.

signified a momentous shift in American political thought. This shift was precipitated by widespread disillusionment with congressional government. With the war won, it soon became clear that the American republics were not moving toward closer union. While unratified, the Articles provided a context for negotiating a definitive peace among the states. But ratification focused attention on unresolved interstate conflicts, most notably over western boundaries, that remained beyond Congress's ordinary jurisdiction. Yet even as the Confederation's defects became conspicuous, the requirement of unanimous consent by the state legislatures for any amendment guaranteed the failure of reform efforts.[8] Under these circumstances, the Articles seemed to work against union, to frustrate cooperative efforts and exacerbate differences. By contrast, Federalists argued, the new Constitution would secure a more perfect union, both by resolving a wide range of outstanding conflicts and by establishing a responsive framework for managing future conflicts and promoting common interests.

During the ratification debates, the authors of *The Federalist* emphasized the discrepancy between the promises made by American diplomats—and ratified by Congress—and the performance of the state governments which alone could fulfill them. "No nation acquainted with the nature of our political association would be unwise enough to enter into stipulations with the United States," wrote Alexander Hamilton, "while they were apprised that the engagements on the part of the Union, might at any moment be violated by its members." Several states clearly had no intention of honoring articles of the peace treaty that were supposed to secure the interests of British creditors and guarantee the rights of returning loyalists.[9]

---

[8]The best discussions of the reform movement—and the mounting desperation of the reformers—are Rakove, *The Beginnings of National Politics*, 360–99; idem, "The Road to Philadelphia, 1781–1787," in Leonard W. Levy and Dennis J. Mahoney, eds., *The Framing and Ratification of the Constitution* (New York, 1987), 98–111; and idem, "From One Agenda to Another: The Condition of American Federalism, 1783–1787," in Jack P. Greene, ed., *The American Revolution: Its Character and Limits* (New York, 1987), 80–103.

[9]*The Federalist*, ed., with an Introduction and Notes, by Jacob E. Cooke (Middletown, Conn., 1961), *Federalist* No. 22 [Hamilton], 136. "The faith, the reputation, the peace of the whole union, are thus continually at the mercy of the

The Confederation's failure to uphold its international obligations would lead inevitably to its collapse. "It is an established doctrine on the subject of treaties," Madison wrote, "that all articles are mutually conditions of each other [and] that a breach of any one article is a breach of the whole treaty."[10] Under the existing regime, Governor Edmund Randolph wrote, "the law of nations is unprovided with sanctions in many cases, which deeply affect public dignity and public justice." "Is it not a political phaenomenon, that the head of the confederacy should be doomed to be plunged into war, from its wretched impotency to check offences against this law?"[11]

Recognition that union was neither spontaneous nor necessary led reformers to argue that the American treaty organization was *not* an improvement on the European system, but rather a radically defective and imperfect constitution for the states collectively. The Revolutionaries may have been dazzled with visions of perpetual peace after the Peace of Paris, but diplomatic setbacks portended perpetual conflict, within the American system as well as in its relations with the world at large. Certainly, the illiberal, short-sighted policies of the old world powers contributed to these setbacks, but disenchanted diplomats like John Adams recognized that the new nation's dilemma was rooted in the faulty organization of the union under the Articles of Confederation.[12]

American diplomacy failed because the union was weak and the states were too much attached to their so-called "sovereignty." Far from securing or promoting union, reformers asserted, the Articles European-

---

prejudices, the passions, and the interests of every member of which it is composed" (144). See also *Federalist* No. 3 [Jay], 14. The most famous challenge to the peace treaty was the New York Trespass Act (1783) which Hamilton argued was in conflict with the law of nations as well as treaty Articles IV, V, and VI. See the excellent discussion of the crucial test case of *Rutgers v. Waddington* (1784) in Julius Goebel, Jr., ed., *The Law Practice of Alexander Hamilton*, 2 vols. (New York, 1964), 1:282–315.

[10]*Federalist* No. 43, *The Federalist*, 297.

[11]*A Letter of His Excellency Edmund Randolph, Esquire, on the Federal Constitution* (Richmond, Oct. 10, 1787), *The Documentary History of the Ratification of the Constitution*, 15: 124.

[12]John R. Howe, Jr., *The Changing Political Thought of John Adams* (Princeton, 1966), 124-32.

ized American politics, authorizing would-be state sovereignties to obstruct and subvert the common interests of enterprising, peaceful, and liberty-loving republicans. The failure of the American union to become progressively more perfect through conventional political and diplomatic means thus led reformers to think increasingly in constitutional terms, to define the union as an inclusive federal polity that should secure the rights and interests of states and citizens alike. Thinking in federal constitutional terms meant that an idealized European republic could no longer be taken as a model for the American union. Only a complete reconstruction of the union would enable the Americans to play an effective role in world politics and thus fulfill the promise of their Revolution.

II. UNION TRANSFORMED

Federalist proponents of a "more perfect union" argued that a Confederation that could not enforce its determinations on its members would disintegrate. The American states were subject to the same political imperatives that governed the European system, regardless of their republican constitutions.[13] With the "dissolution of the confederacy," Hamilton predicted, the "constant apprehension" of war would lead the states to create "standing armies." "Thus we should in a little time see established in every part of this country, the same engines of despotism, which have been the scourge of the old world."[14]

Constitutional reform was imperative, Federalists asserted, because

[13]For a typical example see John Hancock's speech to the Massachusetts General Court, Feb. 28, 1788: "if we are robbed of the idea of our Union, we immediately become seperate nations, independent of each other, and no less liable to the depredations of foreign powers, than to wars and bloody contentions amongst ourselves." *The Documentary History of the Ratification of the Constitution*, 16: 225. For further discussion see Gerald Stourzh, *Alexander Hamilton and Republican Government* (Stanford, 1970), 145–65; Peter S. Onuf, "Anarchy and the Crisis of the Union," in Herman Belz, Ronald Hoffman and Peter J. Albert, eds., *To Form a More Perfect Union: The Critical Ideas of the Constitution* (Charlottesville, 1992), 272–302.

[14]*Federalist* No. 8, The *Federalist*, 46.

America was in danger of becoming Europeanized. Republican constitutions did not eliminate conflicts of interest among the American states
or prevent them from resorting to force. Equating disunion with a state
of war, critics of the Articles of Confederation challenged the Vattelian
belief that enlightened statecraft in a balanced system of sovereign equals
would foster harmony, interdependence, and law. Quite to the contrary, constitutional reformers argued, the states' pretensions to sovereignty jeopardized the American union: the preservation of republican
government therefore depended on curbing the independent authority
of the states.

To justify constitutional limits on the state governments and allay
pervasive fears of consolidated, despotic power, Federalists had to show
that the new federal government itself would be constitutionally limited.
Rising to the rhetorical occasion, proponents of the new constitution—
most notably Madison in his contributions to *The Federalist*—developed
an ingenious rationale for the extended, compound republic. Countless
scholarly commentators, including the present writers, have focused on
the sources, logic, and implications of this conceptual tour de force.[15]
Yet it should be emphasized that the Federalist formulation was compelling precisely because the Revolutionaries' faith in the natural progress
of union was so rapidly eroding.

Madison's extended republic was the inverse image of Vattel's
progressively developing balance-of-power system, where harmony was
predicated on the independence and equality of sovereign states. The
great Swiss writer's vision of Europe's future had inspired Revolutionary internationalists and justified the first tentative steps toward confederal
union. But the Revolutionaries' Vattelian hopes were sorely tested by a
history of diplomatic frustrations, interstate conflict, and rising sectional
tensions. Constitutional reformers concluded that the survival of republican government in America and the attainment of American foreign-
policy goals depended on securing union—before it was too late—by
constituting a true federal republic.

European criticism of the Americans' imperfect union under the
Confederation prefigured Federalist warnings about the Europeaniza-

[15]For discussion and citations see Part I.

tion of American politics. Most conspicuously, Lord Sheffield's disparaging comments about Congress, widely excerpted in American newspapers after their publication in 1783, resurfaced repeatedly during the ratification campaign.[16] The taunts of avowed anti-Americans were echoed by less unfriendly observers, and even by the Revolution's most fervent admirers. European commentators were much less optimistic than the American Revolutionaries about European responsiveness to American diplomatic initiatives, or about the putatively progressive tendencies of the balance-of-power system. "As you have our vices," the Abbé de Mably bluntly warned, so "you will soon have our politics."[17]

The states' republican constitutions did not guarantee their harmonious union. Turgot emphasized the fragility of a union erected upon "the erroneous foundation of the most ancient and vulgar policy, upon the prejudice that nations and states, as such"—however constituted— "may have an interest distinct from the interest which individuals have to be free, and to defend their property." In the absence of union, he warned, any state—regardless of its form of government—was bound to assume a spurious and artificial corporate identity, and then to pursue its supposed "interests" by exercising sovereign powers. Little more than a "discordant . . . jumble of communities," the United States was already too much like Europe.[18] Josiah Tucker was equally convinced that "clashing Interests" would seize control of local governments, thus fostering an endless cycle of "internal Disputes and Quarrels." With "*no Center of Union* among them," it was the Americans' "Fate" to be "A

---

[16]For examples see "Social Compact," *New Haven Gazette*, Oct. 4, 1787; and "Compo," "To the Head of the Wrongheads," *Connecticut Courant*, Nov. 26, 1787, in *The Documentary History of the Ratification of the Constitution*, 3:356, 476. For a good discussion of the importance of Sheffield's book to the development of Madison's thinking, see J. C. A. Stagg, *Mr. Madison's War: Politics, Diplomacy, and Warfare in the Early American Republic, 1783–1830* (Princeton, 1983), 7–16.

[17]Abbé de Mably, *Observations on the Government and Laws of the United States* (English ed., Amsterdam, 1784), 121.

[18]"Letter from M. Turgot to Dr. Price," dated Paris, March 22, 1778, appendix to Richard Price, *Observations on the Importance of the Revolution*, reprinted in Bernard Leach, ed., *Richard Price and the Ethical Foundations of the American Revolution* (Durham, N. C., 1979), 220, 221n, 220.

DISUNITED PEOPLE . . . divided, and subdivided into little Common-Wealths, or Principalities."[19]

Predictions of the imminent Europeanization of American politics underlined the urgency of reform. A negative assessment of European politics also provided common ground for a coalition of reformers who did not necessarily agree on the character of a new federal regime. Yet whatever the framers' intentions, modern Europe served as conceptual antitype and rhetorical foil for their energized, extended republic. The Federalists' "federalism" thus was defined against the bonds of the treaty system that supposedly constituted Vattel's European "republic" as well as against the disintegrating American Confederation. This redefined federalism did not entail the consolidation of all power in the federal government, or the destruction of the state republics.[20] The new system was modelled neither on the European system of states, nor on the consolidation of authority in a single European state.

The crucial conceptual breakthrough in the development of American federalism was the recognition that "state sovereignty"—the monopolization of political power by the state governments—jeopardized republican government as well as the survival of the union.[21] By invoking and implementing "popular sovereignty," Federalists could challenge this monopoly and provide a theoretical rationale for a powerful yet limited government for the federal republic.[22] The result, in theory, was to suppress the notion of distinctive state interests and of sovereign powers in the state governments sufficient to enforce them.

---

[19]Josiah Tucker, *Cui Bono? Or, an Inquiry, What Benefits Can Arise either to the English or the Americans, the French, Spaniards, or Dutch, from . . . the Present War? Being a Series of Letters, Addressed to Monsieur Necker*, 2nd ed. (Gloucester, 1782), 118–19.

[20]On Antifederalist fears of consolidation see Peter S. Onuf, "State Sovereignty and the Making of the Constitution," in Terence Ball and J. G. A. Pocock, eds., *Conceptual Change and the Constitution* (Lawrence, Kans., 1988), 86–93; and Herbert J. Storing, ed., *The Complete Anti-Federalist*, 7 vols. (Chicago, 1981), vol. 1: *What the Anti-Federalists Were For*.

[21]Onuf, "State Sovereignty and the Making of the Constitution."

[22]Gordon S. Wood, *The Creation of the American Republic, 1776–1787* (New York, 1972), 519–64, esp. 536–43; Peter S. Onuf, "Reflections on the Founding: Constitutional Historiography in Bicentennial Perspective," *William and Mary Quarterly*, 3rd ser., XLVI (1989), 364. Also see ch. 3 above.

Confined to their proper sphere, the states would flourish as republics, the primary locus of self-government. Federal supremacy guaranteed that the corporate interests of state governments would always be subordinate to the rights of the sovereign people—the fundamental premise of the states' own constitutions—and that the states would not arbitrarily interfere with the free movement of trade and people across state boundaries. The American founders thus "established a union of interests and of states." It was this double character of the union that guaranteed a perpetually peaceful and ever expanding new world order.[23]

Just as the framers of the federal Constitution sought to banish the dangerous and divisive principle of "monarchical sovereignty" from the American state system, so they dismissed the arguments of apologists for the European "system of war."[24] The behavior of the American republics under the Confederation convinced constitutional reformers that disunion would unleash the forces of state particularism; unchecked by federal obligations, sovereign states would exploit their relative advantages. An *imbalance* of power would then become conspicuous, and the resulting tendency of the system would be to magnify those discrepancies until "the arm of tyranny" finally "impose[d] upon us a system of despotism."[25] The balance of power—the never-ending quest of independent sovereignties for relative advantage—was not, as European theorists suggested, the only alternative to "universal monarchy," the dominion of one great power over all the rest. In America, Federalists argued, the emergence of states as "powers" in the European sense would simply unleash "the dogs of war."[26] The inevitable result would

[23]Joel Barlow, *To His Fellow Citizens of the United States of America* (Philadelphia, 1801), Letter II, 28.

[24]Thomas Paine, *The Rights of Man*, with an Introduction by Eric Foner (New York, 1984), I [1791], 144–45. For an Antifederalist defense of the European "federal republic," see "A Farmer" VII [John Francis Mercer], *Maryland Gazette* (Baltimore), April 15, 1788, in *The Complete Anti-Federalist*, 5:65.

[25]Richard Law's speech to the Connecticut Convention, Jan. 9, 1788, in *The Documentary History of the Ratification of the Constitution*, 3:559.

[26]Edmund Randolph's speech to the Virginia Convention, June 24, 1788, in Jonathan Elliot, ed., *The Debates in the Several State Conventions on the Adoption of the Federal Constitution*, 5 vols. (Philadelphia, 1876), 3:603. Although James Monroe

be the destruction of republican government, the consolidation of power and, finally, the establishment of a "universal" despotism.

Federalists promised that the establishment of the new union would redeem the American experiment in republican government. By forgoing sovereign powers, the exercise of which would be dangerous if not fatal to republican liberty, the states themselves would gain new "energy." Meanwhile, because the states disclaimed sovereignty, the pretext for any serious conflict among them evaporated, and the new federal government could govern the union with a light hand. The perfection of the union—the organization of the states into a compound republic—therefore would *not* result in the creation of the over-mighty, potentially despotic central government so feared by Antifederalists. Opponents of the Constitution had predicted that the consolidation of sovereign powers in the new central government would lead to the obliteration of the states and the destruction of individual liberties. Proponents knew that consolidation was not the point and, more importantly, that sovereignty was not the issue. Skeptics were soon reassured: in fact, Nathaniel Chipman of Vermont wrote in 1793, "solely an impression of the efficiency of the federal government . . . added, at the instant of its organization, a degree of energy to the states governments, and put an end to those factions and turbulent commotions"—such as Shays's Rebellion—"which made some of them tremble for their political existence."[27]

The American experiment in republican government was vulnerable both to the diffusion of power—as in the contemporary European system, or under the Articles of Confederation—and to the concentration of power in a single, despotic and unconstitutional government.

---

opposed ratification, he was convinced that the Confederation Congress was becoming little more than a "diplomatick corps"; he criticized the proposed Constitution because the organization of the Senate, by giving too much scope to "state spirit," reflected "the defective principles" of the Articles. Monroe, "Some Observations on the Constitution" [ca. May 25, 1788], in *The Documentary History of the Ratification of the Constitution*, 9:850, 868–69.

[27] *Sketches on the Principles of Government* (Rutland, Vt., 1793), 278. On the acceptance of the Constitution, see Lance Banning, "Republican Ideology and the Triumph of the Constitution," *William and Mary Quarterly*, 3rd ser., XXXI (1974), 167–88.

Federalists congratulated themselves and their countrymen on avoiding these dangerous extremes by ratifying the new Constitution. "It would hardly have been credible in Europe, or in any Part of the old World," one writer exulted, "that States so different in their Situation, Extent, Habits, and particular Interests" should have been able to overcome "all jealousy and Apprehensions of mischievous Consequences" to form a more perfect union.[28] Friendly foreigners enthusiastically endorsed this happy outcome. "America has emerged from her struggle into tranquillity and freedom," the Scottish critic of Burke, James Mackintosh, averred in 1791. "The authors of her Constitution have constructed a great permanent *experimental answer* to the sophisms and declamations of the detractors of liberty."[29] The establishment of the new federal government vindicated the republican principle that states and their governments existed to serve the people, not the other way around: "it is the spirit of their Government, which encourages not only Agriculture, but Manufactures and Commerce, and discourages War."[30] The "separate states in general exhibit prosperous and respectable governments," another British writer reported in 1793. The very existence of the federal government—the mere "impression" of its "efficiency"—guaranteed against "war and foreign interference."[31]

[28]"A Correspondent," *United States Chronicle* (Providence), Sept. 27, 1787, *The Documentary History of the Ratification of the Constitution*, 13:258–59, cited and discussed in Peter B. Knupfer, *Union As It Is: Constitutional Unionism and Sectional Compromise, 1787–1861* (Chapel Hill, 1991), 32–33.

[29]James Mackintosh, *Vindiciae Gallicae. Defence of the French Revolution and Its English Admirers against the Accusations of the Right Hon. Edmund Burke, Including Some Strictures on the Late Production of Mons. De Calonne*, 4th ed. (London, 1792; original pub. 1791), 170.

[30]Daniel Stuart, *Peace and Reform against War and Corruption. In Answer to a Pamphlet Written by Arthur Young, Esq.*, 2nd ed. (London, 1794), 43.

[31]"A Calm Observer" [Benjamin Vaughan], *Letter on the Subject of the Concert of Princes, and the Dismemberment of Poland and France* (London, 1794), Letter XII, dated June 7, 1793, 229; Chipman, *Sketches on the Principles of Government*, 278.

III. THE EXPANDING UNION

During the ratification debates, Federalists argued that the deterioration of the Confederation jeopardized the states' republican constitutions. In doing so, they reversed the Revolutionaries' conception of the relationship between enlightened republican government and the progress toward union at home and a liberal system of treaties abroad. As Madison suggested when he propounded his "Republican remedy for the diseases most incident to Republican Government," republicanism was a problem, not a panacea.[32] Only by establishing their federal system on a constitutional basis could the American states secure the "perpetual peace" that was essential to the survival of republican government. Only then could the United States participate effectively in international society as a force for progress and civilization.

The federal Constitution would establish a model world order, a system in which the member states eschewed the illusory and destructive prerogatives of "sovereignty" for the solid benefits of republican self-government and civil liberty. The new world order therefore would be radically disjunct from the old world system, and this separation would be made possible precisely because the government of the union would be able to hold its own against the imperial ambitions of European powers. Yet if the vindication of the new world's republican experiment thus depended on embracing the maxims of old world power politics, American "realists" did not therefore repudiate the Enlightenment dream of a more civilized society of states. For James Wilson and other cosmopolitans, the new federal union represented the fulfillment of progressive tendencies that liberal optimists had hoped would work toward the perfection of the European system. The Constitution was the culmination of the great "peace plan" tradition: here at last, Wilson exclaimed, "is accomplished, what the great mind of Henry IV of France had in contemplation."[33] The proposed union would

---

[32]*Federalist* No. 10, *The Federalist*, 65.

[33]James Wilson's speech to the Pennsylvania Convention, Dec. 11, 1787, in *The*

uphold the legitimate claims of "distinct societies" even while combining them "into a new body capable of being increased by the addition of other members."[34] This was indeed "an happy exchange for the disjointed contentious state sovereignties!"[35]

The strength of the union lay in the loyalty of republican citizens who recognized that it was the best guarantee of their rights, including the right to self-government under republican state constitutions. The union was dynamic and expansive precisely because it was voluntary and uncoerced. Settlers in frontier regions would be drawn into the union by self-interest, not by fear of conquest. Joel Barlow believed that expansion depended on preserving states' rights and limiting the power of the central government: "the interest we shall have in inducing new nations to join our union, instead of being our rivals, is a strong argument . . . for preserving at least as much power to our individual states as they now possess, and for not suffering any encroachment from the federal government." Particularly since "their federalizing with us" was a matter of "choice," the terms of union had to be favorable. The principle was equally applicable to settlements organized under federal auspices, but eminently capable of withdrawing from the union should the central government's authority become "oppressive" or even if it "only appears to be so." "We should not forget," Barlow concluded, "that the United States are to be held together by interest, not by force."[36]

Relations among the American states under the federal Constitution

---

Documentary History of the Ratification of the Constitution, 2:583. For other references to the peace plan attributed to Henri IV, see Ezra Stiles, *The United States Elevated to Glory and Honour*, 1783 Connecticut Election Sermon, 2nd ed. (Worcester, 1785), 31; "Aristides" [Alexander Contee Hanson], *Remarks on the Proposed Plan* [Annapolis, Jan. 1, 1788], in Paul Leicester Ford, ed., *Pamphlets on the Constitution of the United States* (Brooklyn, 1888), 248. See also F. H. Hinsley, *Power and the Pursuit of Peace: Theory and Practice in the History of Relations between States* (Cambridge, 1963), 24–27; Stourzh, *Alexander Hamilton and Republican Government*, 126–70, esp. 153–61; Matson and Onuf, *A Union of Interests*, 145–46.

[34] *The Substance of a Speech Delivered by James Wilson*, Nov. 24, 1787, in *The Documentary History of the Ratification of the Constitution*, 2:342.

[35] Wilson's speech to the Pennsylvania Convention, Dec. 11, 1787, in ibid., 2:583.

[36] Barlow, *To His Fellow Citizens of the United States of America*, Letter II, 35, 25, 24.

would be governed by a perfected law of nations. Free American citizens would be equally secure in their liberty and property in any state and therefore would have no interest in promoting or supporting territorial disputes. The acknowledged power of the new Congress to establish a national commercial policy and the elimination of all trade barriers among the states would remove chronic sources of controversy under the Confederation. If issues should nonetheless arise between states, the federal judiciary would render impartial decisions based on legal merit rather than political power: "a tribunal is here founded to decide, justly and quietly, any interfering claim."[37] By these means, relations among the American states would be characterized by the kind of lawfulness and enlightened self-interest that internationalists in Vattel's tradition supposed would characterize the diplomacy of sovereign equals in a developing balance of power.

The renunciation of sovereign powers prevented the American republics from devouring each other, and "plung[ing] us all into the gulf of monarchy, nobility, and priesthood."[38] Rather than contracting and imploding, the union would add new members, thus extending the benefits of peace and security. Because of the principle of state equality—and the absence of a dominant metropolitan core—new states could join the federal union without fear of being overwhelmed by powerful neighbors. The security offered to small and weak states by the federal Constitution was a major incentive for frontier communities to seek membership in the union. Potentially powerful and hostile rivals were thus preempted; the resulting diminution of an old state's relative power *in* the union was more than compensated by the increased power of the union as a whole. There was no limit to the size of the union, Alexander Contee Hanson asserted during the ratification debate: a "true federal republic" was "always capable of accession by the peaceable and friendly admission of new single states."[39]

[37]Wilson's speech to the Pennsylvania Convention, Dec. 11, 1787, in *The Documentary History of the Ratification of the Constitution*, 2:583. See the discussion in William M. Wiecek, *The Guarantee Clause of the U.S. Constitution* (Ithaca, 1972), 11–77.

[38]Barlow, *To his Fellow Citizens of the United States of America*, Letter II, 26.

[39][Hanson], *Remarks on the Proposed Plan*, 248.

The crucial corollary of banishing—or, more accurately, of pre-empting the development of—state sovereignty in America was that state boundaries could be considered contingent and negotiable, as well as permeable. Given the original territorial monopoly of the thirteen states, settlers in distant frontier regions could only hope to enjoy the benefits of reasonably convenient republican self-government if jurisdictional limits were subject to change. But under the new federal republic, boundary conflicts—and the political aspirations of frontier settlers—would not lead to war. Just as American citizens could move from state to state without compromising their rights, so boundaries could be redrawn without adverse effects. Remarkably, British liberal Benjamin Vaughan noted in 1793, "the American republics, in various instances, have even parted with territory and people close adjoining, allowing them to become independent states; and have admitted these offsets to a proportional weight in the general confederacy."[40]

The American federal republic secured the benefits that optimistic internationalists imagined would flow from a more complex and refined balance of power among independent states. Yet the founders' federalism was grounded in their rejection of Vattel's fundamental premise, that the sovereignty of independent states constituted the foundation of an increasingly lawful and harmonious world order. Constitutional reformers could make this crucial conceptual move by developing the federal implications of republican theory. Classical republicanism focused as much on the ascending levels of association in a polity as on the requirements of good citizenship. The "invention of federalism" therefore should not be seen as a deviation from republicanism dictated by a prudent assessment of political and diplomatic realities.[41] On the contrary, the imminent collapse of the union led thoughtful Americans to move beyond the Revolutionaries' faith in the progress of the balance of power or in the sufficiency of republican state constitutions for securing

[40]Calm Observer [Vaughan], *Letter on the Subject of the Concert of Princes*, Letter XI, dated May 21 and 23, 1793, 206.

[41]John M. Murrin, "The Invention of American Federalism," in David E. Narrett and Joyce S. Goldberg, eds., *Essays on Liberty and Federalism: The Shaping of the U.S. Constitution* (College Station, Tex., 1988), 20–47; Onuf, "Reflections on the Founding," 356–64.

a regime of law in their New World. At a time when some disenchanted Revolutionaries were calling for the creation of an American monarchy, the framers and advocates of the new Constitution began to reconceive the union in republican terms.[42]

Madison and his colleagues could propose a truly "Republican remedy" for the crisis of the union because they recognized the interdependence of state and national governments. If a durable union depended on the republican character of its member states, it was equally true that the states as republics depended on a durable union. The American states would have to be "federalized"—subordinated to a perpetual, constitutional alliance—in order to preserve their republican character.[43] An American state would coexist peacefully with its neighbors because the states collectively delegated specific powers exclusively to the government of the union. The states were constitutionally compatible. Defined in terms of their constitutional limitations, republican state governments were also compatible with an energetic national government. The new national government which sustained the state republics was itself "republican," both as the instrument of a more perfect union for the "republic" of American states and, in the more familiar sense, as a constitutionally limited government deriving its authority from the sovereign people.

IV. APOTHEOSIS

In 1799, when the diplomatic system of Europe was in its death throes, the radical Republican pamphleteer Joel Barlow looked forward to the formation of a "general confederation" that would eventually include "every European people." Barlow, who had lived in Revolutionary France for many years, held out little hope for the rehabilitation of the

---

[42]Matson and Onuf, *A Union of Interests*, 86–89; Louise Burnham Dunbar, *A Study of "Monarchical" Tendencies in the United States from 1776 to 1801* (Urbana, 1922); editorial note, *The Documentary History of the Ratification of the Constitution*, 13:168–72.

[43]Barlow, *To His Fellow Citizens of the United States of America*, Letter II, 8n.

old balance of power. Only by abandoning the principle of national sovereignty could a "great union" of European republics guarantee "perpetual harmony among its members" and end the warfare that had so long devastated the continent. The new confederation might appropriately "assume the name of the United States of Europe." The salvation of the Old World, Barlow suggested, depended on following the New World's example.[44]

Barlow's prescriptions constituted an illuminating commentary on the early development of American federalism, however little succor they provided to embattled Europeans. His apotheosis of the federal union is all the more remarkable given his hostility to the Federalist administrations of Washington and Adams. But like his strict-constructionist counterparts at home, Barlow equated oppositionist politics with dedication to fundamental Constitutional principles.[45] By creating a true federal republic, Barlow asserted, the framers guaranteed states' rights and individual liberties—even when Federalists dominated the central government.

In projecting a United States of Europe, Barlow invoked the spirit of 1787, not 1776. Barlow thought that "infinite credit" was due to the Americans for realizing that the construction of a durable federal union was crucial to the survival of their republics. The "two pillars of the edifice, the representative principle and the federal principle, should never be separated." Thus, he concluded, it made no sense to "federalize" the states of Europe without at the same time republicanizing them. This is why the victory of Revolutionary France and the final collapse of the old system of Europe represented such a magnificent opportunity. "Could we flatter ourselves" that, "at the end of the present war," the

[44]Ibid., Letter II, dated Paris, Dec. 20, 1799, 8–9. Barlow followed the convention, which "federalists" like Madison and Hamilton exploited so effectively, of using "federal" and "confederate" interchangeably. For a good brief discussion of Barlow's career at the center of the "Revolutionary Enlightenment," see Henry F. May, *The Enlightenment in America* (New York, 1976), 239–43. Biographies include James Woodress, *A Yankee's Odyssey: The Life of Joel Barlow* (Philadelphia, 1958); and Samuel Bernstein, *Joel Barlow: A Connecticut Yankee in an Age of Revolution* (Cliff Island, Maine, 1985).

[45]Lance Banning, "Republican Ideology and the Constitution;" idem, *The Jeffersonian Persuasion: Evolution of a Party Ideology* (Ithaca, 1978).

Europeans would create a federal republic like that of the Americans, "then we might hope to see the moral force of nations take [the] place of their physical force, the civilization of states keep pace with that of individuals, and their commercial relations established on the principles of peace."[46]

In its brief history, the United States had successfully surmounted formidable obstacles to peace and stability. Its most striking achievement was to demonstrate the falsity of the conventional wisdom that "republicanism is not convenient for a great state." "Not many years will pass," Barlow predicted, before it would be "universally" accepted that "the republican principle is not only proper and safe for the government of any people; but, that its propriety and safety are in proportion to the magnitude of the society and the extent of the territory."[47]

Barlow's brief for the compound, extended federal republic had been previously developed by James Madison and other advocates of national constitutional reform during the great debate over the ratification of the Constitution. Like the Federalists of 1787–88, Barlow transcended the conventional wisdom that republics must be small by reconceiving republicanism in federal terms—and federalism in republican terms. The small-republic idea seemed most compelling when theorists focused on the practical limits of a community of virtuous and vigilant self-governing citizens; a distant government, American revolutionaries agreed, was inevitably despotic. But there were no logical limits to a union of republics, organized on republican principles; thus the Federalists appropriated—and republicanized—a "peace plan" tradition, dedicated to guaranteeing the integrity and interests of the members of international society.

The principle of equality guaranteed harmonious union. As Barlow proclaimed in his poem, *The Conspiracy of Kings*:

> Where equal rights each sober voice should guide
> No blood would stain them, and no war divide.[48]

[46]Barlow, *To His Fellow Citizens of the United States of America*, Letter II, 10, 11, 9–10.

[47]Ibid., 4–5.

[48]Barlow, *The Conspiracy of Kings; A Poem: Addressed to the Inhabitants of Europe, from Another Quarter of the World* (London, 1792), 16.

"Among the several states" of America, he explained in his *Advice to the Privileged Orders* (1792), "the governments are all equal in their force, and the people are all equal in their rights. Were it possible for one state to conquer another state, without any expence of money, or of time, or of blood--neither of the states, nor a single individual in either of them, would be richer or poorer for the event." Jurisdictional controversies which would have driven European states into belligerent frenzies had already been decided "in a few days, by amicable arbitration." The outcome of such disputes was, after all, "a matter of total indifference" to citizens whose rights were secure, "whether the territory on which they live were called New-York or Massachusetts."[49]

The sovereignty of the states in the union was limited by republican constitutions—state and federal—that guaranteed the people's rights, eliminated the distinction between governors and governed, and protected Americans from foreign aggression as well as domestic oppression. As a result, the state governments eschewed violent sanctions in their contests with one another: "the enjoyment of equal liberty has taught the Americans the secret of settling these disputes, with as much calmness as they have formed their constitutions." Just as the state constitutions secured individual rights, the federal Constitution secured the rights of states; these states—as self-governing republics guaranteed against internal subversion and external assault—were much more comprehensively, substantially, and enduringly "equal" than the states of Europe could ever hope to be.[50]

Barlow's sympathetic support of the French Revolutionary cause survived the turbulent upheavals of the 1790s because it was not simply predicated on his hostility to monarchy and aristocracy or on his enthusiasm for French experiments in republican government. Barlow was more profoundly inspired by a vision of a reconstructed European state system, organized on the model of the American federal republic. Thus, as war spread across the European continent, he could confidently assert that "the principles of this revolution are those of universal

[49]Barlow, *Advice to the Privileged Orders, in the Several States of Europe* (New York, 1792), 75–76, 77, 76.
[50]Ibid., 76.

peace."[51] "Monarchical sovereignty, the enemy of mankind, and the source of misery, is abolished," Barlow's friend Thomas Paine proclaimed; "sovereignty itself is restored to its natural and original place, the Nation. Were this the case throughout Europe, the cause of wars would be taken away."[52] "Purge the earth of its tyrants," Barlow urged the people of Piedmont, "and it will be no more tormented with war."[53] Old world monarchs, grasping selfishly and blindly for riches and power in a never-ending contest for relative advantage, brought the scourge of war on their innocent subjects. "The kings of modern Europe are the authors of war and misery," Barlow told the French Convention in 1792.[54] But "if all the nations of Europe were as free as the French, and every individual member of society were equally independent of every other individual, the question respecting the boundaries of any particular government would become in a great measure indifferent, both to the people of that government and to all their neighbours." Such predictions were not the idle speculations of closet-philosophers; in the United States of America, "this theory has been carried into practice."[55]

Only the most visionary Jeffersonians would follow Barlow in applying American lessons to the rapidly deteriorating European situation. By 1799, when he elaborated his proposal for a European federal republic, Barlow himself was hard-pressed to sustain his own original enthusiasm for France's republican revolution. But Barlow recognized that the establishment of republican government in France—even the republicanizing of every European state—could not guarantee peace: the outbreak of war across Europe and France's belligerent challenge to monarchical government everywhere were only to be expected. As the American experience first showed and the French Revolutionary wars now amply confirmed, the international context of republican experiments in particular states ultimately determined their prospects for success.

[51]Barlow, *A Letter Addressed to the People of Piedmont* [1792] (New York, 1795), 27.
[52]Paine, *Rights of Man*, 144.
[53]Barlow, *A Letter Addressed to the People of Piedmont*, 27.
[54]Barlow, *A Letter to the National Convention of France, on the Defects in the Constitution of 1791* (New York, 1792), 9.
[55]Barlow, *A Letter Addressed to the People of Piedmont*, 42–43.

Barlow's proposed United States of Europe only made sense if the old diplomatic system collapsed completely, and in the increasingly unlikely event that a victorious French republic would dictate a peace curbing its own power and securing the liberty and independence of all European states. But the effect of juxtaposing the American and European systems, intended or not, was to emphasize the radical differences between them. The European system as it was actually organized was the antitype of the American federal union. When Barlow celebrated federalism, he condemned and rejected a collapsing European diplomatic system--a system that optimistic American Revolutionaries had once hoped to manipulate and improve. The European conflagration was the most eloquent and persuasive testimony imaginable to the wisdom of the framers of the federal Constitution.

Part Three

CHANGING
WORLD

The outbreak of the French Revolutionary wars demolished American hopes for the continuing improvement of the European diplomatic system. The new federal government soon abandoned efforts to negotiate advantageous commercial treaties that had given such a powerful impetus to Constitutional reform. Frustrated by Federalist unwillingness to challenge British maritime power, Jefferson resigned as Secretary of State. With Madison, Jefferson galvanized the emergent republican opposition, charging that Jay's "English Treaty" of 1794 compromised American neutrality and the Franco-American alliance of 1778. The ultimate effect of Anglo-American rapprochement would be to draw the United States into Britain's anti-republican coalition. The quasi-war with France (1798–1800) fulfilled Republican prophecies. It also reinforced a growing revulsion to European diplomatic connections that subverted the Republicans' Vattelian hopes for the balance of power.

The leading premises of Republican foreign policy were developed during the years of Federalist ascendancy. Increasingly, Republicans linked American independence and security to the vindication of the new nation's neutral rights at sea. The resumption of British assaults on

American shipping in 1805 revealed the vulnerability of neutral traders. In response, Jefferson as president and Madison as secretary of state sought to uphold American rights through commercial diplomacy, implementing retaliatory sanctions that Federalists had eschewed in the 1790s. The Republicans now had no illusions about inaugurating a new world order. They simply wished to preserve the new nation's standing in world politics and promote economic development through trade in order to fuel westward expansion and strengthen intersectional ties. Identifying national sovereignty with neutral rights, Republicans saw the union as the only guarantee of American independence.

European turmoil reinforced the Republican commitment to federalism. As Britain and France struggled, Jeffersonians began to see what was left of the old balance-of-power system as the antitype of their own federal union. If Republicans advocated states' rights and a federal government of limited powers, the federal government nevertheless needed—and used—those powers to function as a state in a world of states. The federal republic was the ultimate, practical embodiment of the dreams of visionary theorists who had long sought to reconstitute the European system for peace and prosperity.

The Republican apotheosis of the federal union reflected a pervasive disenchantment with the balance of power on both sides of the Atlantic. Sympathetic with the French Revolution, British liberals argued for recognition of the new republic and against counter-revolutionary coalitions that only multiplied threats to national interests. They rejected Vattel's premise that the balance of power could sustain a regime of law among nations even as the British government aggressively pursued alliances in the name of the balance of power and European civilization.

Where could legal constraints come from, if not from the balance of power? During the final years of the Napoleonic wars, the balance collapsed. Britain dominated the sea, France the continent. America's rights as a neutral power required a different foundation. Lawlessness among nations was the great theoretical as well as practical challenge to Republican statecraft, which Madison addressed in *An Examination of the British Doctrine, Which Subjects to Capture a Neutral trade, Not Open in Time of Peace* (1806). His challenge was to find a middle ground between

Federalist apologists for British maritime power who argued that neutrals had no rights at all, and natural rights theorists who would enforce law at any cost.

Madison was determined neither to capitulate nor to go to war. Instead he argued for the continuing efficacy of legal principles that constituted the "modern law of nations" despite the collapse of the balance of power. These principles were positive law, *not* ordained by nature, but established through international behavior that Britain itself had repeatedly acknowledged. Madison demonstrated as much by reviewing the opinions of great writers, treaties to which Britain was a party, and British court decisions and ministerial statements. Historically, Britain had acknowledged legal restraints because it recognized that its long-term interests were best served by a regime of law responsive to the larger interests of all nations. But despite his traditional policy orientation—and despite the support of British liberals who advocated a conciliatory posture toward the former colonies—Madison's arguments had no effect on ministerial policy. Troubled by the government's contempt for law, liberals emphasized the common interests of the two nations. Britain should not alienate a potentially friendly power nor begrudge profits to neutral traders who helped sustain Britain's prosperity in wartime. Nor, they insisted, could the mere possession of superior power—the ability to destroy neutrals—justify its exercise. In resisting Napoleon's threat to European civilization, Britain should not abandon civilized standards.

Madison's appeal to British self-restraint could not avert the rapid deterioration of Anglo-American relations that led to the War of 1812. The British government did not respond to the pleas of the Americans or their British friends because of the conviction that the United States was powerless to retaliate. The government assumed that the United States was not an effective polity, that its pretensions to sovereignty and independence were just that. Madison's conception of the modern law of nations presupposed what Britain did not believe—that the United States could function as one of many law-making sovereigns in world society. Only war could settle the point.

Federalist oppositionists weakened the American government's position by publicly questioning the adequacy of the federal Constitution, noting the weakness of American defenses and predicting disunion in the event of war. As they elaborated these themes, Federalists reinforced British determination to make no concessions and Republican concern over the fragility of the federal union. Awareness of vulnerability dictated a circumspect foreign policy but also pushed Republicans toward the threshold of war. If in 1806 Madison had hoped to provide a common ground for Anglo-American accommodation, by 1812 he was prepared for war in defense of American sovereignty.

The war of 1812 was another crisis of the union. The genius of the federal Constitution was to sustain peace in an expanding system of distinct state-republics and free citizens. This more perfect union made the United States the antithesis of the fractious European system. Republicans also recognized that the union was weak and vulnerable: the only justification for risking war was that the failure to fight would itself signal the union's dissolution. If the federal union could survive the test of war, the promise of the Revolution would be redeemed. As a recognized sovereign power, the United States could then take a leading role in promoting the rule of law in the society of nations that would emerge from the wreckage of the Vattelian world.

Chapter Six

The Balance of Power

I. WORLDS APART

"The situation of North America on the chart of the globe, exhibits the strongest imaginable contrast to every other part of the known world," exulted Kentucky lawyer Allan Bowie Magruder. The continent "combines within itself, every kind of relative advantage, which belong to the other parts of the globe." And, unlike the benighted "nations of Asia, Africa and Europe," which could never overcome the "calamities of a barbarous origin," the United States had the "good fortune" to have "commenced her career towards empire, at a period of civilization." The New World therefore would achieve a higher stage of political development than the Old: a prosperous and expanding federal union of free republics represented the antithesis of the European balance of power. Magruder, who soon moved on to Louisiana and served as one of the new state's first senators (1812–13), dedicated these *Reflections* to President Thomas Jefferson.[1] Jefferson's timely diplomacy had extended American control over the heartland of the continent, preempting the

---

[1] Allan Bowie Magruder, *Political, Commercial and Moral Reflections, on the Late Cession of Louisiana, to the United States* (Lexington, Ky., 1803), vii–viii.

establishment of a powerful French presence on the western frontier and securing the new nation's glorious future.

Rumors that Spain had ceded Louisiana to Napoleon by the secret Treaty of San Ildefonso (1800) raised a furor in the Seventh Congress, meeting in the new capital city of Washington in early 1803. Federalists urged an immediate war of conquest, before a French force could assume control. The Jefferson administration hoped that the volatile diplomatic situation would open the way for the peaceful acquisition of the region, or at least for ironclad guarantees against further interruptions of American trade down the Mississippi. Federalists and Republicans alike agreed that the union was at risk: the "contrast" between New World and Old would disappear with Napoleon in control of the Mississippi Valley.[2] "From this corrupted fountain of the moral virtues, the streams of colonization would have flown," Magruder wrote, after the danger had passed. "Louisiana, our own natural territory, in the very neighborhood of the only truly republican people in the world, would have became the great receptacle, the last asylum of human crimes."[3]

Magruder's *Reflections* captured his contemporaries' ambivalent sense of the new nation's moral superiority to Europe and its simultaneous vulnerability to Europeanization. Republican America represented the latest stage in the progress of civilization, but it could flourish only as long as it sustained its natural distance from the Old World, "the great scene of human folly and misfortune."[4] The American Revolution had begun the process of dismantling the old colonial empires and thus of disentangling the New World from the Old. Optimistic expansionists were convinced that Britain's remaining colonies would eventually fall under American control, and that the Spanish empire was on the verge

[2]The standard accounts of the Louisiana crisis are Arthur P. Whitaker, *The Mississippi Question, 1795–1803* (New York, 1934), 189–236, and Alexander DeConde, *This Affair of Louisiana* (New York, 1976), 127–92. For an incisive analysis of the implications of the crisis for American political economy see Drew R. McCoy, *The Elusive Republic: Political Economy in Jeffersonian America* (Chapel Hill, 1980), 196–99. See also the discussion in Peter S. Onuf, "The Expanding Union," in David T. Konig, ed., *Devising Liberty: The Conditions of Freedom in the Early American Republic* (forthcoming).

[3]Magruder, *Political, Commercial and Moral Reflections*, 86.

[4]Ibid., viii.

of complete collapse.[5] In the meantime, the continent offered magnificent opportunities for the growth of American population, prosperity and power that the remnants of colonial regimes—and their native American allies—could not long resist.

Yet this projected movement across space and time would be reversed if the "balance of power," the death-struggle of the European great powers, were extended to America. Had Napoleon established a powerful French presence in Louisiana, asserted Magruder, "the lamentable picture of European wretchedness would serve as a mirror to explain and prognosticate" the new nation's "future destiny. She would be compelled to adopt the same Gothic principles to defend her territory, that have equally disgraced and enslaved the nations of Europe." Even if the Americans successfully resisted French encroachments, the new nation would be Europeanized. "The European policy of keeping up the balance of power in America," Magruder concluded, "would give rise" to standing armies and all the other "evils incident to the system," and antithetical to republican government.[6]

The "more perfect union" created by the federal Constitution, not the superior virtue or peaceful character of their citizens, constituted the crucial advantage of the American states over their European counterparts. The republican Revolutionaries of 1776 had hoped that the end of

[5]According to Virginia Senator George Nicholas, "we have nothing to fear from the colony of any European nation on this continent; they ought rather to be considered as a pledge of the good conduct of the mother country towards us; for such possessions must be held only during our pleasure." Speech of Feb. 25, 1803, *Annals of the Congress of the United States, 1789–1824*, 42 vols. (Washington, 1834–56), 7th Cong., 2nd Sess., 233. For similar sentiments see also speech of Senator De Witt Clinton, Feb. 23, 1803, ibid., 133.

[6]Magruder, *Political, Commercial and Moral Reflections*, 38, 42. "To maintain an army," David Ramsay explained, would require "heavy taxes, and an extensive executive patronage. These would, gradually, have undermined our republican forms of government, and paved the way for the concentration of power in the hands of an hereditary monarch." *Oration on the Cession of Louisiana, to the United States* (Charleston, S.C., 1804), 14. On the origins and implications of the Jeffersonian aversion to standing armies see Lance Banning, *The Jeffersonian Persuasion: Evolution of a Party Ideology* (Ithaca, 1978). For Jeffersonian ambivalence on war see Reginald C. Stuart, *The Half-way Pacifist: Thomas Jefferson's View of War* (Toronto, 1978).

monarchical rule and the institution of popular governments would lead to peace and prosperity; but domestic unrest, interstate conflict and diplomatic embarrassments in the "critical period" convinced their reform-minded successors that the survival of republican government in America depended on the reconstitution of the union. The apparent collapse of the European system in the 1790s reinforced the importance of federalism in America: republics, as Alexander Hamilton argued in *The Federalist* and the belligerent career of Revolutionary France soon confirmed, were no more peaceful in practice than monarchies.[7] Ironically, the transformation of France into a republic unleashed the "dogs of war," subverting the intricate structure of alliances—the "classic," old-regime balance of power—that supposedly had secured the liberties of member states.

For Magruder and fellow Jeffersonians, the European balance was no longer the potentially progressive force it had been for optimistic Revolutionaries. "The history of that quarter of the world," he explained,

> furnish[es] a summary of the evils which America has escaped.—Europe is cut up into innumerable independent sovereignties; some powerful and others feeble, and whose interests, are in many respects, dissimilar. These circumstances combine to render a balance of power to prevent the strong from subjugating the weak, an object of absolute necessity. . . . A single state does not, in every instance, possess adequate power to maintain its stand unaided by the resources of others. Treaties of alliance are formed under the most frivolous pretences with the rest. . . . By this means, and with the design of protecting the balance of power . . . all Europe is sometimes then in a blaze at once.

Magruder acknowledged that these "gothic principles" had for many centuries secured the independence of most states, if not the lives and liberties of their subjects. But the French Revolution "changed the aspect of affairs." With the "secondary states of the continent" subjugated by France, "the balance of power was destroyed" and "Britain is now engaged singly, and unaided by former coalitions, in defending her

[7]*Federalist* Nos. 6–8, *The Federalist*, ed., with an Introduction and Notes, by Jacob E. Cooke (Middletown, Conn., 1961), 28–50. For further discussion of this point see Gerald Stourzh, *Alexander Hamilton and the Idea of Republican Government* (Stanford, 1970), 149–53.

crown, and in repelling a series of encroachment that threatens her own and the independence of all nations." In the meantime, "liberty has been banished from the Eastern shores of the Atlantic, and the fugitive only finds an assylum in America."[8]

Perhaps at some distant date, Magruder conceded, "a convention of the states of Europe" might follow the advice of the French King Henri IV and adopt a peace plan and so put "an end to the horrors of war." But if the self-interest of warring states dictated peace, the "inveterate policy" of despotic regimes was too deep-rooted "in the habits of mankind" to fulfill the "fondest dreams of philosophy and benevolence."[9] Of course European sovereigns would resist the creation of republican governments that would destroy their power—and that alone could sustain a durable union. The French for their part had betrayed the promise of their own revolution, exchanging republican liberty for imperial glory and foreign conquest.

Magruder lauded the American founders for securing peace, the great desideratum of international politics. "The Federal orb, like the sun in the physical hemisphere, supports and maintains each revolving satellite." Individual states, "too weak to be secure and too small to be respectable," were protected from the ambition of more powerful neighbors. In contrast, the alliances that characterized old regime statecraft threatened the sovereignty and independence of even the most powerful states. But the endless cycle of European wars, justified in the name of an elusive, ever-receding "balance" would not be visited on America, where "by the Federal Union, all the qualities of strength, wisdom and virtue, move in one consolidated mass to the accomplishment of every great measure upon which our happiness depends." "Upon this liberal plan of government," Magruder concluded, "the whole world might be regulated in peace and harmony."[10]

[8]Magruder, *Political, Commercial and Moral Reflections*, 35–36.
[9]Ibid., 37. For further discussion of the peace-plan tradition see Joel Barlow, *To His Fellow Citizens of the United States of America* (Philadelphia, 1801), Letter II, dated Paris., Dec. 20, 1799, 16–17. See also F. H. Hinsley, *Power and the Pursuit of Peace: Theory and Practice in the History of Relations between States* (Cambridge, 1963), 13–80, esp. 24–27 (on Henri IV).
[10]Magruder, *Political, Commercial and Moral Reflections*, 73, 74, 73.

II. REPUBLICAN FOREIGN POLICY

Republican foreign policy was shaped by the great party battles of the 1790s. Fears of Hamiltonian consolidation and corruption led Jefferson and his allies to defend states' rights and strict construction of the federal Constitution. Administration policies, they claimed, jeopardized the founders' great achievement, the creation of a compound republic. As they sought to defend what they considered to be the original federal balance, Republicans increasingly identified national independence and security with sustaining and expanding the union. At the same time, the collapse of the Vattelian world forced Republicans to reassess their faith in the efficacy of conventional diplomacy to achieve progressive ends. As Magruder and his allies celebrated the union, they became increasingly conscious of the distinctiveness of the American state system and the overriding need to avoid dangerous European entanglements.[11]

The Republicans' fundamental commitment was to preserve the federal union from internal and external threats. They portrayed the United States as an exemplary world order, a higher form of political organization that enabled the state republics to fulfill their original ends of association. "The United States have taught the nations of the world that it is possible to terminate disputes by appeals to reason instead of by force," Benjamin Rush wrote when the Constitution was ratified in 1788. "I do not despair of this mode of deciding national disputes becoming general in the course of the approaching century."[12] By

---

[11]For an excellent overview see Richard Buel Jr., *Securing the Revolution: Ideology in American Politics, 1789–1815* (Ithaca, 1972). On the salience of the republican tradition see Banning, *Jeffersonian Persuasion.* For seminal treatments of party conflict in the 1790s see Marshall Smelser, "The Federalist Period as an Age of Passion," *American Quarterly,* 10 (1958), 391–419, and John R. Howe, "Republican Political Thought and the Political Violence of the 1790s," *American Quarterly,* 19 (1967), 147–65.

[12][Benjamin Rush], "Observations on the Federal Procession in Philadelphia," July 9, 1788, in Lyman Butterfield, ed., *The Letters of Benjamin Rush,* 2 vols. (Princeton, 1951), I:473, 475. See also Rush to Madison, Feb. 27, 1790, predicting the eventual

resolving "national disputes" among the American states, the new federal union would secure their fundamental rights and interests and preserve their republican constitutions. Peace would be guaranteed without sacrificing the rights and interests of free citizens.

If the federal Constitution thus resolved the international problem for the American republics, it also gave them collectively the capacity to negotiate and enforce agreements with the unreconstructed sovereignties of the old world.[13] Jeffersonians insisted that one of the original points of creating a more perfect union was to enable the United States to reconstitute the world trading system on a more equitable and liberal basis.[14] Presenting itself to the larger world as a single sovereign power, the new nation could negotiate treaties that would help create a more stable, peaceful, and lawful diplomatic system.

At first revolutionary changes in France promised to reinforce the progressive effects of the American Revolution on world politics. In late 1791 the *National Gazette* reprinted a letter from London enthusiastically endorsing the French Revolution, congratulating the Americans on their new federal charter, and looking forward to a new system of alliances that would "create a vortex of love and concord, which shall attract and involve all God's rational offspring!" As long as the British government pursued an ostensibly neutral course toward the French Republic, British liberals could embrace the Jeffersonian vision. "With you we may speedily associate for preserving the peace and freedom of

adoption by the "courts of Europe" of a system for deciding "national disputes" by peaceful means. Ibid., 1: 540.

[13]For illuminating discussions of the importance of union in Madison's thought see Adrienne Koch, *Madison's "Advice to My Country"* (Princeton, 1966), 103–59, esp. at 132–34; and Drew R. McCoy, *The Last of the Founders: James Madison and the Republican Legacy* (Cambridge, 1989), 134–51, and passim. See also Richard E. Ellis's insightful analysis of states' rights thinking in *The Union at Risk: Jacksonian Democracy, States' Rights and the Nullification Crisis* (New York, 1987).

[14]Merrill Peterson, "Thomas Jefferson and Commercial Policy, 1783–1793," *William and Mary Quarterly*, 3rd ser., XXII (1965), 183–202; Drew R. McCoy, "Republicanism and American Foreign Policy: James Madison and the Political Economy of Commercial Discrimination, 1789 to 1794," *William and Mary Quarterly*, 3rd ser., XXXI (1974), 633–46; J. C. A. Stagg, *Mr. Madison's War: Politics, Diplomacy, and Warfare in the Early American Republic, 1783–1830* (Princeton, 1983), 3–47.

all mankind," this Briton assured his American correspondent, "and may one nation and another be continually added to the compact."[15]

Republican hopes for changing the world depended both on the new federal government's willingness to assume an aggressive diplomatic posture, most notably in pursuit of a commercial treaty with Britain, and on the responsiveness of the powers to American initiatives. It is a mistake to emphasize the importance of anti-British sentiment in shaping Republican foreign policy. A commercial treaty that opened up the British West Indies and confirmed American neutral rights would have given a much different tone to Republican rhetoric, however deep-seated Jefferson's Anglophobic prejudices. After all, an equitable Anglo-American accord was the first and most crucial step toward constituting a more liberal world order. Nor were the Republicans prepared to offer substantial aid to the French Revolutionaries, particularly after Citizen Genet's controversial filibustering tour through the states in 1793.

Over the course of their protracted political exile, Jefferson and his followers argued forcefully that Hamilton's opposition to their commercial diplomacy had subverted the new nation's standing in the international community. Republicans agreed that the Treasury Secretary's successful opposition to a discriminatory tariff, proposed by Madison in 1791 and 1794 as a bargaining chip to gain more favorable terms of trade with the British West Indies, was one of the Federalists' original sins against the new federal union. The promise of the federal Constitution was betrayed: perfecting the American union would *not* lead to advantageous and equitable commercial alliances with Britain and other foreign powers.[16] Secretary of State Thomas Jefferson was thus frustrated in his

[15]Letter, dated London, Sept. 26, 1791, *National Gazette*, Dec. 8, 1791. For similar sentiments see the "Toast by Dr. [Richard] Price," on the first anniversary of the French Revolution, July 14, 1791, urging a "confederation" between Britain and France "for extending the blessings of peace and liberty throughout the world"; other powers, including the United States, would be drawn into this union. *National Gazette*, Nov. 3, 1791. "The time is, I Hope, coming, when a conviction will prevail of the folly as well as the iniquity of wars," Price wrote in *A Discourse on the Love of Our Country. Delivered on November 4, 1789, in the Meeting-House in the Old Jewry* (London, 1789), 29–30.

[16]Lawrence Kaplan, "The Consensus of 1789: Jefferson and Hamilton on Ameri-

efforts to implement the crucial foreign policy objectives that independence required and the adoption of the Constitution made possible. Jefferson's goal, "to have met the English with some restrictions which might induce them to abate their severities against our commerce," had been thwarted by Hamilton's interference.[17]

Hamilton's successful opposition to Jefferson's and Madison's commercial policy—and their goal of reconstructing the Atlantic trading system through a new system of commercial treaties—helped lay the foundation for the party battles of the 1790s. Thrown on the defensive by Hamilton, the Republicans soon displayed their characteristic enthusiasm for strict construction, states' rights and the compact theory of the Union. Yet the original and fundamental complaint was not that the federal government had exceeded its powers, but that it had *failed* to act vigorously in promoting American interests abroad. In his "Political Observations" of April 1795, Madison justified his proposals for commercial discrimination against Britain as a fulfillment of the founders' original intentions:

> Had the present federal government, on its first establishment, done what it ought to have done, what it was instituted and expected to do, and what was actually proposed and intended it should do; had it revived and confirmed the belief in Great-Britain, that our trade and navigation would not be free to her, without an equal and reciprocal freedom to us, in her trade and navigation, we have her own authority for saying, that she would long since have met us on proper ground.[18]

For Jeffersonian oppositionists, the framers' original intentions had been perverted and betrayed by Federalist administrations that capitulated to British maritime supremacy and willingly accepted a degrading, dependent, neo-colonial relationship with the old mother country.

Union, not an aversion to power as such, had the highest priority in Republican thinking. In the critical years after the Revolution, Repub-

can Foreign Policy," in *Entangling Alliances with None: American Foreign Policy in the Age of Jefferson* (Kent, Ohio, 1987), 67–78.

[17]Jefferson to Washington, Sept. 9, 1792, in Julian Boyd et al., eds., *The Papers of Thomas Jefferson*, 25 vols. to date (Princeton, 1950–), 24:354.

[18]"Political Observations," April 20, 1795, in J. C. A. Stagg et al., eds., *The Papers of James Madison*, 19 vols. to date (Chicago and Charlottesville, 1962–), 15:519–20.

licans agreed, the survival and perfection of the union depended on redefining the federal balance and creating a more energetic and effective central government; once installed, that government could secure the integrity and independence of the union by negotiating advantageous treaties with foreign powers. But when the Federalists instead used the federal government's power to promote the particular interests of privileged groups, preservation of the union depended on resisting corruption and consolidation and upholding states' rights. By favoring eastern merchants who imported British manufactures and federal creditors who were also disproportionately from the eastern states, Hamilton's fiscal policy exacerbated sectional tensions in the new national government and set the stage for partisan controversy over foreign policy.

Jefferson set forth the leading features of his commercial policy in his final report to the House of Representatives in December 1793. This was the frustrated Secretary of State's farewell address. It was also a valedictory statement for optimistic Revolutionaries who hoped to reconstruct the world through the expansion of trade and the progressive development of the law of nations. And it was a preview of the commercial diplomacy that would be pursued by Jefferson and Madison more than a decade later. "The numbers of mankind would be increased, and their condition bettered," promised Jefferson, if trade were "relieved from all its shackles in all parts of the world." Every country would then "be employed in producing that which nature has best fitted it to produce, and each be free to exchange with others mutual surpluses for mutual wants." As a result, "the greatest mass possible would then be produced of those things which contribute to human life and happiness." Yet, as the framers of the Constitution recognized, it was vain to rely on the enlightened self-interest of Old World powers to remove the "piles of regulating laws, duties, and prohibitions" that embarrassed world trade. "It is not to the moderation and justice of others we are to trust for fair and equal access to market with our productions," Jefferson explained, "or for our due share in the transportation of them." Instead, the United States must be prepared to pursue "defensive and protecting measures" to force commercial concessions from "particular nations"— namely Britain—that would otherwise "grasp at undue shares."[19]

[19]Secretary of State Jefferson's Report to the House of Representatives, Dec. 16,

The creation of a more perfect union should have enabled the American states to secure their fair share of the world's trade. That trade in turn guaranteed the strength and independence of the union. But if the new nation renounced its maritime rights and submitted to another power's naval superiority, "it will be disarmed of its defence, and its productions" would be at that power's "mercy." The most dangerous and insidious consequence of such a supine policy was that American "politics may be influenced by those who command its commerce." The unwillingness to pursue an aggressive foreign policy and to exploit "our own means of independence"—discriminatory tariffs and other commercial sanctions—was to jeopardize the union by fostering party divisions and sectional tensions.[20] The same complex of concerns that would later characterize the Republican response to the Louisiana crisis was already apparent in Jefferson's 1793 report: American union and independence were inseparable, and they depended equally on insulating the new nation from foreign influence and interference. As Drew McCoy has shown, however, Republican solicitude for the union did not imply withdrawal from all connections with the Old World. Just as Republicans believed that territorial expansion—at the expense of the new nation's imperial neighbors—was the only alternative to division and disunion, so too the liberalization of world trade and the vigorous defense of neutral rights would guarantee the expanding markets that would sustain American prosperity and power.[21]

Jefferson's 1793 report previewed Republican arguments in the bitter congressional struggle over the Jay Treaty a year later. Republi-

---

1793, in *American State Papers: Documents, Legislative and Executive, of the Congress of the United States*, 38 vols. (Washington, 1832–61), *Foreign Relations*, 1:303. The case for discrimination was made by Madison in a series of speeches to the House, Jan. 3, 14, 30, and 31, 1794. *The Papers of James Madison*, 15:167–71, 182–201, 210–24, 224–43. "Trade ought to be *free* before it could find its *proper* channel," he told his colleagues (Jan. 31, at 236); but "it was not free at present, it could not, therefore, find the channels in which it would most advantageously flow. The dykes must be broken down before the waters could pursue their natural course." For the history of earlier efforts to gain commercial reciprocity see Vernon G. Setser, *The Commercial Reciprocity Policy of the United States, 1774–1829* (Philadelphia, 1937), esp. 59–113.

[20]Jefferson's Report of Dec. 16, 1793, *American State Papers: Foreign Relations*, 1:303.

[21]McCoy, *The Elusive Republic*, 185–235.

cans were prepared to see any retreat from their leader's bold program as a craven capitulation to British power. They traced every foreign policy disaster, beginning with British assaults on American neutral rights during the first phase of the French Revolutionary wars, to the Federalists' failure to negotiate an equitable commercial treaty with Britain. John Jay's controversial treaty of 1794, Republican critics charged, was the logical outcome of Federalist cowardice, a public acknowledgement of the new nation's subservience to the old mother country and its unwillingness to stand up for its rights as a neutral power. Far from securing American rights, Jay formally renounced any future use of discriminatory duties or other commercial sanctions, the favored instruments of Republican foreign policy. At the same time, Anglo-American accord—notwithstanding its defective, unequal terms—alienated the embattled French republic and prepared the way for the Quasi-War (1798–1800).

The Republicans' primary objection to the Jay Treaty was that it jeopardized American neutrality and independence by drawing the United States into tacit alliance with the counter-revolutionary coalition headed by Britain. Although most historians agree that Jay could not have done much better, Republicans were convinced that his failure to gain more favorable terms was more a function of the self-defeating nature of Federalist foreign policy than of a realistic assessment of the international situation.[22] By forfeiting its standing as a neutral power, Jay guaranteed that the new nation would become entangled in the expanding European conflict. At the same time, the Jay Treaty discredited the Jeffersonian conception of treaties as instruments of a liberal foreign policy that would unshackle commerce and promote peace. Given the

[22]Charles R. Ritcheson, *Aftermath of Revolution: British Policy toward the United States, 1783–1795* (Dallas, 1969), esp. 317–59; Jerald A. Combs, *The Jay Treaty: Political Battleground of the Founding Fathers* (Berkeley and Los Angeles, 1970); and Robert W. Tucker and David C. Hendrickson, *Empire of Liberty: The Statecraft of Thomas Jefferson* (New York, 1990), 69–72, have all discounted the efficacy of commercial sanctions and emphasized Britain's determination to preserve its maritime supremacy; failure of the treaty project would have led to a war which the Americans could not have sustained. On the beneficial effects of the treaty for Anglo-American relations see Bradford Perkins, *The First Rapprochement: England and the United States, 1795–1805* (Philadelphia, 1955).

radically deteriorating international situation, the hope that treaty guarantees of neutral rights could limit the scope of conflict—and permit neutral trading powers to exploit new commercial opportunities—was undoubtedly visionary. Neutrals could only look forward to a comprehensive peace settlement when the belligerents finally recognized the futility of their self-destructive course. In the meantime, Republicans concluded, it was much better to have no treaty at all. In Madison's words, "a Treaty thus unequal in its conditions, thus derogatory to our national rights, thus insidious in some of its objects, and thus alarming in its operation to the dearest interests of the U. S. in their commerce and navigation, is in its present form unworthy the voluntary acceptance of an Independent people."[23]

The ratification of the Jay Treaty decisively thwarted Jeffersonian hopes for constructing an improved world order. This frustration—the sense that the new nation could no longer hope to promote progressive change in the European state system—was apparent in Republican warnings about the dangers of the "balance of power." The American Revolutionaries could conflate their conception of their own "more perfect union" with a belief that treaty compacts with other nations would ultimately constitute a naturally harmonious world order. This republican teleology, buttressed by the Enlightenment's recognition of the unnaturalness and irrationality of war and faith in the civilizing and harmonizing effects of expanding commerce, knew no upper limit: why shouldn't the whole world be embraced in a still more perfect union, a union of perfect unions? But the French Revolutionary wars soon gave the lie to these hopes.

For enlightened Europeans the collapse and ruin of the Vattelian order demolished any lingering images of a republic of Europe that could sustain separate sovereignties. Jeffersonians like Barlow and Magruder agreed that the absence of a true union was the root of Europe's troubles: now more clearly than ever, American federalism represented the only solution to the classic problems of international

---

[23]Draft of the Petition to the General Assembly of the Commonwealth of Virginia [Sept. 1795], in *The Papers of James Madison*, 16:75–76. Madison dismissed the Federalist argument that rejection of the treaty "will be made the pretext of a war on us."

politics. At the same time, however, the disintegration of the European system subverted the sense of world historical development that had inspired the American Revolutionaries. In 1776, Americans had been prepared to take a leading role in a community of states that was already becoming more refined and civilized, a world in which a more rational diplomatic system and an expanding regime of law were supported by an increasingly complex and stable balance of power. Within two decades, the international situation was completely, disastrously different. There was now no possibility that the United States—negotiating from a position of conspicuous weakness—could deflect the belligerents from their mutually destructive, lawless course. Instead, Republican critics argued, the first imperative of American foreign policy should be to avoid all European political entanglements. The balance of power was the "vortex" of death and destruction, not a sensitive mechanism that could be made to work for neutral rights, free trade and world peace.[24]

The Jeffersonians' revulsion to the balance of power reflected growing disenchantment with the French Revolution and wariness about the motives of progressively more despotic and less republican French governments. Anxious to protect a still-fragile union from internal stresses and external threats, the Republicans heeded Washington's injunction to avoid "entangling alliances." In fact, they argued, it was Washington's failure to uphold this principle when he endorsed the controversial Jay Treaty of 1794 that led to escalating depredations against American shipping in the Quasi-War with France. By the terms of that treaty the United States had forfeited its neutrality, submitting to British maritime superiority and violating the spirit—if not the letter— of the Franco-American alliance of 1778. For Republicans the great lesson of Federalist foreign policy was not that the new nation had chosen the wrong allies, but rather that all alliances jeopardized American independence. Jefferson therefore did not seek closer ties with France. On the contrary, the formal abrogation of the 1778 alliance in the Franco-American Convention of 1800 relieved the Republicans of a chronic source of embarrassment. Determined to avoid compromising

---

[24]Sen. Robert Wright (Md.), speech of Feb. 24, 1803, *Annals of Congress*, 7th Cong., 2nd Sess., 165.

connections with either great power, Jefferson resisted subsequent Federalist agitation for a formal Anglo-American rapprochement, despite a growing community of interests between the two nations. The Republicans' memory of what they considered the disastrous effects of the Jay Treaty combined with their realistic assessment of the French emperor's imperial ambitions to guarantee their commitment to American neutrality.[25]

Disgusted by Jay's Treaty and disillusioned by the European wars, Jeffersonians retreated from Jefferson's idea that the world could be made safe for neutrals through treaties. While their Federalist opponents insisted that the new nation's weakness and vulnerability required a prudent submission to British power, Republicans replied that America's independence could only be guaranteed by avoiding alliances that would draw the United States into European controversies. American independence would not have been compromised if the Federalists had recognized and exploited the opportunities afforded by the establishment of a federal government that used its powers to regulate trade and impose commercial sanctions. Because the Federalists measured American power in conventional military terms, Republicans charged, they failed to recognize the new nation's potential influence in world politics. Union made—or should have made—the American states impregnable. But the Jay Treaty jeopardized union by drawing the new nation into the expanding European conflict.

Rejection of the Jay Treaty, Federalists argued, would have led to war with Britain, "civil war" in America, and the "dissolution of the union." According to John Adams, asserting the rights of "a poor and divided nation" risked potentially disastrous British reprisals.[26] But to

[25]The best account is Albert Hall Bowman, *The Struggle for Neutrality: Franco-American Diplomacy During the Federalist Era* (Knoxville, 1974), 360–435. See also Kaplan, *Entangling Alliances*, esp. ch. 6.

[26]John Quincy Adams to Charles Adams, June 9, 1796; John Adams to Abigail Adams, April 18, 1796, both quoted in Combs, *The Jay Treaty*, 183. By contrast, J. C. A. Stagg et al. suggest that Madison's draft of the Virginia Assembly's Petition against the Jay Treaty [Sept. 1795], "was singularly free of any appeal to narrowly sectional interests." Editorial note, *The Papers of James Madison*, 16:67. On the prevalence of disunion sentiment see Memorandum from John Taylor, May 11, 1794, ibid., 15:328–31.

Republican critics the Federalists' failure to threaten or invoke commercial sanctions betrayed a lack of faith in the union itself. The Federalists' willingness to "sacrifice . . . the dearest interests of our Commerce, as the most sacred dictates of national honor," thus reflected their sense that the union was an *imperfect* form, that conflicts of interest were exacerbated by the division and diffusion of political authority.[27] Ironically, as partisan controversy over foreign policy became increasingly virulent, Republican efforts to mobilize the states against the administration seemed to confirm Federalist fears.

At the same time, of course, the Republicans' commitment to federalism—their devotion to the compound republic—was strengthened and deepened. Republicans became convinced that Federalist efforts to muzzle opposition sentiment with the Alien and Sedition Acts were simply the opening round of a comprehensive campaign against states' rights that would weaken and ultimately destroy the union.[28] These assaults on what the Republicans considered the fundamental principles of the reconstituted and perfected American regime flowed logically from the Anglophile Federalists' determination to draw the New World into the Old World's balance-of-power politics.

[27]Madison to Robert R. Livingston, Aug. 10, 1795, ibid., 16:47.

[28]For a comprehensive history of the Alien and Sedition laws see James Morton Smith, *Freedom's Fetters: The Alien and Sedition Laws and American Civil Liberties* (Ithaca, 1956). Madison set forth the compact theory of the federal union in the Virginia Resolutions, Dec. 21, 1798, and at greater length in the Virginia General Assembly's Report of 1800 [Jan. 7]. *Papers of James Madison*, 17:185–91 and 303–51, esp. at 308–12. See also ch. 1, above. For a brief discussion of Jeffersonian antipathy to the balance of power see Daniel G. Lang, *Foreign Policy in the Early Republic: The Law of Nations and the Balance of Power* (Baton Rouge, 1985), 142–45. See also Lawrence S. Kaplan, "Jefferson, The Napoleonic Wars, and the Balance of Power," in *Entangling Alliances with None*, 111–26.

III. END OF THE OLD WORLD

Convinced that the corrupt old alliance system had sucked Britain into a destructive and self-defeating counter-revolutionary coalition, British liberal reformers denounced the balance of power as furiously as their American counterparts. Indeed, the Jeffersonian critique of the European system was to a large extent prefigured in polemical assaults by the "Friends of Peace" on British ministerial policy.[29] For the Friends, sympathy for the French republicans—particularly during the early stages of the revolution—combined with continuing agitation for domestic constitutional reform to dictate withdrawal from continental entanglements. By waging war against France and refusing to undertake reform at home, the ministry of William Pitt the Younger (1783–1801) jeopardized the stability of the British state. The prominent Yorkshire reformer Christopher Wyvill warned that the government could only avoid a "great concussion" by correcting "abuses of recent introduction" and "restor[ing] our Parliament to the purity of its original institution."[30] Liberals therefore urged the ministry to normalize relations with France. Recognition of the French republic and withdrawal from the counter-revolutionary alliance would secure Britain's fundamental interests as a sovereign state.

Opposition to alliance politics had a profound impact on international thought on both sides of the Atlantic. The "conspiracy of kings" may have failed to destroy republican France, but it did demolish the faith of Vattelian internationalists in the progressive development of the balance-of-power system and the law of nations which it supported.[31] Long before the Jay Treaty taught a similar lesson to Republican

[29]J. E. Cookson, *The Friends of Peace: Anti-War Liberalism in England, 1793–1815* (Cambridge, 1982).

[30]Rev. Christopher Wyvill, *A Letter to the Right Hon. William Pitt* (York, n. d. [1793]), 20–21.

[31]Thomas Erskine, *A View of the Causes and Consequences of the Present War with France* (London, 1797), 49.

oppositionists in America, British liberals concluded that alliances desta-
bilized European politics, multiplied causes for war, and violated fundamental claims to national independence and sovereignty. Liberal antipathy to the balance of power was reinforced by rhetorical exigencies:
defenders of ministerial policy justified an interventionist stance by
extolling the balance and linking it to the preservation of a civilized legal
order in the European republic. In effect, counter-revolutionary forces
appropriated—and thus helped discredit—the leading tenets of Vattelian
internationalism. The resulting dissociation of a developing law of
nations from the balance-of-power system constituted the great conceptual crisis of post-Revolutionary internationalism. How could there be
any "law" at all in an anarchic world?

The internationalists' conceptual crisis was predicated on a critical
reassessment of recent developments in European history. British liberals, drawing on an isolationist tradition in debates over foreign policy,
anticipated the Republicans' belated, but no less decisive rejection of the
system of alliances that Vattel said made Europe a "sort of republic."
From the perspective of the French Revolutionary wars, the progressive
refinement of the balance—the main premise of Vattelian thought—
seemed increasingly problematic. If no major power had been able to
achieve continental supremacy, or "universal monarchy," the so-called
balance had not secured weaker states such as Poland against the
encroachments of powerful neighbors.[32] British oppositionists and their
Republican counterparts in America concluded that the European
diplomatic system was fundamentally flawed. Progress toward a more
liberal world order therefore required withdrawal from foreign entanglements and non-interference in the domestic affairs of other states.

[32]For an attack on the balance and "the plunderers of Poland," see "A Lover of
Peace" [Benjamin Vaughan], *Comments on the Proposed War with France, on the State of
Parties, and on the New Act Respecting Aliens* (London, 1793), 106. On the European
states system see Derek McKay and H. M. Scott, *The Rise of the Great Powers, 1648–1815*
(London, 1983); T. C. W. Blanning, *The Origins of the French Revolutionary Wars*
(London, 1986); and, for the classic account from the French perspective, Albert Sorel,
Europe and the French Revolution: The Political Traditions of the Old Regime [1885], trans.
and ed. by Alfred Cobban and J. W. Hunt (London, 1969). See also Edward Vose
Gulick, *Europe's Classical Balance of Power: A Case History of the Theory and Practice of
One of the Great Concepts of European Statecraft* (Ithaca, 1955).

Recognition of the fundamental principle of national self-determination was the precondition for enlightened diplomacy. For Jeffersonians this meant vindication of American independence and preservation of a federal union that was the antitype of the European balance.

Britain's role in European affairs had been controversial throughout the eighteenth century. Critics of the British alliance system questioned the relevance of the continental balance to a maritime power with extensive colonial interests. In response, policy-makers invoked the conventional wisdom, that Britain "held the balance" on the continent, to justify interference in continental affairs whenever a status quo that was so beneficial to British interests was jeopardized.[33] Through the manipulation of old alliances or the fabrication of new ones, the British government could maintain an active role in European politics while avoiding direct involvements and thus placating insular opinion. Reformers decried this interventionist tradition, charging that balance-of-power diplomacy drew Britain into conflicts involving no authentic national interest. As one oppositionist put it, Britain could "derive but little benefit from an intimate connexion with states, linked together in a complicated chain of alliances, deriving their consequence from the pursuit of military achievements, and established by the principles of arbitrary government and the divine right of kings."[34]

Secrecy, subsidies, and subterfuge enabled irresponsible governments to pursue their ambitious designs heedless of an ill-informed and easily misled political public. Worst of all, these gratuitous diplomatic entanglements perverted and retarded natural progress toward a cosmopolitan harmony of interests. As a result, the increasing intercourse of

[33]On Britain's role as "the natural guardian of the balance of power in Europe," see John Bowles, Esq., *Reflections on the Political and Moral State of Society, at the Close of the Eighteenth Century* (London, 1800), 63; and Geoffrey Mowbrar, Esq., *Remarks on the Conduct of [the] Opposition during the Present Parliament* (London, 1798), 103. See the discussions in Felix Gilbert, *To the Farewell Address: Ideas of Early American Foreign Policy* (Princeton, 1961), 19–43; and M. S. Anderson, "Eighteenth-Century Theories of the Balance of Power," in Ragnhild Hatton and M. S. Anderson, eds., *Studies in Diplomatic History* (London, 1970), 183–98.

[34]*Considerations on the Causes and Alarming Consequences of the Present War, and the Necessity of Immediate Peace. By a Graduate of the University of Cambridge* (London, 1794), 29.

nations had *not* led to peace and understanding; instead, Dr. James Currie wrote in 1793, the proliferation of "treaties offensive and defensive" had caused wars to become far more "general, bloody, and expensive." Adherence to the outmoded precepts of the old diplomacy was therefore "a principal cause both of the frequency and extensiveness of modern wars."[35] According to liberal Benjamin Vaughan, a member of parliament who soon afterward fled to France and then America, the "very principle of a balance . . . leads every one to take a part" in every war.[36] A European community predicated on a constantly shifting balance of power was in fact no community at all, but rather a scene of "universal desolation."[37]

The system of alliances with which Pitt and his colleagues sought to overthrow Revolutionary France inspired the most furious liberal denunciations. This "connected chain of despotism" threatened to extinguish liberty everywhere;[38] the "concert of princes" was itself responsible for calling into existence the "concert of peoples" which now terrorized the old regimes of Europe.[39] "Branded in the face of all Europe as a standing plague, abomination, and reproach," France was forced to assume a belligerent role, and so to spread its revolution across the continent. As Whig barrister and member of parliament Thomas Erskine wrote in 1797, ministerial warmongers who would not allow the French to choose their own form of government thus became "the practical founders of republics all over Europe."[40]

Yet if oppositionists took violent exception to the old diplomacy, they strongly supported its ostensible goal, the vindication of national sovereignty and independence. Traditionally, British commentators saw

---

[35]Jasper Wilson [Dr. James Currie], *A Letter, Commercial and Political, Addressed to the Right Hon. William Pitt, in Which the Real Interests of Britain, in the Present Crisis Are Considered* (Dublin, 1793), 5.

[36]Lover of Peace [Vaughan], *Comments on the Proposed War with France*, 25.

[37]Jasper Wilson [Dr. Currie], *A Letter, Commercial and Political*, 6.

[38]Ibid., 59.

[39]Lover of Peace [Vaughan], *Comments on the Proposed War with France*, 26. See also *Two Speeches of the Right Honourable Charles James Fox . . . January 31st and February 11th, 1793* (London, 1793).

[40]Erskine, *A Causes and Consequences of the Present War with France*, 75, 115.

Bourbon pretensions to universal monarchy as the leading threat: the question now was whether the Revolutionaries had succeeded to these imperial ambitions. At first, liberals could make a plausible case that the counter-revolutionary powers were more intent on foreign conquests than the French.[41] The preservation of British independence depended on remaining aloof from the "concert of Princes": if the British King "means . . . to remain his *own master* at home and abroad, he must beware of contributing to form a foreign tribunal *superior to himself.*"[42] "Should we once concur in the establishment of a precedent, by which the internal arrangements of individual states are rendered amenable to the regulation of a general confederacy," another liberal isolationist warned, "how soon may our present conduct be converted into the instrument of our destruction!"[43]

The collapse of the first coalition in 1796 put such exaggerated anxieties to rest. It was then incumbent on anti-war liberals to explain, and dissociate themselves from, the French republic's increasingly obvious belligerent tendencies. Typically, liberals blamed France's enemies for deflecting the Revolution from its original, constitutionalist goals and thereby creating a monster in their own image. The plea for negotiation and accommodation did not therefore imply any endorsement of successive French regimes: as early as 1793 Wyvill was "willing to concede . . . that the designs of the National Convention are probably as unjust and ambitious as the views of Louis the XIVth."[44] Nonetheless, liberals insisted, the French were free to form *any* kind of government they pleased and the British had no right to interfere. Noninterference

---

[41]On allied designs to "conquer France," see *A Letter from the Right Honourable Charles James Fox, to the Worthy and Independent Electors of the City and Liberty of Westminster* (Dublin, 1793), 40–41. James Mackintosh emphasized France's peaceful intentions in *Vindiciae Gallicae. Defence of the French Revolution and its English Admirers against the Accusations of the Right Hon. Edmund Burke*, 4th ed. (London, 1792).

[42]"A Calm Observer" [Benjamin Vaughan], *Letters on the Subject of the Concert of Princes, and the Dismemberment of Poland and France* (London, 1794), first published in *Morning Chronicle*, Letter IX, April 29, May 2 and 4, 1793, 159–60; Letter II, July 25, 1792, 30–31, emphasis in original.

[43]*Considerations on the Causes and Alarming Consequences of the Present War*, 138.

[44]Wyvill, *A Letter to the Right Hon. William Pitt*, 25.

was in turn the best guarantee against reciprocal challenges to British independence by the revolutionary regime, as well as against the more insidious dangers of "political" connections with the corrupt continental powers which sought to restore the French monarchy.

The liberals' goal was to extricate Britain from unholy alliances with the despotic, anti-revolutionary powers of the continent. A few optimists hoped that the end of hostilities would lead to "a cordial and sincere friendship with France and her allies."[45] But growing disenchantment with the revolution as its "republican" credentials became progressively more suspect reinforced a powerful isolationist tendency in oppositionist circles. On one hand, Britain had no right to interfere in the domestic concerns of another state: "crimes committed in one state," Whig leader Charles James Fox insisted in 1793, "were not cognizable in another."[46] On the other, Britain should assiduously avoid diplomatic connections with corrupt, despotic regimes which inevitably implicated it in a criminal conspiracy against French sovereignty and independence. The financial power of the British state was also its greatest potential weakness: the temptation to fight wars by subsidizing proxies too often proved irresistible. As a result, Benjamin Vaughan charged, Britain found itself propping up allied regimes which would otherwise have long since collapsed. By "keeping hospitals for all the incurable governments on the continent of Europe," Britain interfered with the progress of freedom abroad, and jeopardized its survival at home.[47] The elaborate fiscal machinery of the modern war-making state bore increasingly heavily on taxpayers while enlarging the dangerously corrupting power of state creditors and financiers. The relentless persecution of British "Jacobins" further demonstrated the incompatibility of British liberty with a perpetual state of war.[48]

---

[45]George Edwards, Esq., *The Political Interests of Great Britain* (London, 1801), 172.

[46]*Two Speeches of the Honourable Charles James Fox*, 5.

[47]Lover of Peace [Vaughan], *Comments on the Proposed War with France*, 17.

[48]For an attack on the *"funding-system"* that kept Europe in a state of perpetual war see Jasper Wilson [Dr. Currie], *Letter Addressed to Pitt*, 4–6. On the persecution of the Jacobins see E. P. Thompson, *The Making of the English Working Class* (London, 1963), 102–85; Albert Goodwin, *The Friends of Liberty: The English Democratic Movement in the Age of the French Revolution* (London, 1979), 359–415, and passim; and Cookson, *The Friends of Peace*.

The agenda of British anti-war liberals was always centered on domestic constitutional reform or, in the darkest days of "patriotic" repression, on simply preserving a modicum of liberty. The best assistance British sympathizers could offer the French Revolutionaries was to promote Britain's withdrawal from contaminating continental connections. Rehabilitation of the British constitution would subvert the counter-revolutionary coalition. "The confederacy formed against France," the most "dangerous" that had ever "existed in Europe," would not survive without British support. When the "combined powers" came to terms with France, the revolutionary republic would curb its own undoubted excesses and peace would reign across the continent.[49] The great lesson of the French Revolution, Erskine concluded, was that states must "confine their interferences with the affairs of other countries within the bounds which are calculated to secure their own territories and independence."[50] The British should tend their own garden, just as the French—recognized as a truly sovereign, independent people—should be allowed to tend theirs.

The Vattelian principle of noninterference combined with a decidedly un-Vattelian skepticism about alliances and the traditional balance-of-power assumptions on which they were based dictated a withdrawal from world politics and a diminishing concern for the common good of the entire system, thus pointing toward the apotheosis of the nation-state. The liberals' project thus ultimately converged with their opponents' efforts to mobilize British power against the French menace. As the conquests of the French Directory prepared the way for Napoleonic imperialism, British liberals began to argue that constitutional reform was the key to mobilizing national resources and guaranteeing popular loyalties. "Public liberty," the prolific reformer George Edwards wrote in 1801 in an illuminating explication of the emerging liberal position, was the basis of "national strength." So long as the British constitution was "preserved and supported" and the government pursued its "proper objects," "domestic happiness and internal improvement," Britain would successfully repel any external threat.[51] The

[49] *Two Speeches of the Honourable Charles James Fox*, 5.

[50] Erskine, *A View of the Causes and Consequences of the Present War with France*, 136–37.

[51] Edwards, *Political Interests of Britain*, 238, 246, 82.

notion that constitutional reform was not a subversive activity sponsored by the French, but was instead the best guarantee of the British state against foreign invasion provided a patriotic cover for the return of the liberals from the political wilderness.

Liberal solicitude for British national security prepared the way for a meeting of the minds with their erstwhile opponents. If respect for another country's independence precluded preemptive interference in its domestic affairs, the same principle justified military preparedness and a determination to rebuff all external threats. Beginning from different premises, ministerial proponents of "perpetual war" against France and liberal peace advocates arrived at remarkably similar conclusions. First, the bankruptcy of the old diplomatic system of Europe was apparent to all. The history of the anti-French coalitions was one of "disjointed politics . . . follies, and dissensions"; "mutual jealousies" had prevented the so-called allies from "acting in concert."[52] Whether this failure was rooted in the constitutional defects of the allies' governments or, as ministerial writers suggested, was instead a function of poorly defined, mutually contradictory war aims, was a distinction that increasingly made little difference.

Edmund Burke's diatribe against the "spirit of aggrandizement" and "mutual jealousy" that animated "all the coalesced Powers," written in bitter disgust after the collapse of the first coalition in 1796, was an ironic refrain to a chorus of anti-administration writers who had been arguing for years that "old rooted animosities" were bound to subvert any anti-revolutionary alliance.[53] If French Republicans demonstrated a sovereign contempt for their international obligations, Britain's allies proved equally faithless and perfidious. The "object" of the "grand Alliance" against France, Fox's political associate Robert Adair thus

---

[52]William Hunter, Esq., *A Short View of the Political Situation of the Northern Powers: Founded on Observations Made during a Tour through Russia, Sweden, and Denmark* (London, 1801), 4, 8. For the diplomatic history see McKay and Scott, *The Rise of the Great Powers*, 272–302.

[53]Edmund Burke, "Second Letter on a Regicide Peace" [1796], in Paul Langford, ed., *The Writings and Speeches of Edmund Burke*, 9 vols. to date (Oxford, 1981–), vol. IX (ed. R. B. McDowell): 269. For "old rooted animosities," see Daniel Stuart, *Peace and Reform against War and Corruption*, 2nd ed. (London, 1794), 106.

charged in 1802, was "either to plunder France against her consent, or to plunder Europe with it." "The cause of the Monarchy for its own sake, was absolutely indifferent to them; that of the balance of power for its own sake, was nearly the same." As a result, Adair concluded, "the great fellowship of states is gone and extinguished forever."[54]

Recognition that the European republic and its system of public law had been completely superseded reinforced the importance of national independence and sovereignty but led commentators away from Vattel to a Hobbesian conclusion: each state would have to enforce its own rights without concern for the rights of others or the common good. The resulting conceptual transformation in the liberal position is most strikingly apparent in George Edwards's *Political Interests of Great Britain*, published in 1801. Edwards still hoped for rapprochement with France; a union of interests between the two great powers would break down the artificial restraints and distinctions fostered by war. "All the different nations are united together by mutual ties of humanity, fraternity, and peace," he proclaimed; one day, "universal friendship" would draw all mankind into "the universal republic of the world." Yet a "system of permanent peace" depended on "a sufficient armed force in every country"; such a force, combined with the pursuit of liberal domestic policies, would make any state "sufficiently formidable" to resist any foreign aggression.[55]

In several crucial respects, the development of British liberal thinking in the 1790s anticipated and paralleled that of their Jeffersonian counterparts in America. British liberals denounced the balance of power while Secretary of State Jefferson still hoped to promote its progressive potential through commercial diplomacy; British sympathizers with the French Revolution warned against "entangling alliances" long before American Republicans drew similar lessons from Jay's English Treaty. Republican efforts to secure the American Constitution against Hamiltonian corruptions were matched by liberal efforts

[54]Robert Adair, Esq., *The Letter of the Honourable Charles James Fox to the Electors of Westminster, Dated January 23rd, 1793. With an Application of Its Principles to Subsequent Events* (London, 1802), 109–12.
[55]Edwards, *The Political Interests of Britain*, 71–72, 144, 132, 131.

to reform the British constitution—until the anti-Jacobin repression drove the most prominent reformers into exile or retirement. Federalist efforts to suppress the Republican opposition proved much less effective, even counter-productive, as they prepared the way for Jefferson's rise to power. But the Republicans were by then as thoroughly disenchanted with France as were the many British Friends of Peace who now rallied to their embattled nation's cause. Although the new nation's weakness and remote situation dictated a neutral course, the ascendant Jeffersonians were no less committed to the vindication of national sovereignty and independence.

Of course, Jefferson's "Revolution of 1800" was not duplicated in Britain. The continuing weakness of liberal, pro-American elements was increasingly apparent as mounting tensions ultimately led to the War of 1812. Yet, despite apparently irreconcilable differences over maritime rights, Anglo-American thinking about law and order in the society of nations was moving toward convergence. The point of departure was a general agreement on both sides of the Atlantic, representing a wide range of ideological perspectives, that the old diplomatic system of Europe was defunct. As a result, Vattel's conception of the law of nations, grounded in the balance of power, could no longer be sustained. Bemoaning the passing of the old regime, spokesmen for the British ministry depicted an unbalanced, anarchic and lawless world. Proceeding from similar premises, Republican defenders of the American union and its rights as a neutral power sought to establish a new foundation for an international legal regime.

IV. UNION AND INDEPENDENCE

The new Jefferson administration's overriding concern was to sustain and strengthen the union, the foundation of America's future greatness and the best guarantee of national sovereignty and independence. The electoral purge of Anglophiles and consolidationists in the "Revolution of 1800" helped redress the federal balance while a brief period of peace in Europe minimized external threats to American rights and interests. But Jefferson's union remained vulnerable at home and abroad. Driven into opposition, the Federalists would combine divisive sectional appeals with their continuing agitation for a national constitution on the British model. As soon as the European war resumed, the new nation would face renewed challenges from hostile European powers, both at sea and along the extended northern and western frontiers.[56]

The ascendant Republicans had few illusions about the progressive potential of what remained of the European diplomatic system. Yet it was neither possible to withdraw into a "Chinese" isolation, nor to become entangled in a political and military alliance with one of the great powers. Republicans concluded that national security depended on territorial expansion—to preempt frontier separatism as well as incursions from neighboring powers—and on the concomitant expansion of foreign markets for American staples.[57] Toward these ends, Republican administrations exploited all the opportunities the collapsing balance afforded, even while insisting on their moral superiority to European diplomatic practices.[58] Scholarly debate over Jeffersonian foreign policy focuses on these opportunistic—and often apparently misguided—initiatives and responses.

Republican diatribes against the balance of power reflected the pervasive recognition that the European diplomatic system could no longer provide the context for a progressive foreign policy. Revolutionaries such as Jefferson and Paine had looked forward to greater civility and lawfulness in the conduct of diplomacy, which they defined in terms

[56]For further discussion see Onuf, "The Expanding Union."

[57]On "Chinese" isolation see Jefferson to G. K. van Hogendorp, Oct. 13, 1785, in *The Papers of Thomas Jefferson*, 8: 633. The best treatment of Jeffersonian foreign policy and political economy is McCoy, *The Elusive Republic*.

[58]For Robert Tucker and David Hendrickson, the discrepancy between moralistic professions and ethically dubious motives was most conspicuous in blundering efforts to annex West Florida. They describe the Republican campaign to vindicate maritime neutral rights as premised on a similar, self-deluding confusion of idealism and self-interest. In this case, however, the implications for national security were, as the War of 1812 demonstrated, potentially disastrous. *Empire of Liberty*, 145–56, 222–28, passim.

of converging personal and political ethical standards, because they believed in a progressively developing balance of power.[59] Such exalted expectations could not survive the collapse of the system that had sustained them.

The Republicans confronted a different, much more hostile world than did their Revolutionary predecessors. Yet they did not necessarily abandon internationalist goals. With the creation of a more perfect union, the American founders had already begun to direct their hopes away from Europe and toward the American hinterland. These tendencies were powerfully reinforced by the disintegration of the European system in the 1790s. Thus when, in the aftermath of the Louisiana crisis, Republican orators condemned the balance of power, they portrayed the federal republic as a perfected international system, a durable and dynamic peace plan for the New World. This celebratory rhetoric suggested that American exceptionalism was not a function of the moral superiority of virtuous republicans but rather of the founders' success in preempting disunion and guaranteeing peace and harmony among the American states. Indeed, as Magruder and other writers argued, the union was the only effective barrier against the Europeanization of American politics.[60] In the absence of federal union, it followed, republics could not pretend to act on a higher ethical plane than other polities.

---

[59]Paine, *Letter Addressed to the Abbé Raynal on the Affairs of North-America* (Philadelphia, 1782), 43–49, on the progressive development of the "national mind." Jefferson wrote Madison, Aug. 28, 1789: "I know but one code of morality for man whether acting singly or collectively." *The Papers of James Madison*, 12: 363. Jefferson's most famous statement on international morality is in his Second Inaugural, March 4, 1805: "we act on that conviction, that with nations as with individuals our interests soundly calculated will ever be found inseparable from our moral duties." James D. Richardson, ed., *A Compilation of the Messages and Papers of the Presidents*, 10 vols. (Washington, 1903), 1:378. On the discrepancy between this standard and Jeffersonian practice, see Tucker and Hendrickson, *Empire of Liberty*, 11–17, and passim. For more sympathetic accounts of Jefferson's ambivalent attitudes toward "reason of state" see Stuart, *The Half-Way Pacifist*, 61: "Jefferson remained firmly cemented in the pragmatism of the Enlightenment." Charles A. Miller establishes the limits of his naturalism—and of his identification of personal and national morality—in a thoughtful discussion of Jefferson's approach to the law of nations. *Jefferson and Nature: An Interpretation* (Baltimore, 1988), 189–96, and passim.

[60]Magruder, *Political, Commercial and Moral Reflections*, 37–38.

Jeffersonians thus happily endorsed the teaching of their nemesis Hamilton in *Federalist* No. 11: because, in a state of nature, republics were not naturally peaceful—and republicans were not morally superior—the creation of a more perfect union was imperative, and all means to preserve it were justified.[61]

The Jeffersonian conception of the federal republic—as a plurality of distinct states in perfect union—required that the United States act effectively and energetically—as a single sovereignty—in the larger world. The virulent partisanship of the 1790s showed how disputes over foreign policy could exacerbate sectional tensions and jeopardize the union. Jeffersonians therefore were unwilling to recognize the Federalists as a loyal opposition: the survival of a union of equal, self-governing state republics depended on sustaining a unified posture toward inevitably hostile foreign powers. At the same time, Jeffersonians insisted, union was the foundation of American prosperity and power and therefore was essential for preserving American independence. Union and independence became virtually synonymous and interchangeable terms in the Republicans' lexicon, epitomizing both their sense of American distinctiveness—the multiplicity in unity of the federal republic—and of their recognition of the need to protect the New World from the corrupting influences of the old.

The Republicans' indictment of the balance of power reflected their determination to insulate the New World. At first, European developments favored the new Jefferson administration. While the Peace of Amiens (1801) held, the former belligerents no longer threatened American rights and interests as a neutral trading power. But the interval in the European conflict also offered Napoleon the opportunity to redeploy his forces and extend his power in the New World. As a potential rival for control of the Mississippi watershed, France represented a much greater and more immediate threat to the American union than did Britain.

---

[61]Hamilton wrote: "Let the thirteen States, bound together in a strict and indissoluble union, concur in erecting one great American system, superior to the controul of all trans-atlantic force or influence, and able to dictate the terms of the connection between the old and the new world!" *The Federalist*, 73. For Republican references to No. 11, see James Madison to Robert R. Livingston, Aug. 10, 1795, and Madison to Unidentified Correspondent, Aug. 23, 1795, *The Papers of James Madison*, 16:47, 57.

After the resumption of the European wars in 1802—and before the British renewed their assaults on neutral carriers—Jeffersonians like Magruder, despite their traditional Anglophobia, could identify the cause of British and American "independence" against the threat of Napoleon's quest for "universal monarchy."[62]

Republican sympathy for embattled Britain did not justify an alliance against France. For Republicans, American "independence" was incompatible with diplomatic ties that entangled the new nation in European balance-of-power politics. During the Louisiana crisis, Federalist publicists combined belligerent rhetoric about descending on New Orleans with pleas for an Anglo-American alliance. "We ought to look around for some natural, permanent, and powerful ally," exhorted "Coriolanus" (William Stephens Smith), before Napoleon "has completed his arrangements to dismember the United States of America."[63] But the Jeffersonians argued that any American effort to restore the global balance of power would simply draw the new nation "into the vortex of European politics and perpetual war."[64] The Federalists invite us to "join in the crusade for restoring the lost balance of power," quipped Virginia Senator Stevens T. Mason, and "do ourselves the honor of leading the van in a new coalition!"[65] Federalists should remember that the independence of all the secondary powers of Europe had been sacrificed in the name of a "visionary balance of power."[66]

The successful outcome of the Louisiana crisis reinforced the

[62]On the Jeffersonian tilt towards Britain in the Louisiana crisis see the critical account in Tucker and Hendrickson, *Empire of Liberty*, 135.

[63]"Coriolanus" [William Stephens Smith], *Remarks on the Late Infraction of Treaty at New-Orleans* (New York, 1803), 39, 3.

[64]Sen. Robert Wright (Md.), speech of Feb. 24, 1803, *Annals of Congress*, 7th Cong., 2nd Sess., 165. John Taylor accused the Federalists of a "settled plan to make the United States a party in the bloody scenes and ceaseless collisions of the old world." Taylor, *A Defence of the Measures of the Administration of Thomas Jefferson* (Washington, 1804), 93.

[65]Sen. Stevens T. Mason (Va.), speech of Feb. 25, 1803, *Annals of Congress*, 7th Cong., 2nd Sess., 219.

[66]Rep. William C. C. Claiborne (Tenn.) to his constituents, Jan. 9, 1799, in Noble E. Cunningham, Jr., ed., *Circular Letters of Congressmen to Their Constituents, 1789–1829*, 3 vols. (Chapel Hill, 1978), 1:144.

Jeffersonian commitment to neutrality. Exultant republican orators counterpointed diatribes against "the European Hydra, denominated the *Balance of Power*," with celebrations of the harmony and stability—the true balance of popular liberty and energetic government—guaranteed by the federal union of the American states.[67] The preservation of American independence depended on preserving the union. With sufficient time to grow and prosper, the union would be proof against the "wars and intrigues" of "the European world."[68] As the new nation's "pacific system" extended across the American continent, Republican editor William Duane predicted, Europeans "will consider us as a chosen portion of mankind, thrown on this hemisphere by Providence, to repair by our example, by our industry, and the blessings of our government and country, the havock and destruction so often experienced in Europe, by the collision of ambition, and frequent and destructive wars."[69]

Republican orators celebrated the Louisiana Purchase not only because it vindicated their leader's "pacific system," but also because they knew that the United States was ill-prepared to wage or win a conventional war. Not surprisingly, Federalists charged their foes with "feebleness and pusillanimity." If anything, Jefferson's dumb luck in the Louisiana affair simply reinforced the administration's unpreparedness in the face of future threats.[70] Critics of the administration—and most foreign observers—were persuaded that further expansion would disperse an already scattered population, multiply conflicting interests, and shift the regional balance of power: a weak union would grow weaker. More significantly, they questioned the Jeffersonian assumption that the United States could remain aloof from the global balance of power, or

[67]Orasmus Cook Merrill, *The Happiness of America. An Oration Delivered at Shaftsbury, on the Fourth of July, 1804* (Bennington, Vt., 1804), 9.

[68]Robert R. Livingston and James Monroe to Sec. of State James Madison, May 13, 1803, *Annals of Congress*, 7th Cong., 2nd Sess., Appendix, 1146.

[69]"Camillus" [William Duane], *The Mississippi Question Fairly Stated, and the Views and Arguments of Those Who Clamor for War, Examined* (Philadelphia, 1803), 39.

[70][Alexander Hamilton], "Purchase of Louisiana," *New-York Evening Post*, July 5, 1803, in Harold C. Syrett, ed., *The Papers of Alexander Hamilton*, 27 vols. (New York, 1961–87), 26: 131. For an incisive critique of Jefferson's handling of the Louisiana crisis, see Tucker and Hendrickson, *Empire of Liberty*, 145–56.

that—even in the absence of European interference—the union itself could survive unless "those egregious baubles of sovereignty, those pestiferous incitements to demagogy, the State Governments" were more adequately controlled, if not "abolished."[71] For many Federalists, the compound republic was simply a stage in the development of a conventional nation-state that could hold its own in a world at war. For them the American federal union did not constitute an alternative to the European balance of power, but rather a dangerous impediment to military preparedness and the negotiation of diplomatic ties essential to the new nation's security.[72]

Foreign policy debates of the Napoleonic era focused on the character and prospects of the American union as well as on the implications of the European balance of power for the national interest. The collapse of the European balance into a struggle between Britain and France, the two remaining great powers, strengthened the Jeffersonian commitment to neutrality abroad and the expansion of the federal union at home. Congressman George W. Campbell of Tennessee reaffirmed these Jeffersonian tenets in 1805: "rapidly progressing in population, wealth, and consequent importance—and freed from the ravages of war that threaten to lay waste the fairest nations of Europe, we are permitted in quiet to enjoy the inestimable blessings of a free and enlightened government."[73] "Let honorable peace continue twenty years more," Campbell's colleague John Rhea wrote his constituents a year later, and "the prosperity, happiness and power of the United States of America will remain fixed on a basis not to be moved by the united efforts of nations."[74] No European power, no coalition of powers, then would be able to challenge the new nation's vital interests.

[71][John Ward Fenno], *Desultory Reflections on the New Political Aspects of Public Affairs in the United States of America, since the Commencement of the Year 1799* (New York, 1800), 52, excerpted approvingly in *Anti-Jacobin Review and Magazine* (London), VI (July 1800), 542–43.

[72]In Jefferson's view, Hamiltonians "espoused our new constitution, not as a good and sufficient thing in itself, but only as a step to an English constitution." Jefferson to Marquis de Lafayette, June 16, 1792, in *The Papers of Thomas Jefferson*, 24:85.

[73]Rep. George W. Campbell (Tenn.) to his constituents, Feb. 26, 1805, in *Circular Letters of Congressmen to Their Constituents*, 1:392.

[74]Rep. John Rhea (Tenn.) to his constituents, April 8, 1796, ibid., 1:429.

The American federal union might be the antithesis of the European balance of power, but sustaining the difference depended on avoiding diplomatic and military entanglements. Napoleon's designs on Louisiana demonstrated the new nation's vulnerability: a well-situated European power could exploit partisan differences and conflicting sectional interests to destroy the union. With control of the river trade, Napoleon could draw frontier settlements into alliance and so destroy the union. As David Ramsay wrote in 1804, "our nearest neighbours, would have become our enemies," and the sordid history of the European balance of power would have been repeated on the American continent.[75]

Jeffersonians believed that the United States would soon grow strong enough to guarantee its freedom from old world entanglements. Vermonter Orasmus Cook Merrill looked westward to the "immense fields" now opened to "enterprize" and offering "new excitements to union and independence, and new granaries for the securing of peace, and for the supply of nations."[76] "In the course of a few years," Magruder promised, "the nation will become so wealthy by the peaceable accumulations of commerce, and so powerful in point of population, that she may be the arbiter of nations, and the dispenser of peace to the universe."[77] Here were the key premises of Jeffersonian policy: union was predicated on expansion; a strong union was impregnable; and a prosperous union would be able to enforce its will on the less enlightened powers of the world. By the same logic, of course, "union and independence" were in jeopardy whenever territorial expansion and economic development were blocked, as they would have been by French colonization in the Mississippi Valley. This is why, before Napoleon was deflected from his North American designs, the Louisiana affair presented such an excruciating dilemma for the Jefferson administration. But the Purchase "insulated" the United States "from the rest of the world." "We have not only averted the impending danger of an immediate war with France," wrote "Sylvestris," "but we have obtained a perpetual guarantee against similar danger from the same

---

[75]Ramsay, *Oration on the Cession of Louisiana*, 9.
[76]Merrill, *The Happiness of America*, 10.
[77]Magruder, *Political, Commercial and Moral Reflections*, 65.

quarter in future; a quarter, where we were weakest, and on many accounts most vulnerable."[78]

Republican writers acknowledged that as long as the bonds of union remained weak the United States would be vulnerable to challenges from European powers. The European balance defined the boundaries of the American federal union both on land and at sea, and those boundaries would remain dangerously permeable until the new nation grew populous, prosperous and powerful enough to defy the world. But Europe would not wait for the Americans to achieve the prosperity and power—or the full recognition of their common, interdependent interests—that would guarantee their union. With the resumption of assaults on neutral shipping in 1805, American national security was again in jeopardy. Resisting pressure to capitulate to British maritime power, Republicans increasingly identified neutral rights with American independence. Only by preserving a true neutrality, Republicans insisted, could the new nation hope to avoid being sucked into the "vortex" of old world power politics.[79] At the same time, as Federalist critics charged, the vast expansion of neutral trade exposed American shipping to assault, and so endangered that very neutrality.

Jefferson and Madison did not expect Britain explicitly to acknowledge American neutral rights claims. Under war conditions, any formal agreement with a belligerent was bound to compromise American pretensions as an independent power. For Republicans, neutral rights claims were equivalent to a continuing declaration of independence, precluding any alliance that would actually or constructively draw the new nation into the European conflagration. Republican statesmen insisted that recognition of neutral rights, which they equated with national sovereignty, was the necessary precondition for the constitution of a lawful world order.

[78]"Sylvestris," *Reflections, on the Cession of Louisiana to the United States* (Washington, 1803), 13, 11.

[79]Paul A. Varg, *Foreign Policies of the Founding Fathers* (East Lansing, Mich., 1963); Roger H. Brown, *The Republic in Peril: 1812* (New York, 1964); Burton Spivak, *Jefferson's English Crisis: Commerce, Embargo, and the Republican Revolution* (Charlottesville, 1979); Tucker and Hendrickson, *Empire of Liberty*, 175–228.

Federalist critics charged that Jeffersonians jeopardized national security by confusing the presumably negotiable interests of American producers and shippers in exploiting Europe's distress with non-negotiable first principles.[80] Yet however much the Republicans misjudged the implications of neutral rights claims for national security, their approach to foreign policy proceeded from accurate assessments of the new nation's insecurity, the tenuousness of American loyalties, and the weakness of the union. The Republicans sought to construct a consensus on vital national interests by extending the union and by defending American commercial interests abroad. The aggressive assertion of maritime rights would broaden the Jeffersonian coalition and thereby strengthen intersectional ties; at the same time, neutrality was supposed to insulate a fragile union from the cross-pressures of the European conflict in much the same way the Louisiana Purchase provided "an almost insuperable barrier to any nation that may be inclined to disturb us in that quarter."[81]

During the Napoleonic wars, Republicans linked "neutrality" with "independence and union" as they constructed an expansive definition of the national interest. Federalists challenged them at every point, insisting that neutrality was impossible, independence illusory, and union a frail reed. Britain stood alone in the climactic phase of the great struggle against Napoleonic designs for world domination. In juxtaposition to the Jeffersonian vision of a liberal world order implicit in neutral rights rhetoric, Federalists invoked a Burkean conception of Britain as the embattled defender of western civilization.[82] Convinced of the futility of the administration's recourse to commercial sanctions in

---

[80]These criticisms are recapitulated in Tucker and Hendrickson, *Empire of Liberty*, 222–28.

[81]Rep. Joseph H. Nicholson (Md.), speech of Oct. 25, 1803, *Annals of Congress*, 8th Cong., 1st Sess., 466.

[82]"Your protection must be found in the navy and power of England," according to a typical Federalist exhortation. Britain was "the only check to the overwhelming armies of France, the common protector of America, and of all that is yet to be saved of the liberty of Europe or the world." [Independent American], *An Inquiry into the Present State of the Foreign Relations of the Union, as Affected by the Late Measures of Administration* (Philadelphia, 1806), 42.

behalf of American rights and doubtful that the union could survive any direct assault, Federalists appeared all too eager to fulfill their own dire prophecies.

Republican commercial diplomacy, particularly an increasingly punitive Embargo, controverted Republican solicitude for civil liberties. The irony is that commercial sanctions never would have been invoked if the Jefferson administration had not been determined to cultivate northern support by protecting the carrying trade. Jefferson's efforts to transcend sectionalism by promoting the growth of the Republican party in New England were, up to a point, successful. But resistance to the Embargo demonstrated the tenuousness of the union as much as the ineptitude of Jeffersonian diplomacy.

Administration blunders notwithstanding, it is not clear that any line of policy could have secured national unity or prevented British assaults on American shipping. This does not mean that the outcome of Anglo-American conflict was predetermined. It is a mistake to assume that the British position was necessarily fixed—or to neglect the Federalists' crucial role in undercutting Republican initiatives. The Jeffersonians' commitment to the union and determination to vindicate neutrality and independence may ultimately have led to war, but the Federalist opposition reinforced the prevailing sense in Britain of the union's weakness, and therefore of the minimal risks entailed by depredations on American shipping. In the event, it was not so much the administration's exaggerated claims to neutral rights that prevented accommodation with Britain as it was the British government's conviction that there was no need to make any concession at all.

Chapter Seven

The New Law of Nations

I. LAWLESSNESS

Before they were silenced in the great anti-Jacobin repression, British opposition writers had proclaimed the bankruptcy of alliance politics. The balance of power was not a reliable premise or goal of enlightened diplomacy; it did not and could not secure peace and law among nations. French Revolutionaries and American Republicans also condemned the balance, so renouncing any hopes they may have had in the progressive potential of the old diplomatic system. In the end, however, it was defenders of the British government's belligerent stance against France who pronounced the death sentence of the old regime, even while extolling its virtues. Spokesmen for the ministry argued that the collapse of the European balance subverted the law of nations and thus inaugurated a new epoch of lawlessness. Threatened with extermination, Britain was freed from all legal restraints: neutral carriers who helped sustain the French war effort—however indirectly—were subject to capture and condemnation.

British anti-Jacobin writers argued that the political practices and principles of Revolutionary France precluded the restoration of the old European order. What was most disturbingly "revolutionary" about the French Revolution was its challenge to the "liberties" and constitutions of other European states. As a British ministerial writer complained in 1806, "it was the first mischief of the French Revolution, during the reign of Jacobinism, to introduce a distinction between Kings and their People." By appealing to supposedly oppressed peoples and ignoring the constitutional authority of kings "as representatives of their people and kingdoms," France's new rulers destroyed "all established forms of political intercourse."[1] As long as monarchs had governed Europe, another anti-Jacobin explained, "the world had . . . the best security— that of personal interest and self-preservation." A king would never "employ, even against his worst enemies, such dangerous weapons, nor seek to dissolve the ties which constitute the strength of regular Government."[2]

French violations of the "public law of Europe" were amply chronicled by defenders of British ministerial policy. The Revolutionaries "have arrogated to themselves the right of giving laws to Europe," trespassing "in the most wanton manner" on the rights of neighboring neutral states.[3] "By a vague and fictitious reference to natural rights," complained John Bowles, one of the most prolific anti-Jacobin writers, the French "pretend not only to set aside the most positive [treaty] stipulations, but also to absolve other nations from their authority."[4] The French argument for "natural frontiers" infuriated Edmund Burke: "she construed the limits of Nature by her convenience," thus "establishing the convenience of a Party as a rule of public Law."[5] The Revolutionar-

[1] *The State of the Negotiations; With Details of Its Progress and Causes of Its Termination, in the Recall of the Earl of Lauderdale* (London, 1806), 90.

[2] John Bowles, Esq., *Reflections on the Political and Moral State of Society, at the Close of the Eighteenth Century* (London, 1800), 51.

[3] Josiah Dornford, Esq., *The Motives and Consequences of the Present War Impartially Considered* (London; reprinted Dublin, 1793), 13–14. "Who vested in France the right of punishing foreign sins?" asked John Casper Lavater of Zurich. Lavater, *Remonstrance Addressed to the Executive Directory of the French Republic, against the Invasion of Switzerland* (London and Dublin, 1793), 8.

[4] Bowles, *The Real Grounds of the Present War with France* (London, 1794), 7. According to another writer, "the new invented *rights of nature*" invoked by France were nothing more than "*their own interest.*" John Gifford, Esq., *A Letter to the Earl of Lauderdale, Containing Strictures on His Lordship's Letters, to the Peers of Scotland*, new ed., with additions (London, 1800), 46.

[5] Edmund Burke, "Fourth Letter on a Regicide Peace" [1795], in Paul Langford,

ies "not only annulled all their old treaties," wrote Burke, "but they have renounced the law of nations from whence treaties have their force."[6]

There could be no peace with France because its rulers were determined to export anarchy and confusion. "Unexpected victories have made them drunk with arrogance and ambition," ministerial writer Geoffrey Mowbrar complained in 1798, and they now "aspire to the unqualified dominion of Europe."[7] "They will not make peace with you," another commentator warned, "they will exterminate you."[8] The French were "savages" whose "unbounded licentiousness" and contempt for the conventions of civilized behavior had returned Europe to a brutal state of nature.[9] In this hideous anti-community, the "all-paramount principle of self-preservation," the first law of nature, was routinely invoked.[10] "The preservation of our political existence" justified all appropriate measures, including interference in the domestic affairs of other nations.[11]

---

ed., *The Writings and Speeches of Edmund Burke*, 9 vols. to date (Oxford, 1981–), vol. IX (ed. by R. B. McDowell): 92–93.

[6]Burke, "First Letter on a Regicide Peace" [1796], in *The Writings and Speeches of Edmund Burke*, IX:240. For Citizen Hauterive it was the formation of an anti-French coalition that signalled the destruction of a "general system of public law in Europe." [Citizen Hauterive], *State of the French Republic, at the End of the Year VIII*, trans. Lewis Goldsmith (Dublin, 1801), 30.

[7]Geoffrey Mowbrar, Esq., *Remarks on the Conduct of [the] Opposition during the Present Parliament* (London, 1798), 101.

[8]*Reform or Ruin: Take Your Choice! In Which the Conduct of the King, the Lord Lieutenant, the Parliament . . . Is Considered: and That Reform Pointed Out, Which Alone Can Save the Country*, 2nd ed. (Dublin, 1798), 10.

[9]Bowles, *The Real Grounds of the Present War with France*, 5; Bowles, *Objections to the Continuation of the War with France Examined*, 2nd ed., (London, 1794), 56; Gifford, *A Letter to the Earl of Lauderdale*, 5; [Nicholas Vansittart], *Reflections on the Propriety of an Immediate Conclusion of Peace* (London, 1793), 8. George Dallas concluded that "a republican form of government . . . animate[s] a nation more to the pursuits of war, than . . . to the arts of peace." *Thoughts upon Our Present Situation with Remarks upon the Policy of a War with France* (Dublin, 1793), 34.

[10]John Gifford, *A Letter to the Honourable Thomas Erskine; Containing Some Strictures on His Views of the Causes and Consequences of the Present War with France* (Dublin, 1793), 34.

[11]Dornford, *The Motives and Consequences of the Present War Impartially Considered*,

France's alleged contempt for the "publick law of Europe" gave its antagonists the right to punish its crimes.[12] Because "men are never in a state of *total* independence of each other," Burke explained, and their actions always have some corresponding "effect upon others," "there is a *Law of Neighbourhood*." If men—and nations—stood in isolation from one another, there would be no such right. But the nations of Europe were in fact interdependent—historically the continent was "virtually one great state"—and "the grand vicinage of Europe [has] a duty to know, and a right to prevent, any capital innovation which may amount to the erection of a dangerous nuisance."[13]

The fundamental problem was that the old balance of power had disintegrated. The "balance of Europe" was, as one writer put it, the basis of its "system of civilization."[14] Balance, explained Bowles, was the "vital principle of European polity, and the soul of union, harmony, and order, among the states of which Europe is composed. It is the grand design and scope of the laws of nations, and the principal aim of those treaties, by which the respective rights and interests of European states have been regulated and secured."[15] "The balance of power," Burke agreed, "had been ever assumed as the common law of Europe at all times, and by all powers."[16] But "the balance of Europe is gone," Robert

44. See also Gifford, *A Letter to the Earl of Lauderdale*, 86, citing Vattel, *The Law of Nations*, II, iv, on the right of interference: "a more complete justification of the conduct of England, and the other belligerent powers, could not have been offered."

[12]Burke, "Third Letter on a Regicide Peace" [1797], in *The Writings and Speeches of Edmund Burke*, IX:339.

[13]Burke, "First Letter on a Regicide Peace" [1796], in ibid., 249–50, 248, 251.

[14][William Gregory], *Some Remarks on the Apparent Circumstances of the War in the Fourth Week of October, 1795* (Dublin, 1795), 6. See also Dornford, *The Motives and Consequences of the Present War Impartially Considered*, 22, quoting oppositionist Charles Grey on "the duty of every member of the commonwealth of Europe to support the established system of the balance."

[15]John Bowles, *The Dangers of Premature Peace* (London, 1795), 7. The treaties "which have long constituted the public code of Europe . . . were at once the guardians and expositors of the Law of Nations." Bowles, *Reflections at the Conclusion of the War* (London, 1801), 7.

[16]Burke, "Third Letter on a Regicide Peace" [1796], in *The Writings and Speeches of Edmund Burke*, IX:338. "All of Europe was bound together in one federal chain, sustaining the weak and confining the powerful." [Judge Day?], *Considerations upon the State of Public Affairs at the Beginning of the Year 1796*, 4th ed. (London, 1796), 3.

Adair concluded in 1802, and "the great fellowship of states is gone and extinguished forever."[17] According to Bowles, "no new fangled scheme of barriers and counterpoises" could ever have the "solidity" of the "ancient" balance of power the Revolution had destroyed.[18]

Burke provided the classic account of the Revolutionary assault on the constitutions of Europe's old regimes in his "Letters on a Regicide Peace" (1795–97). While demolishing "the whole body of that jurisprudence which France had pretty nearly in common with other civilized countries," successive Revolutionary governments consistently pursued "their old steady maxim of separating the people from their Government." Before the Revolution, liberty flourished in every country of Europe, even "under monarchies stiled absolute." "In all these old countries the state has been made to the people, and not the people conformed to the state."[19] But the genius of the French Revolution was to concentrate power. Because the French had eliminated all traditional "obstructions" to the mobilization of state power, including guarantees of personal liberty and the public welfare, the "whole force of the nation" could be brought to bear on "one point."[20] The disproportionate power of republican France in turn subverted the balance of power that historically had functioned as the "constitution" of the European republic. Lesser powers could no longer hope to negotiate favorable terms of alliance, nor would belligerents respect neutral rights. The two great powers now laid down the law in their respective spheres and all previously "established forms of political intercourse" were abandoned.[21] By 1807, according to a typical assessment, "there are but two indepen-

[17]Robert Adair, Esq., *The Letter of the Honourable Charles James Fox to the Electors of Westminster, Dated January 23rd, 1793. With an Application of Its Principles to Subsequent Events* (London, 1802), 101.

[18]Bowles, *Reflections on the Political and Moral State of Society*, 114.

[19]Burke, "First Letter on a Regicide Peace" [1796], in *The Writings and Speeches of Edmund Burke*, IX:240, 204; "Second Letter on a Regicide Peace" [1796], in ibid., 287.

[20]Ibid., 287. A later writer attributed the durability of the old balance of power to an "*equilibrium of weakness in* [the] . . . *military constitutions*" of the European states before the French Revolution. *A Letter on the Genius and Dispositions of the French Government, Including a View of the Taxation of the French Empire. By an American*, 9th ed. (Philadelphia; reprinted London, 1810), 5.

[21]*The State of the Negotiations*, 90.

dent states" left in Europe: "from the continent which he has subjugated, Buonoparte has banished all neutrality."[22]

Anti-Revolutionary British polemicists played a crucial, if negative,
role in the development of international legal thought. In celebrating
the old law of nations they illuminated the premises of Vattelian
internationalism: the connections between the balance of power and the
law of nations had never before been so systematically elaborated. But
when the French Revolution destroyed the balance and subverted
conventional conceptions of world order, Enlightenment internationalism gave way to Burkean organicism and reactionary nostalgia. In this
ideological context, the apotheosis of the lost balance only reinforced
the skepticism of oppositionist Friends of Peace who insisted that the
devastation of Europe resulted from fundamental flaws in the old
diplomatic system, not from French lawlessness and savagery. Yet if, as
these critics insisted, the law of nations was not grounded in the balance
of power, how else could a lawful world order be constituted? The
question was particularly urgent and compelling for Jeffersonian Republicans in America who identified national sovereignty and independence
with the vindication of neutral rights. Recognizing that neutrality was
inconceivable in a lawless world, Republicans were forced to elaborate
a new conception of the sources of a new law of nations.

II. NEUTRAL RIGHTS

Anti-Jacobin eulogies to the lost balance of power and the old law of
nations were invoked to justify the British ministry's non-recognition of
the French republic and its apparent determination to interfere in
France's internal affairs. Liberal critics questioned the ministerial inter-

---

[22] *The Crisis. By the Author of Plain Facts; or a Review of the Conduct of the Late
Ministers* (London, 1807), 26, 31. According to James Stephen, Britain was the only
"independent Power . . . left in the civilized world" that could still challenge French
hegemony. [Stephen], *The Dangers of the Country. By the Author of War in Disguise*
(London, 1807), 92.

pretation of recent history. If, as Friend of Peace Benjamin Vaughan wrote in 1793, "the boasted old law of nations generally lay a dead letter in the books of civilians," France's enemies had only themselves to blame.[23] The counter-revolutionary coalition was ultimately responsible for the European conflagration: the "royal principle of *interference*" brought forth its revolutionary equivalent, "the popular principle of *fraternity*."[24] As the conflict deepened, the "concert of princes" set new standards of lawlessness. Efforts to induce "famine" in France by blocking food shipments constituted "a strange relapse into systems, from which the philanthropy of modern writers of all nations, and the softening principles of the age, had once seemed to have delivered us."[25] Whatever crimes might be charged to the Revolutionary regime, it was a "palpable absurdity" not to "treat with any potentate, who is in a position to levy war against us."[26] Nonrecognition of the Revolutionary regime, and the ministry's apparent unwillingness to come to terms, was itself a kind of interference in the domestic affairs of another nation.[27] "A Lover of Peace" complained that England "falsely pretend[ed] to be *neutral* in the interior concerns of France" when, in fact, "by acknowledging no power of foreign communication existing there, but in its degraded king," it "takes a decided part in them."[28]

The cumulative effect of the debate over the origins of the French Revolutionary wars was to strip away any illusions about the continuing

[23]"A Lover of Peace" [Vaughan], *Comments on the Proposed War with France, on the State of Parties, and on the New Act Respecting Aliens* (London, 1793), 26, 19. See J. E. Cookson, *The Friends of Peace: Anti-War Liberalism in England, 1793–1815* (Cambridge, 1982).

[24]"A Calm Observer" [Benjamin Vaughan], *Letters on the Subject of the Concert of Princes, and the Dismemberment of Poland and France*, first published in the *Morning Chronicle*, Letter IX, April 29, May 2 and 4, 1793 (London, 1794), 171.

[25]Ibid., Letter IX, April 29, May 2 and 4, 1793, 168.

[26]*Considerations on the Causes and Alarming Consequences of the Present War, and the Necessity of Immediate Peace. By a Graduate of the University of Cambridge* (London, 1794), 126.

[27]Jasper Wilson [Dr. James Currie], *A Letter, Commercial and Political, Addressed to the Right Hon. William Pitt, in which the Real Interests of Britain, in the Present Crisis are Considered* (Dublin, 1793), 49.

[28]Lover of Peace [Vaughan], *Comments on the Proposed War with France*, 97.

rule of law in the "European Community."[29] British oppositionists were particularly troubled by the government's increasingly conspicuous contempt for all legal restraints. "SELF-DEFENCE," "the primitive, and most sacred right of mankind," now justified all policy expedients.[30] The most distinguished writers" agreed that a nation's fundamental obligation was to secure itself against external threats.[31] In times of national emergency "the all-paramount principle of self-preservation" superseded all other obligations. This *"right of Security,"* according to John Gifford, historian of France and leading anti-Jacobin writer, "only gives to States that right and that power which are vested in every individual by the laws of nature, confirmed by the laws of society."[32] In effect, the law of nations imploded: to the extent of its effective powers, each state was a law unto itself. Because they had been forced to abandon "the system and public law of Europe," the British "are as much compelled, as political robbers, by the wisdom of injustice, and the necessity of wrong, to keep our full share of the conquests."[33] Britain was in no position to uphold legal standards: "if others suffer from this change in our conduct, we are not to blame."[34]

Defenders of the British government's belligerent policy toward France juxtaposed Revolutionary lawlessness to the civilized intercourse of the old regime. This bias toward an organic, customary law of Europe was most eloquently articulated by Burke: treaties and compacts had no

---

[29]Bowles, *Reflections at the Conclusion of the War,* 7, refers to Great Britain "as a member of that European Community, of which she necessarily forms a part." See also *Considerations upon the State of Public Affairs at the Beginning of the Year MDCCXCVIII. Part the First. France* (Dublin, 1798), 44: "the revolution of France is the wreck of the moral world, and the conquests of France are the dissolution and destruction of the political order."

[30][Two Gentlemen at Halifax], *The Present Claims and Complaints of America Briefly and Fairly Considered* (London, 1806), Letter II, 55.

[31]William Hunter, Esq., *A Short View of the Political Situation of the Northern Powers: Founded on Observations Made during a Tour through Russia, Sweden, and Denmark* (London, 1801), 56, citing Grotius, Bynkershoek, Pufendorf, Vattel, and Il Consolato del Mare.

[32]Gifford, *A Letter to the Honourable Thomas Erskine,* 87-88, also citing Vattel.

[33][Judge Day?], *Considerations upon the State of Public Affairs,* 55.

[34]*The Crisis,* 27.

more real force than the underlying sense of community they expressed. "Nothing is so strong a tie of amity between nation and nation as correspondence in laws, customs, manners, and habits of life." It was "the secret, unseen, but irrefragable bond of habitual intercourse," Burke insisted, that held men and states together, "even when their perverse and litigious nature sets them to equivocate, scuffle, and fight, about the terms of their written obligations." A regime of law depended on the persistence of *artificial* conditions—a balance of power, a community of interests among sovereigns, a common set of values—which the French Revolutionaries had irrevocably destroyed.[35]

Writers who did not share Burke's nostalgia for the old regime were nonetheless similarly pessimistic about the prospects for international law-making. Imposing what amounted to municipal-law standards on the law of nations, these commentators offered little scope for the creation of new law. For instance, Robert Ward, a leading British authority on the law of nations, insisted that treaty stipulations could provide no workable definition of contraband which, because of its "fluctuating nature; must be independent of institution." "No general proclamation having ever been agreed upon by the different States which compose the world," any specific enumeration of contraband items—or any other definition of neutral rights—failed to meet Ward's rigorous test for lawfulness.[36] The community of states was not so constituted that any authoritative source of law could be identified: "Over the actions of independent States," another commentator as-

[35]Burke, "First Letter on a Regicide Peace," *The Writings and Speeches of Edmund Burke*, IX:247.

[36]Robert Ward, Esq., *An Essay on Contraband: Being a Continuation of the Treatise of the Relative Rights and Duties of Belligerents and Neutral Nations, in Maritime Affairs* (London, 1801), 209, 176. Ward was the author of *An Inquiry into the Foundation and History of the Law of Nations in Europe from the Times of the Greeks and Romans to the Age of Grotius* (London, 1795). Also see "Alfred," *Letters on the Real Causes and Probable Consequences of the Present War with Russia* (London, 1801), 34–35: treaties "can nowise affect or alter the established law of nations." American diplomat Robert Goodloe Harper, an Anglophile Federalist, agreed that treaties "could make no alteration in the general law of nations," but could only "modify that law with respect to the contracting parties themselves." *Observations on the Dispute between the United States and France*, 4th ed. (Boston, 1798), 17.

serted, "there can be no sovereignty" and therefore "no permanent tribunal."[37]

The arguments for universal consent or for a customary international law pointed to the same conclusion: the European states-system was not—and perhaps could not be—governed by law. British writers thus turned the contradictory premises of the old law of nations against the very possibility of legal obligations. The collapse of the balance of power—and, with it, the myth of a European community bound "together in the strictest intimacy . . . by the closest ties" and observing the "same public law"—left the sovereigns of Europe in a lawless state.[38] In the absence of "any Amphictionic council in Europe able to redress the wrongs of nations," Gould Francis Lecky concluded, "the only means left us are anticipating injuries by injuries, or avenging them by retaliation." Britain could only follow the French example, and neutrals beware the consequences: "*it is for us to seize the sword and buckler, to whomsoever it belong, and convert it to our own advantage and preservation.*"[39] Or, as the author of "The Crisis" succinctly put it, Britain must "not only assert our antient and acknowledged rights," but also, "as this eventful crisis" demanded, "at once interdict all neutral trade whatever."[40]

British writers set forth a conception of the source and development of the law of nations fundamentally at odds with neutral-rights claims. They privileged the customary practices of states over more recent efforts to formulate legal principles. During a period of international upheaval it was absurd to suppose, as the Americans did, that neutral states could generate new law through expansive assertions of their "rights." "Our naval rights and ancient maritime jurisprudence" were "the firmest bulwark of our safety and prosperity" and could never be "the subject of discussion and infringement."[41] The claims of neutral

[37] *The Crisis*, 46.

[38] John Bowles, *The Dangers of Premature Peace*, 52n–53n.

[39] Gould Francis Lecky, Esq., *An Historical Survey of the Foreign Affairs of Great Britain, with a View to Explain the Causes of the Disasters of the Late and Present Wars* (London, 1808), 106, 103; emphasis in original.

[40] *The Crisis*, 43–44.

[41] *A Letter to William Roscoe, Esq. Containing Strictures on his Late Publication Entitled*

powers constituted "progressive . . . encroachments . . . on *our* maritime rights."[42] During periods of peace, "the extreme rigour of the law has, by treaty, been frequently dispensed with," but because the "right" of the most powerful maritime states to give the law to others "already existed . . . , the abandonment of it is purely conventional."[43] Neutrals confused "the indulgences and relaxations" which Britain "may, from time to time, have granted" with pretended rights. But the very notion of neutrality was suspect in wartime when any sort of commerce between a so-called neutral power and a belligerent could be construed as "assistance."[44]

James Stephen's *War in Disguise*, first published in 1805, was the most exhaustive and influential legal justification for the British government's narrow definition of neutral rights. "Neutrality" was simply a pretext for Britain's secret enemies to collude with France: "the flag of the United States" was thus used "to protect the property of the French planter" by carrying on a trade between France and its West Indian colonies that had been legitimately interdicted. Only by preventing "the frauds of the neutral flags" could Britain's "maritime rights" as a belligerent power be effectively restored. Stephen drew a crucial distinction between the apparent self-interest of neutral traders and the true interests of the civilized world, including neutral states, in repelling the French menace: "the fall of this country [Britain], or what would be the same in effect, the loss, at this perilous conjuncture, of our superiority at sea, would remove from before the ambition of France almost every obstacle by which its march to universal empire could be finally

---

"Considerations on the Causes, Objects, and Consequences of the Present War" (Liverpool, 1808), 117.

[42] *The Crisis*, 40. See the extended discussion in [James Stephen], *War in Disguise; Or, The Frauds of the Neutral Flags* (London, 1805).

[43] Hunter, *A Short View of the Political Situation of the Northern Powers*, 56. For an earlier formulation of this position by an American Federalist, see Harper, *Observations on the Dispute*, 16. In his view, France could not have relinquished a right to search neutral vessels "if she did not believe herself to have possessed" such a right "by virtue of the law of nations."

[44] [Two Gentlemen at Halifax], *The Present Claims and Complaints of America*, Letter I, 24.

impeded."[45] At least according to the narrow constructions favored by Stephen and other British writers, the law of nations authorized British maritime supremacy, and that supremacy was critical to reestablishing a lawful world.

The identification of the British cause with the survival of western civilization was invoked to justify suspension of the legal restraints that supposedly made Europe a civilized community of states. The paradox did not escape liberal commentators who feared that Britain would forfeit its moral advantage by sinking to Napoleon's level. William Roscoe, Whig member for Liverpool and a prominent opponent of slavery, recoiled at the British assault on the Danish fleet in Copenhagen harbor in 1807. "The example of France is now no longer *a warning*," wrote Roscoe, "but *a pattern* for Great Britain." Britain was increasingly cut off from the European community and its contemptuous disregard for the rights of neutral states only exacerbated its isolation. Nations, like individuals, were "accountable . . . for their moral conduct," Roscoe warned, and British lawlessness promised to unleash the wrath of the Lord.[46]

By 1807, even James Stephen, the British government's most eloquent and influential apologist, betrayed misgivings about Britain's moral superiority over its adversary. It was a "foul libel" "that we promote wars, for the sake of our trade in Europe," Stephen wrote in his new pamphlet, *The Dangers of the Country*. But it was also "unquestionably true" that British involvement in the slave trade was responsible for "miseries" in Africa "far greater and more durable than those of Europe."[47] The punishments inflicted on Africa should be taken as a warning. Europe had already become "a second Africa," as "order,

---

[45]Stephen, *War in Disguise*, 20, 119, 4. See also Lord Sheffield, *Strictures on the Necessity of Inviolably Maintaining the Navigation and Colonial System of Great Britain* (London, 1804), 40–41, and passim. For a discussion of Stephen's pamphlet in historical context see Bradford Perkins, *Prologue to War: England and the United States, 1805–1812* (Berkeley and Los Angeles, 1961), 77–79.

[46]William Roscoe, Esq., *Considerations on the Causes and Consequences of the Present War, and on the Expediency, or the Danger of Peace with France* (London, 1808), 84–85, 75.

[47][Stephen], *The Dangers of the Country*, 171, 174. Stephen was the brother-in-law of British antislavery leader William Wilberforce. David Brion Davis, *The Problem of Slavery in the Age of Revolution, 1770–1823* (Ithaca, 1975), 366–68.

security, public morals, [and] the sacred principles which mitigate the horrors of war, and regulate the intercourse of nations" vanished "from this civilized quarter of the globe." In view of European crimes against Africa, there was a poetic justice in this result: "the public law of the Slave Coast may soon be upon a level with that of polished Europe."[48]

Yet if, as Stephen suggested, European sins in Africa had called forth a divine judgment, "the hand of Providence" was equally apparent in blessings simultaneously conferred on the United States. "Those revolutionary tempests which have laid waste the ancient realms of Europe" had given an extraordinary boost to the new nation's prosperity and power. For Stephen, the explanation was clear: by moving to end its own involvement in the international slave trade, and by steps toward the abolition of slavery in the northern states, "the United States have alone, of all nations on earth, during the same period, done much to redeem themselves from those sins to which, I chiefly ascribe the calamities of Europe." From this perspective, the Americans' unwitting support of "the pestilent ambition of France" paled into relative insignificance. Although Britain was in no position to sacrifice "our most essential belligerent rights," a conciliatory policy toward the former colonies was imperative. Ultimately "a nation which thus honourably respects the sacred rights of humanity and justice" would see that British victory was "the only remaining hope of liberty in Europe"—particularly once Britain had assumed a position of moral leadership in suppressing the slave trade.[49]

III. THE "EXAMINATION"

The rapid deterioration of Anglo-American relations prompted efforts on both sides of the Atlantic to preserve peace and secure mutual rights and interests. In Britain, liberal proponents of a conciliatory policy toward the former colonies gained support from commercial groups

[48][Stephen], *The Dangers of the Country*, 170, 178, 222.
[49]Ibid., 223, 224, 225, 224, 225.

with interests in the American and West Indies trade. A misplaced jealousy of American prosperity provoked escalating assaults on neutral rights which, they argued, would eventually drive the United States into alliance with Napoleon. As the editors of the *Edinburgh Review* warned in 1807, "both nations would suffer more from a war than from any other event which can happen to them."[50] Peace was in their "mutual interest," Macall Medford explained: "perhaps no two countries were ever better situated for making each other rich and happy than England and the United States of America."[51]

By providing access to world markets, neutral carriers played a key role in sustaining a prosperous British economy that could support the enormous costs of the war against France. Echoing the earlier arguments of anti-mercantilists who had welcomed American independence, pro-American writers now asserted that the United States best served British interests by remaining neutral. According to Alexander Baring, a Whig member of parliament with strong American connections, neutral trading partners were "necessary to countries at war, and particularly to those whose resources are derived from commerce." Because they were "commercially . . . dependent" on Britain, the Americans offered an especially useful sort of neutrality, despite their increasing sensitivity to encroachments on their sovereignty and independence.[52] The British national interest therefore dictated a prudent and circumspect policy toward the new nation. "The neutrality of the New world is our best safeguard," another writer concluded in 1809. "While America covers the ocean with her ships, England may defy the conqueror of Europe."[53]

[50]"Randolph and Others on the Neutral Questions," *Edinburgh Review*, XI (Oct. 1807), 9.

[51]Macall Medford, *Oil without Vinegar, and Dignity without Pride: Or, Britain, America, and West-Indies Interests Considered*, 2nd ed. (London, 1807), 3.

[52]Alexander Baring, Esq., M.P., *An Inquiry into the Causes and Consequences of the Orders in Council; and an Examination of the Conduct of Great-Britain towards the Neutral Commerce of America* (New York, 1808), 15. See also *The Speech of Henry Brougham, Esq. before the House of Commons, Friday, April 1, 1808, in Support of the Petitions from London, Liverpool and Manchester, against the Orders in Council* (London, 1808), 33. For a discussion of Baring's role as a spokesman for a conciliatory policy see Perkins, *Prologue to War*, 18–20.

[53]"Lord Sheffield and Others on Foreign Affairs," *Edinburgh Review*, XIV (July 1809), 475.

Liberal writers accused the ministry of confusing the British Naviga-tion Acts with the "general maritime law of nations."[54] This tendency was most conspicuous, British and American critics charged, in the interpretation and enforcement of commercial regulations by British prize courts. British admiralty law and the law of nations were virtually indistinguishable in Sir William Grant's controversial *Essex* decision in 1805. Grant sanctioned strict enforcement of the so-called "Rule of 1756," a British edict banning neutrals from any wartime trade forbid-den to them in time of peace. Prior to this time, the Rule had been only sporadically enforced; in the *Polly* decision of 1800 Admiralty judge Sir William Scott had effectively neutralized the ban by sanctioning the reexport of French colonial produce from American ports to the conti-nent. Grant's resuscitation of the Rule of 1756 reflected the growing conviction in government circles that the neutral carrying trade was sustaining the French war effort. Whether or not this conclusion was justified, critics rejected the claim that the Rule—as an edict of the British government—could have any standing in the law of nations.[55]

No other power had acknowledged Britain's authority to regulate neutral trade, nor could any do so without conceding its rights of sovereignty. "Can it be maintained that a court of admiralty is to sit in judgment upon the mutual claims of sovereign states?" asked the *Edinburgh Review*.[56] With the promulgation of successive orders-in-council, the ministry itself abandoned any pretense that Britain would acknowledge legal restraints. On the contrary, the *Review* complained, "many people have lately been seduced into a contempt of the whole idea of the rights of states"; to them, "a measure is rather recommended by any proof of its repugnance to the law of nations."[57] The British government's contempt for law, American commentators agreed, signi-

[54]Medford, *Oil without Vinegar*, 21.

[55]Christopher Robinson, *Reports of Cases Argued and Determined in the High Court of Admiralty*, 6 vols. (London; reprinted Philadelphia, 1801–10), II:295–304 [*Polly*], V:349–66 [*William*], reviewing *Essex* at 362–66. For discussion, see Perkins, *Prologue to War*, 77–91. For challenges to the Rule of 1756, see *An Inquiry into the Causes and Consequences of the Orders in Council*, 22; "War in Disguise," *Edinburgh Review*, VIII (April 1806); "Randolph and Others on the Neutral Questions," 25.

[56]"Randolph and Others on the Neutral Questions," 15.

[57]"Examination of the Late Orders in Council," *Edinburgh Review*, XI (Jan. 1808), 487.

fied a determination to sweep "all neutrals from the ocean."[58] Because
British mercantile interests envied the prosperity of their American
counterparts, "it is proposed to make war" on the last neutral power,
"not in *disguise*, but open and flagrant."[59]

In the wake of such assaults, it is hardly surprising that spokesmen
for the American government should articulate increasingly circumspect
neutral rights claims. The Republicans' overriding concern had always
been to vindicate American sovereignty and independence. "*Suffer no
nation to interfere with your internal affairs*," exhorted Republican editor
William Duane in 1803.[60] After 1805, however, the Jefferson administration began to retreat from expansive definitions of what constituted a
neutral power's "internal affairs." American writers conceded that because the principle of "free ships, free goods" was not yet established in
the law of nations, belligerent powers could legally seize enemy goods
from neutral ships on the high seas.[61] But this did not mean that there
were no legal limits on British searches, or that British prize courts could
settle controversial questions—on the scope of lawful trade between
neutrals and belligerent powers, the extent of blockades, and definitions
of contraband—simply according to the British government's convenience. Thrown on the defensive by such pretensions, neutral rights
advocates called on the belligerents to recognize and respect the sovereignty and independence of nonbelligerents. Tench Coxe, a leading
Jeffersonian political economist, thus insisted that "foreign municipal

[58]Charles Jared Ingersoll, *A View of the Rights and Wrongs, Power and Policy, of the
United States of America* (Philadelphia, 1808), 98.

[59][Gouverneur Morris], *An Answer to War in Disguise; Or, Remarks upon the New
Doctrine of England, concerning Neutral Trade* (New York, 1806), 67.

[60]"Camillus" [William Duane], *The Mississippi Question Fairly Stated, and the Views
and Arguments of Those Who Clamor for War, Examined* (Philadelphia, 1803), 39;
emphasis in original.

[61][Morris], *An Answer to War in Disguise*, 37; [James Madison], *An Examination of
the British Doctrine, Which Subjects to Capture A Neutral Trade, Not Open in Time of Peace*
(Philadelphia, 1806), reprinted in Gaillard Hunt, ed., *The Writings of James Madison*, 9
vols. (New York, 1900–1910), 7:366. On the retreat from "free ships, free goods" as a
potential "bargaining counter," see Donald R. Hickey, "The Monroe-Pinkney Treaty
of 1806: A Reappraisal," *William and Mary Quarterly*, 3rd ser., XLIV (1987), 82–83.
Hickey suggests that the principle was of diminishing importance to American
shippers, who now "had sufficient capital to purchase any goods they transported."

laws do not affect neutral ships." "If our government must yield any part of the law of nations, we can have no security for the remainder."[62]

Secretary of State James Madison's extended legal brief, *An Examination of the British Doctrine, Which Subjects to Capture a Legal Trade, Not Open in Time of Peace* (hereinafter, the *Examination*), published in 1806, represents the fullest and most authoritative statement of the Jefferson administration's position on neutral rights. An exhaustive demonstration of the illegality of the Rule of 1756, Madison's pamphlet had little impact on the course of events and generally has been ignored or dismissed by scholars.[63] But the *Examination* provided the conceptual framework for Henry Wheaton's landmark treatise on international law (1836), and through it the subsequent development of international legal thought.[64] Significantly, Madison eschewed the extreme natural rights arguments that would have justified expansive neutral rights claims. As the leading legatee of Vattelian internationalism, Madison instead em-

[62]"Juriscola" [Tench Coxe], *An Examination of the Conduct of Great Britain, Respecting Neutrals, since the Year 1791*, 2nd ed. (Boston, 1808), 49, 27. On Coxe's role as unofficial adviser to Madison and Jefferson during this period, see Jacob E. Cooke, *Tench Coxe and the Early Republic* (Chapel Hill, 1978), 453–62.

[63]The most extensive discussion of the *Examination*'s genesis and its "mixed" reception is in Irving Brant, *James Madison: Secretary of State, 1800-1809* (Indianapolis, 1953), 295-302 and 314–16. See also the dismissive treatments in Ralph Ketcham, *James Madison: A Biography* [1971] (Charlottesville, 1990), 442–44; Perkins, *Prologue to War*, 43; Robert W. Tucker and David C. Hendrickson, *Empire of Liberty: The Statecraft of Thomas Jefferson* (New York, 1990), 192–93. For a more favorable assessment see Paul A. Varg, *Foreign Policies of the Founding Fathers* (East Lansing, Mich., 1963), 179-80. The *Examination* is not discussed in either of the two leading recent treatments of Madison's foreign policy, Drew R. McCoy's *The Elusive Republic: Political Economy in Jeffersonian America* (Chapel Hill, 1980) or J. C. A. Stagg's *Mr. Madison's War: Politics, Diplomacy, and Warfare in the Early Republic, 1783–1830* (Princeton, 1983).

[64]*Elements of International Law with a Sketch of the History of the Science* (Philadelphia, 1836), I, i, §§ 14–15, 46, 48–50. Wheaton's definition of international law—"those rules of conduct which reason deduces, as consonant to justice, from the nature of society existing among independent nations; with such definitions and modifications as may be established by general consent" (46)—is taken word for word from *An Examination of the British Doctrine*, with one omission and no acknowledgment (238). Wheaton's treatment of the several sources of international law follows Madison's closely and in the same order, again without acknowledgment. Later editions of the *Elements* cite the *Examination* on the definition of international law and quote it inaccurately on treaties as a source of law.

phasized the progressive tendencies of the law of nations during the "modern" period and elaborated a broad conception of the sources of its continuing development. In a period of world war, when most commentators were skeptical about the very possibility of law, Madison discovered evidence of law everywhere: in learned treatises, treaties, customary ministerial practices, and even judicial decisions. No longer was nature the direct source of the law of nations; nations made law suiting their collective interests and nature's design.

The search for a viable law of nations was crucial for Madison because the balance of power, which for Vattel constituted the foundation of a civilized and lawful European community, had collapsed. Madison's challenge was to sustain the development of law in the absence of a progressively more elaborate and refined distribution of power. Law could be grounded neither in immutable first principles, as natural rights advocates claimed, nor in the mere exercise of preponderant power, which was the British government's barely disguised premise. As Madison sought to vindicate the sovereignty of a weak and increasingly vulnerable neutral power, he had to seize a disappearing middle ground between violently opposed, but equally skeptical conceptions of world law and order. Radical Republican naturalists agreed with British proponents of power politics that the law of nations was now defunct—if it had ever existed at all. In the face of such pervasive skepticism, Madison's quest for positive law consistent with natural principles represented an heroic reaffirmation of the internationalist faith.

Most naturalists insisted that the "law of nations" was no law at all, and that a true law had to be grounded in nature and reason. "By a misapplication of terms," Joel Barlow wrote in 1795, a "system of robbery and plunder" was "called the law of nations."[65] Inspired by French efforts to revive the Armed Neutrality of 1780—and thus to neutralize British maritime supremacy—Barlow, Thomas Paine, and William Barton all proposed schemes for establishing a "new code of public law."[66] Jefferson's election in 1800 and the coincidental interval

---

[65]Joel Barlow, *A Letter Addressed to the People of Piedmont* (New York, 1795), 41.

[66]Barlow, "Memoir on Certain Principles of Public Maritime Law Written for the French Government," Paris, Dec. 5, 1799, *To His Fellow Citizens of the United States of*

in the European war apparently presented an extraordinary opportunity to construct a new world order. The reformers' first task was to discredit the historic sources of legal rules: treatises, custom and usage, even treaties. Apologists for the old regime were fundamentally mistaken, wrote Paine, in conflating "the idea of a law of treaties with the idea of a law of nations." He correctly asserted that treaties did not bind nonsignatories, thus implying that treaties could not produce general rules. Even among signatories, treaties were unenforceable.[67]

Proceeding from first principles, radical Republican theorists denied the legality of any rule that did not meet the test of reason. According to Barton, an "invariable standard of natural equity . . . constitutes the only true basis of the LAW OF NATIONS."[68] Vattel's fundamental premise was flawed: there could be no connection between law, which must be grounded in nature and reason, and the power of distinct sovereignties to enforce their will. Given the collapse of the balance of power, such a conclusion may have seemed irresistible. But the implications were unacceptable to Madison, particularly when British hardliners invoked similar logic to justify renewed depredations on neutral rights.

America (Philadelphia, 1800), Letter II, appendix; Thomas Paine, *Compact Maritime* (Washington, D.C., 1801); William Barton, *A Dissertation on the Freedom of Navigation and Maritime Commerce, and Such Rights of States, Relative Thereto, as Are Founded on the Law of Nations* (Philadelphia, 1802). Barton's book was dedicated to Thomas Jefferson; Barlow wrote Jefferson from Paris, Oct. 26, 1801, Jefferson Papers (Library of Congress, Washington; microfilm ed.), that if "no convention for an Armed or unarmed Neutrality can be relied on, the prospect for civilization is frightful. We must all turn pirates abroad and tax gatherers at home." For similar sentiments see J. F. W. Schlegel's influential, *Neutral Rights; Or, an Impartial Examination of the Right of Search of Neutral Vessels under Convoy,* trans. from the French (Philadelphia, 1801), 48: "it is clear that if the neutral powers should seriously unite to prevent prizes made on their subjects, privateering would cease by degrees." The Francophilia of all three writers was well known. Barton explicitly acknowledged the inspiration of Citizen Hauterive's *State of the French Republic,* 28, which advocated "*a general system of public law . . . for Europe*" (emphasis in original). Federalist George Cabot anticipated that "good use" could be made of Barlow's *To His Fellow Citizens of the United States of America,* because it proved "the connection between our Patriots & the Directory." Cabot to Timothy Pickering, Pickering Papers (Massachusetts Historical Society, Boston; microfilm ed.), 25:263.

[67]Paine, *Compact Maritime,* 3.
[68]Barton, *A Dissertation on the Freedom of Navigation and Maritime Commerce,* 6.

By emphasizing and exaggerating the discrepancy between power and right, the naturalists proclaimed the impossibility of law in an imperfect world of contending sovereign states. Naturalist polemics may have offered a compelling critique of British lawlessness, but in denying that Britain could give law to other states they also effectively denied the law-making capacity of *any* state. In effect, naturalists invoked a municipal-law standard: as British ministerial writers insisted, the existence of law depended on universal consent.[69] But Madison had to show that there could be legal restraints on the British government in the *absence* of its explicit consent. Similarly, he had to show that the United States, despite its limited power and vulnerability, could participate in making a new law of nations.

Madison's disagreement with doctrinaire naturalists on the source of law was underscored by his determination to preserve American independence against mounting foreign threats. When naturalists called for a new law of nations, "founded in justice, approved by reason, and sanctioned by humanity," they necessarily challenged conventional conceptions of sovereignty.[70] Invoking the fundamental legal maxim that "no party is a competent judge in his own cause," the naturalists denied that any state had the right to determine and enforce its claims against other states.[71] The collapse of the balance of power—and the increasingly apparent opposition of law and power—now justified naturalists in their iconoclastic assault on the Vattelian concept of sovereignty. The "rival states" of the old world might "call themselves *independent*," sneered Barlow, but this was simply "another word for the ferocity of savage life, and a license for organized violence."[72] Yet the same developments that prompted the naturalists to reject the concept of sovereignty reinforced the Jefferson administration's commitment to defend the new nation's sovereignty. The collapse of the European

[69]See, e.g., Ward, *An Essay on Contraband*, 176.

[70]Chapman Johnson, *An Oration on the Late Treaty with France, by Which Louisiana Was Acquired: Delivered in Staunton on the Third of March, 1804* (Staunton, Va., 1804), 19.

[71]Ingersoll, *A View of the Rights and Wrongs*, 34.

[72]Barlow, *To His Fellow Citizens of the United States of America*, Letter II, 26, his emphasis.

system unleashed threats to vital national interests that jeopardized American independence.

Ironically, naturalist schemes for a renovated law of nations represented a logical extension of Jeffersonian ideas about interstate organization and collective security in the American federal republic. Barlow made the connection most explicitly in his *Letters to His Fellow Citizens*, when he called for the creation of a "United States of Europe."[73] But Paine and Barton agreed that the only hope for establishing a rule of law in Europe was for every European state to renounce its pretensions to sovereignty and combine in a true federal system. Paine invoked the Armed Neutrality of 1780 as "the only thing that has any pretension of right to be called and considered as a law of nations." The Armed Neutrality approached this exalted status not only because its definition of neutral rights was grounded in natural right, but because it was "signed and ratified by a large majority of the maritime commercial nations of Europe" who thereby bound themselves to uphold its provisions by force of arms.[74] "The great *desiderata*," Barton agreed, were "*a definitive recognition and establishment of those [national] rights, and the adoption of an efficient guarantee for their protection.*"[75] By emphasizing the need for explicit consent and coercive sanctions, both writers suggested that a true law of nations could only exist when the "sort of republic" conceived by Vattel was transformed into the more perfect federal union advocated by Barlow.

The naturalists' prescriptions for world order represented the logical corollary and extension of the Jeffersonians' apotheosis of union and condemnation of the balance of power. Radical Republicans exulted in the juxtaposition of the degeneracy of the European states system and

---

[73]Ibid., 9. See also *Address of the National Assembly of France to the People of Ireland* (Dublin, 1790), 21–22, where every free nation was invited to join a "great federal republic" that would "substitute a balance of freedom in place of a balance of power." In *Rights of Man*, Paine looked forward to the formation of a "European Congress, to patronize the progress of free government, and promote the civilization of Nations with each other." Thomas Paine, *Rights of Man*, with an Introduction by Eric Foner (New York, 1984), I [1791], 146–47.

[74]Paine, *Compact Maritime*, 4.

[75]Barton, *A Dissertation on the Freedom of Navigation*, 288, his emphasis.

the perfection of the American system. Yet the radicals' broad definition of neutral rights in fact jeopardized American neutrality. Because they were primarily concerned with curbing Britain's preponderant naval power, proponents of a new Armed Neutrality—or a "United States of Europe"—necessarily favored French interests. But it was politically and diplomatically imperative for the Jefferson administration to suppress any French bias, whatever its leaders' ideological predilections, and avoid any potentially disastrous entanglement in European affairs. Only by adhering to a strict neutrality could the administration preempt a Federalist counter-insurgency and secure its political position throughout the union. Jefferson and Madison also understood that a more modest formulation of neutral rights—defined in terms that the British government had itself historically acknowledged—would facilitate Anglo-American diplomacy. To define neutral rights in more expansive terms would challenge traditional British conceptions of the law of nations while committing the United States to coercive sanctions. In the absence of universal consent to "first principles," the determination to enforce natural rights signified a willingness, even eagerness, to go to war.

In his *Examination*, Madison eschewed natural rights, but not first principles—for principled as well as prudential reasons. Just as participation in an armed neutrality would draw the new nation into war, such an alliance would compromise American sovereignty and independence. Significantly, Madison discussed the various treaties that constituted the Armed Neutrality of 1780 as a source of law, not as a model world order. "With the exception of Great Britain alone," he wrote, "all the powers of Europe, materially interested in the maritime law of nations, have given a recent and repeated sanction to the right of neutrals to trade freely with every part of the countries at war." The neutrality treaties did not have the force of law because the signatories had merged their sovereignties in a more perfect federal union, but rather because of the relation of these treaties to other treaties—and other sources of law—in the development of the "modern code of nations." For Madison "the progress of the law of nations" was predicated on growing respect for the sovereignty of neutral as well as belligerent states.[76] Far from sustaining

[76] *An Examination of the British Doctrine*, 264, 210, 207. Naturalists rejected the very

this progress, the naturalist assault on sovereignty threatened to subvert neutral rights: in anything short of a perfect world, naturalist logic suggested, the only hope for a weak, would-be nonbelligerent was submission to superior force.

Madison asserted that treaties could only establish law if they were the voluntary acts of independent sovereigns. It followed that any treaty that limited the capacity to enter into further agreements either was legally defective or was the higher law of a formal constitution. But when states acted as true sovereigns, and where their agreements were "sufficiently general, sufficiently uniform, and of sufficient duration, to attest that general and settled concurrence of nations," treaties may be considered "as *constituting* a law of themselves" (Madison's emphasis). According to this formulation, the ongoing equilibrium of the powers— Vattel's balance of power—was *not* the foundation of the law of nations. International law-making was instead a progressive, social process, depending on accumulating expressions of consent to "principle[s] or rule[s] of conduct."[77] "This august code," as Tench Coxe later wrote, "is the *federal constitution* of the civilized world."[78]

Madison drew critical comparisons among the various sources of a revived law of nations. "Usage or practice," he argued, "is evidence for the most part by *ex parte* ordinances issued by belligerent governments, in the midst of the passions or policy of war," while "the spirit of treaties is, with few, if any exceptions, at all times more just, more rational, and more benevolent, than the spirit of the law derived from practice only." Yet the lawfulness of specific practices, treaty provisions, or formulations of treatise-writers was *not* immanent in the source itself, even if these different sources commanded varying degrees of respect, but instead depended on compatibility with emergent legal standards. The need to make judgments about lawfulness thus set a premium on the act of interpretation, and this is where "reason" played a key role in Madison's scheme. Madison's "reason" should not be confused with the transcendent, immutable principles invoked by the naturalists. Reason

---

idea of a "modern" law of nations, "as if there existed an ancient law on a contrary principle." Paine, *Compact Maritime*, 4.

[77] *An Examination of the British Doctrine*, 238.

[78] "Juriscola" [Coxe], *Examination of the Conduct of Great Britain*, 27, Coxe's emphasis.

might be "the main source from which the law of nations is deduced," but its importance for the progressive development of the law—toward greater reasonableness—was as a rule of interpretation, a means of distinguishing what was lawful in the broad stream of state practice.[79]

Madison sought to synthesize Republican commitments to American sovereignty and independence with the tenets of Vattelian internationalism. The challenge was to articulate a broad, progressive conception of the modern law of nations that would restrain belligerent depredations on neutral states. Madison understood that the United States was powerless to impose its own *"ex parte"* definitions of neutral rights on the belligerents. Instead, he sought to persuade his British counterparts to recognize the capacity of all independent states to participate in the ongoing formulation of new law. Madison thus argued against the equation of power and right—the tendency of British policy to deduce the "law of nations" from the "comparative state of naval armaments"—without embracing the alternative absolutism of the naturalists.[80] If might did not make right, neither did natural rights claims justify a resort to arms—until they were translated into accepted legal principles through the general concurrence of nations. Madison thus concluded that legal principles were *not* transparently accessible to reason, but were instead the result of the protracted, progressively more enlightened deliberations of the society of sovereign states. Reason was immanent in this process; it was not an absolute, external standard, but rather the key to nature's design.

Madison's *Examination* was designed to foster peaceful coexistence on the basis of well-established legal principles, thus averting a confrontation over neutral rights that would risk American independence.[81] The

---

[79] *An Examination of the British Doctrine*, 239, 240, 331–32.

[80] Ibid., 346.

[81] Richard Rush's tribute to Henry Wheaton's treatise on the law of captures applies equally well to Madison's *Examination*: "he takes the ground of the most eminent writers, and dwells upon the enlightened adjudications of the tribunals of his own country. He does not push the neutral right to the extent of either Martens or Schlegel; nor does he carry the belligerent claim, or the belligerent justification, to that pitch of rapacious rigor which it assumes when such decrees as the orders in council are declared to be sanctioned by public law." [Rush], *American Jurisprudence, Written and Published at Washington, Being a Few Reflections Suggested on Reading "Wheaton on Captures"* (Washington, 1815), 50–51.

desideratum was British respect for American sovereignty, the minimal requirement of an international legal regime. Madison knew that any attempt to force the British to acquiesce in broad neutral rights claims would be counterproductive. A diplomatic crisis would lead either to war with Britain or to an alliance that would draw the United States into Britain's wars. Treaties served peaceful and progressive purposes only when they were dissociated from balance-of-power politics, and therefore expressed the unimpaired sense of independent sovereigns. But neutral powers jeopardized their independent capacity to participate in international society when they negotiated formal agreements with nations at war—even when those agreements ostensibly guaranteed neutral rights.

Madison juxtaposed law-making treaties to alliances that actually or prospectively expanded the scope of belligerence. Peace treaties were effective law-making instruments because, in the aftermath of wars, "hostile passions and pursuits have spent their force"; similarly, "treaties of commerce . . . are necessarily founded in principles of reciprocal justice and interest."[82] For Madison, law was reducible neither to the treaties that supposedly constituted the balance of power nor to the transcendent "first principles" that naturalists sought to impose on all powers. Balance-of-power theorists conflated the law of nations with an inherently unstable alliance structure, thus promoting the pretensions of belligerents at the expense of peace-loving neutrals. In response, naturalists concluded that in the inevitably anarchic conditions of international society there was no direct connection at all between treaties, or any other form of independent state practice, and the principles of natural law that ought to govern nations.

Madison's goal was to demonstrate that there was a progressive, if necessarily problematic, relationship between state practice generally, and treaties particularly, and legal development. "The question concerning the treaty must be decided by the law," he argued, "not the question concerning the law by the treaty."

> Treaties may be considered as simply repeating or affirming the general law: they may be considered as making exceptions to the general law, which are to be a particular law between the parties themselves: they may

[82]Ibid., 239.

be considered as explanatory of the law of nations, on points where its meaning is otherwise obscure or unsettled.[83]

Even when treaties were freely negotiated under the most optimal conditions, the relation between specific treaty provisions and the law of nations was circumstantial and therefore subject to interpretation. Wartime agreements met none of Madison's criteria of lawfulness.

Madison's emphasis on the importance of treaties for the development of the modern law of nations was, in the circumstances, an argument *against* a new Anglo-American accord.[84] Far better to leave some controversial issues unresolved than to risk involving the United States in the European conflagration. In the meantime, Madison insisted, the belligerent powers must acknowledge and uphold legal principles previously established by "the general and settled concurrence of nations." The Napoleonic wars constituted the ultimate test of European civilization: could the rule of law survive the collapse of the old diplomatic system, the so-called "balance of power"? Madison answered affirmatively, despite mounting contradictory evidence: "under the influence of science and humanity," he proclaimed, the law of nations "is mitigating the evils of war, and diminishing the motives to it, by favoring the rights of those remaining at peace, rather than of those who enter into war."[85]

In retrospect, Madison's optimism seems hopelessly misguided. But in its contemporary diplomatic context the *Examination* constituted a realistic admission of American weakness and a plea for British forbear-

[83]Ibid., 237, 236.

[84]On the Jefferson administration's reluctance to negotiate a new accord to replace the Jay Treaty see Hickey, "The Monroe-Pinkney Treaty of 1806," 73, 86–87, 88. Hickey concludes that the aborted agreement was "far superior to the Jay Treaty and in all likelihood would have benefited the United States." See also Varg, *Foreign Policies of the Founding Fathers*, 183–86: Madison was confident "that the United States could achieve its goals by means other than treaties involving compromises."

[85]*An Examination of the British Doctrine*, 238, 207. For similar sentiments see the extended review of "War in Disguise," *Edinburgh Review*, VIII (1806), 1–35. "There is nothing chimerical in the idea of confining our maritime wars within the same limits with those which are waged on land, and completing, all over the civilized world, the distinction between an armed enemy and a pacific trader." Unfortunately, "the wars which have affected Europe for the last fifteen years, have not been of a character favourable to the development of such liberal principles" (p. 15).

ance. Madison defined American rights and interests in circumspect terms, in effect offering to recognize British maritime supremacy in exchange for a genuine recognition of American sovereignty and independence. Rather than threatening reprisals, he appealed to Britain's self-interest. The shape of the peace, he suggested, was implicit in the conduct of the war: failure to adhere to accepted legal principles would perpetuate a state of war, even when exhausted combatants laid down their arms during intervals of "peace," and thus subvert all future hopes for a durable rule of law among nations. Britain's true interests, Madison argued, depended on respecting a system of law that Britain, as the leading maritime power, had helped create. The crucial question was whether Britain, in acknowledging the restraints of law, would recognize and respect the sovereignty and independence of the new American nation. Or, as liberal critic Alexander Baring later asked, was the British government determined to show the Americans that the "abuse of absolute power is inseparable from its existence"?[86]

IV. NEUTRALITY AND THE WAR OF 1812

Madison's plea for British forbearance and peaceful coexistence fell on deaf ears. Even when the younger Pitt's death in January 1806 led to a brief period of Whig rule, efforts to normalize Anglo-American relations faltered. The Tories' return to power in March 1807 guaranteed a hostile posture toward the former colonies. The *Essex* decision may have jeopardized neutral rights that Madison claimed were already established in the "general law of nations," but subsequent orders-in-council betrayed an open contempt for legal standards. "England has chosen, for the first time," the *Edinburgh Review* sadly concluded in 1808, "to abandon the high ground on which she has stood, and to strive with [France] . . . in the pernicious, as well as despicable race of injustice

---

[86]Baring, *An Inquiry into the Causes and Consequences of the Orders in Council*, 71.

to unoffending and unprotected states."[87] The questions Madison raised in the *Examination* were now moot: whatever the British government meant by claiming to defend European civilization from Napoleonic despotism, it clearly did not mean to uphold a rule of law among nations. Republican editor William Duane was convinced that Britain fomented war as a "pretext for annihilating the trade of neutrals" and thus securing the "commercial monopoly" that sustained its global power. Britain now "asserts a right of giving law to all commercial states."[88]

The disastrous deterioration of Anglo-American relations in the last phases of the Napoleonic wars is a familiar story that does not require yet another telling.[89] We find it somewhat curious, however, that historians have focused so much attention on the blundering efforts of successive Republican administrations to preserve American sovereignty and independence without going to war. The gist of the historical literature is that Jefferson and Madison should have carried a bigger stick, while at the same time recognizing that the nation's true interest lay in submitting to Britain's superior power. This "realist" interpretation has a certain after-the-fact authority: the community of interests and values between the two nations, already apparent to contemporary observers, would grow much stronger in the postwar years, and Napoleon's quest for "universal monarchy" was undoubtedly a graver threat to the independence of sovereign nations than British maritime depredations. Nor should the national security risks of diffuse and decentralized authority, administrative incompetence, and military unpreparedness be discounted. But the case against the Republicans is based on a mistaken premise, that "Mr. Madison's War" was the logical result of their exaggerated, gratuitously provocative pretensions to "neutral rights." As we have shown in our reading of the *Examination*, Madison by 1806 had already disclaimed an expansive definition of neutral rights. He instead hoped to avoid confrontation by developing a flexible, positivist con-

[87]"Examination of the Late Orders in Council," *Edinburgh Review*, XI (Jan. 1808), 498.

[88]William Duane, *The Law of Nations, Investigated in a Popular Manner. Addressed to the Farmers of the United States* (Philadelphia, 1809), 98.

[89]Reginald Horsman, *The Causes of the War of 1812* (Philadelphia, 1962); Burton Spivak, *Jefferson's English Crisis: Commerce, Embargo, and the Republican Revolution* (Charlottesville, 1979); Stagg, *Mr. Madison's War*; Donald R. Hickey, *The War of 1812: A Forgotten Conflict* (Urbana, 1989).

ception of the law of nations compatible with British state practice. Peaceful coexistence would be possible, Madison suggested, if the two nations acknowledged common legal standards while agreeing to postpone efforts to resolve controversial issues not yet settled in the law of nations.

Why did the British government fail to respond more favorably to Madison's invitation? As British liberals repeatedly argued, the Americans could have been placated without seriously jeopardizing British national security. The war seemed pointless to the *Edinburgh Review*:

> So little is to be gained, and so much to be lost by an American war, that though our preposterous policy has at last brought the disputes between the two nations to this issue, no class of politicians seems wholly satisfied with the result. Strictly speaking, we have no real quarrel with America; our Contest with that power arising incidentally out of our main quarrel in Europe. America invades us in no substantial interest—she crosses us not in any favourite walk of policy—she aims no blows at our prosperity and independence.[90]

Jefferson and Madison had always assumed that British policy-makers, as they sought to promote Britain's commercial and strategic interests, would recognize the importance of preserving peaceful relations with the United States. But the prevailing contempt toward the former colonies in high government circles guaranteed an unsympathetic response to American overtures. Madison's invocation of common interests and shared legal values may have laid the groundwork for a future regime of Anglo-American comity and cooperation, but the immediate effect was to link neutral rights arguments to the selfish interests of manufacturers, transatlantic traders, and West Indian planters. In any case, Madison undoubtedly exaggerated the importance of the American trade to the British economy, and therefore the influence of pro-American critics of ministerial policy. But Madison's chief mistake was not to grasp the strength and extent of the British belief in American impotence. If the United States was powerless to support its pretensions—no matter how reasonable they might be—why should Britain settle for anything less than complete capitulation?[91]

---

[90]"War with America," *Edinburgh Review*, XX (Nov. 1812), 451–52.
[91]British attitudes toward the United States are ably summarized in Perkins, *Prologue to War*, 11–18, and Horsman, *The Causes of the War of 1812*, 189–203.

British commentators assumed that the American union was on the verge of collapse, that "the slender tie which holds [the Americans] together would burst at once in the tumult of war." The "weakness and instability" of the federal Constitution gave it the appearance "rather of an experiment in politics, than of a steady, permanent government."[92] American Federalists reinforced the British perception of American weakness by calls for military preparedness, proposals for constitutional reform, and thinly veiled threats to bolt the union.[93] The Federalist perspective was so pervasive in Britain that even the most sympathetic commentators assumed the union's ephemerality. Baring thus urged the ministry to respect American rights and interests, not because the present government was capable of retaliating, but because any regime that came to power with "the dissolution of the present Federal Government in America" was bound to be more formidable. "The constitution of the United States ensures to the world a general adherence to a system of peace," precisely because it was so "evidently not calculated for the support of large naval and military establishments, which views of ambition would require."[94] The *Edinburgh Review* agreed: "it is almost as ridiculous to be jealous of America as of Turkey—of a nation three thousand miles off—scarcely kept together by the weakest government in the world."[95]

---

[92]"Hillhouse on Amendment of American Constitution," *Edinburgh Review*, XII (July 1808), 472, 471. Federalist Sen. James Hillhouse of Connecticut, later a member of the Hartford Convention, sought to curb executive power by having the president drawn by lot from the cohort of retiring senators for a one-year term. *Amendments to the Constitution of the United States, Submitted for Consideration, by Mr. Hillhouse. April 12th, 1808* (Washington, 1808). See also "True Picture of the United States of America," *British Critic*, XXX (1808), 557, urging the ministry to take a hard line in further "transactions with the government (if government it can be called) of the American states."

[93]For a good analysis of Federalist attitudes, see Richard Buel, Jr., *Securing the Revolution: Ideology in American Politics, 1789–1815* (Ithaca, 1972), 263–79; on Federalists and the union, see James M. Banner, Jr., *To the Hartford Convention: The Federalists and the Origins of Party Politics in Massachusetts, 1789–1815* (New York, 1970), 84–121.

[94]Baring, *An Inquiry into the Causes and Consequences of the Orders in Council*, 76.

[95]"Lord Sheffield and Others on Foreign Affairs," *Edinburgh Review*, XIV (July 1809), 47

Predictions of the union's imminent demise echoed assaults on the Articles of Confederation during an earlier "critical period." The same themes were elaborated and embellished: the states were too powerful, the union was too large, the center could not hold. By allowing the state governments dangerously "disproportionate strength and efficacy," the federal constitution virtually guaranteed "the dismemberment and dissolution of the general government."[96] When the "feeble and shadowy texture of the federal government" finally gave way, various outcomes were possible: "a cluster of independent and rival republics," or "two or three consolidated masses." Or, "by some grand revolutionary effort," Americans might "be finally incorporated into one nation, with one name, and one government."[97] The Europeanization of American politics did not necessarily depend on European aggression. In "a great federal republic," equal in size to Europe, "the local interests of the states and the ambition of powerful individuals, will sow the seeds of division among them." The likelihood of separatism and disunion guaranteed American impotence. "The leaders of the American government may menace and talk big," wrote Gould Francis Lecky, "but they are conscious within themselves that they have not strength sufficient to concentrate the powers of the states in their own hands, and be able to wield it with any effect." Regardless of their bluster about "neutral rights," the Republicans would never dare risk war with Britain.[98]

Madison's circumspect policy suggested that American leaders were themselves anxious about the durability of the union and were indeed reluctant to risk war, for prudential as well as principled reasons. Yet the Republicans most emphatically did not see the federal republic as a bastard form of government, or as a way station toward a more effective and energetic system. If the new nation remained vulnerable because conflicting sectional and class interests were not yet fully harmonized and, more immediately, because of the treasonous tendencies of Anglo-

[96]"Hillhouse on Amendment of American Constitution," 476.

[97]"Lives of Washington," *Edinburgh Review*, XIII (Oct. 1808), 168–69. For similar predictions during the critical period of the 1780s see Cathy D. Matson and Peter S. Onuf, *A Union of Interests: Political and Economic Thought in Revolutionary America* (Lawrence, Kans., 1990), 83–86, 137–41.

[98]Lecky, *An Historical Survey of the Foreign Affairs of Great Britain*, 150–51, 153.

phile Federalists, the federal Constitution nonetheless was the "pattern of perfection."[99] The founders had created a union that secured peace among the American republics and thus guaranteed the continent's future population, prosperity and power. Identifying America's greatness with the preservation of the union, Republicans saw themselves as defenders of a unique legacy of peace and freedom. The collapse of European state system only served to reinforce their appreciation of the founders' achievement.

Historians have noted that, at least from the perspective of Republican policy-makers, the diplomatic crisis leading to the War of 1812 recapitulated the central issues of the first American war for independence.[100] Just as grievances about violations of rights led reluctant Revolutionaries to decide for independence, British assaults on American ships, sailors, and sovereignty provoked equally reluctant Republicans to mobilize for another war. But the Republicans fought—however ineptly—to vindicate union, the great achievement of 1787, as well as the independence gained by the Revolutionaries of 1776. For Madison, who eschewed natural rights claims, the primary concern was to sustain a federal republican union within which individual rights could be fully enjoyed. In order for the United States to hold its own in a world where rights were imprecisely defined and imperfectly secured, the union had to be preserved inviolate. Toward this high purpose, to preserve republican government in its most developed form, it was imperative that the federal government exercise the full powers of sovereignty, including the power to make war.

The diplomatic crisis culminating in the War of 1812 presented a fundamental challenge to the Jeffersonian conception of the federal union as well as to the sovereignty and independence of the new American nation. Federalist opponents of the war effort expected the union to collapse, and some actively sought to fulfill their own prophecy. They remained unconvinced that the federal republic was a solution to the classic problem of size and over-extension. The Federalists

[99]Such pretensions were contemptuously dismissed in "Hillhouse on Amendment of American Constitution," 477.
[100]Roger H. Brown, *The Republic in Peril: 1812* (New York, 1964).

assumed that the tendency of American politics was centrifugal, toward escalating conflicts of interest among increasingly hostile states and sections.[101]

European commentators agreed that European political experience and political theory were normative for the new world. According to Talleyrand's widely circulated analysis, the commercial motives of Americans and the opportunities afforded by "a vast and new country" provided a temporary interval of peace before the pressures of growing population and frustrated enterprise re-created European conditions.[102] Comparisons between the American and French revolutions emphasized these exceptional environmental circumstances. The most conspicuous contrast was between an impotent American government that, for the time being at least, did not have to govern, and a powerful French revolutionary state that threatened to extend its sway across the European world. Significantly, no European writer, no matter how sympathetic to the American cause, saw the federal union as an effective solution to the long-term challenges of American politics, much less as a model for Europe. Republicans thus celebrated the more perfect union of 1787, the great American contribution to republican theory and practice, in the face of nearly universal skepticism and incomprehension—and of their own anxious misgivings.

The diplomatic crisis leading to war in 1812 illuminated the vulnerability of a fragile union. Republicans were determined to guarantee the

[101]According to Joseph H. Daveiss, "the centripetal power diminishes according to the increase of distance, and the centrifugal tendency is increased in the same ratio." [Daveiss], *An Essay on Federalism* (Frankfort?, 1810?), 47. See the discussion in Onuf, "The Expanding Union," in David T. Konig, ed., *Devising Liberty: The Conditions of Freedom in the Early American Republic* (forthcoming).

[102]Citizen Talleyrand, *Memoir Concerning the Commercial Relations of the United States with England. Read at the National Institute, the 15th Germinal, in the Year V. To which is added an Essay upon the Advantages to be Derived from New Colonies in the Existing Circumstances* (Boston, 1809), 16. The French edition was discussed in "Talleyrand, sur les Colonies, &c.," *Edinburgh Review*, VI (1805), 63–79, see esp. 65–66. The same conclusions, also attributed to Talleyrand, were reached in "Gifford's Life of the Rt. Hon. W. Pitt," *Quarterly Review*, IV (1810), 237–38: "the infant republic of America was nearly precluded from warlike exertion, by the combined effect of its weakness and remoteness from the great theatre of political contention."

integrity of the federal republic against the contaminating influence of the European balance of power. This meant that the government of the union would have to uphold American sovereignty and independence against foreign threats, even at the risk of war. Madison's challenge in the *Examination* was to develop a conception of law for sovereign states that would minimize and mitigate the threat of war without compromising national sovereignty. In contrast to the federal union, which secured the rule of law for the American republics by curbing their independent authority and establishing the supremacy of the federal government in its own sphere, Madison's law of nations was predicated on the independence of sovereign states and the absence of an effective superintending authority. Madison's great contribution, in elaborating on the diverse sources of law in a world of independent states, was to establish the foundation for liberal internationalism after the diplomatic system of the old regime had collapsed.

V. FEDERAL UNION, MODERN WORLD

James Madison played crucial and complementary roles in the conception and construction of a new law of nations and of a federal constitutional order for the United States. As Madison was uniquely situated to know, the conceptual foundations of these two orders were fundamentally different. Seeking to sustain the federal union as a radical alternative to the balance of power, Madison recognized the danger of conceptual confusion as well as of diplomatic entanglements. The federal republican solution could not be extended to international relations, as Joel Barlow and other natural rights theorists suggested, without sacrificing American sovereignty and independence to an "armed neutrality" and drawing the United States into the European conflagration. Thus, if there were to be any law at all in the world, it would have to flow from the initiatives and practices of independent states, not from "nature" or "reason"—or from the federal republic of all states that implementing natural rights would require.

Yet if the conceptual foundations of a modern law of nations and American constitutional law were diametrically opposed, their subsequent development was frequently and fruitfully linked. This, indeed, was the genius of Madison's scheme, to make the modern law of nations responsive to diverse sources, including the decisions of federal courts that sought to interpret, apply, and elaborate legal principles. In practice, the issues routinely faced by the federal judiciary were of the same sort that often arose among nations. The impartiality of federal judges and their adherence to fundamental constitutional principles gave their decisions an authority and credibility that other forms of international law-making so often lacked.[103] Madison's campaign for neutral rights and a new law of nations thus converged with the development of jurisprudence in the federal constitutional order, which Madison had helped establish, to lay the foundations of a legal order for the modern world.

European powers built on these foundations at the Congress of Vienna, not to restore the Vattelian world, with its untenable dependence on the balance of power, but to create a "balance of rights."[104] In Paul Schroeder's compelling interpretation, "the stable, peaceful political equilibrium Europe enjoyed from 1815 to 1848 rose not from a balance of power, but from a mutual consensus on rules and norms, respect for law, and an overall balance among the various actors in terms of rights, security, status, claims, duties and satisfactions rather than power."[105] With the world largely at peace, the issue of neutral rights receded in importance. Trade expanded at an unprecedented rate; liberal internationalism began its remarkable ascent.

American diplomats pursued the liberal quest for commercial treaties to assure national prosperity and secure America's place in this new world order. Maritime supremacy enabled Great Britain to thwart these

[103]Benjamin Munn Ziegler, *The International Law of John Marshall* (Chapel Hill, 1939).

[104]Paul W. Schroeder, "Did the Vienna Settlement Rest on a Balance of Power?" *American Historical Review*, 97 (1992), 698.

[105]Ibid., 694. Concerned only with European political relations, Schroeder neglected to ask where a "respect for rights and the rule of law" (696) came from and why it was so important after 1815.

initiatives. British practice made custom the dominant source of international law, thereby guaranteeing that no law could emerge without Britain's silent assent. Americans responded in Madison's spirit. An American diplomat and constitutional lawyer, Henry Wheaton, wrote the first great treatise on the law of nations—now known as international law—since Vattel's. Wheaton's *Elements of International Law* and American practice gave full scope to all of Madison's sources from the great treatises of the past to treaties and judicial decisions—along with custom. At mid-century the liberal legal framework of international relations bore a distinctively American stamp.

Index